PEOPLE,
RESOURCES,
and
POWER

Gorsebrook Studies in the Political Economy of the Atlantic Region

General Editor: Ian McKay

1. Gary Burrill and Ian McKay, eds., *People, Resources, and Power: Critical Perspectives on Underdevelopment and Primary Industries in the Atlantic Region* (1987).

The Gorsebrook Research Institute for Atlantic Canada Studies was formed in 1982 to encourage and support interdisciplinary research concerned with a variety of socio-economic, political, environmental, and policy issues specific to Canada's Atlantic region. Closely allied to the Atlantic Canada Studies program at Saint Mary's University, Halifax, the Gorsebrook Research Institute encourages interdisciplinary co-operation across the Atlantic region.

PEOPLE, RESOURCES, and POWER

**Edited by Gary Burrill and Ian McKay
with an afterword by Rick Williams**

GORSEBROOK
RESEARCH
INSTITUTE

Published for the Gorsebrook Research Institute of
Atlantic Canada Studies by Acadiensis Press,
Fredericton, New Brunswick.

Published for the Gorsebrook Research Institute by Acadiensis Press, Fredericton, New Brunswick.

Canadian Cataloguing in Publication Data

Burrill, Gary, 1955-
McKay, Ian, 1953-

People, Resources, and Power: Critical Perspectives
    on Underdevelopment and Primary Industries in
    the Atlantic Region

(Gorsebrook studies in the political economy of
Atlantic Canada; no. 1)
Revised versions of essays originally published in
New Maritimes.
Includes bibliographies.
ISBN 0-919107-10-9

1. Natural resources - Atlantic Provinces.
2. Atlantic Provinces - Industries. 3. Atlantic Provinces - Economic conditions. 4. Atlantic Provinces
- Economic policy. I. McKay, Ian, 1953-   .
II. Burrill, Gary Clayton, 1955-   . III. Gorsebrook Research Institute for Atlantic Canada Studies.
IV. Series.

HC117.A8P46 1987   338.09715   C8R-094065-1

Printed in the Maritimes by union labour.

Contents

Acknowledgements

Sharon Ingalls and Sharon Martell, who worked on the secretarial tasks associated with the preparation of this collection, J.W. Johnson, our designer, and Douglas Beall, our copy editor, deserve credit for work done well under pressure. We would like to express our thanks to the New Maritimes Editorial Council for permission to reprint articles from *New Maritimes*, and to express our gratitude to Lorraine Begley, Ken Clare, and Scott Milsom for their work as our co-editors on the magazine. We would also like to thank Ken MacKinnon, Martha MacDonald, and Gene Barrett of the executive committee of the Gorsebrook Research Institute for Atlantic Canada Studies for their advice and encouragement.

G.B.
I.M.

Dependency and Resources in the Atlantic Region: An Introduction

This book is about resources and the reasons why the working people of the Atlantic region have derived so little benefit from the natural wealth which surrounds them. Bringing together articles on agriculture, fishing, forestry, and mining and energy, it looks at the hidden wounds capitalism has inflicted on the region's people and the damage it has done to the region's environment. One article comes from *Round One*, a series which taught many people their first lessons on regional underdevelopment in the 1970s, and fifteen were first published in *New Maritimes*, an independent, regional left publication which has continued to develop a critical perspective on regional development in the 1980s.

This book is intended to be a useful guide for students and others who have an interest in understanding the region from a critical, progressive perspective. As a set of radical readings, it does not claim to be either comprehensive or neutral. Each of the main resource sectors—agriculture, fishing, forestry, and mining and energy—is discussed separately, and the reader looking for more materials (often written from a perspective very different from that of this book) is provided with suggestions for additional reading at the end of each section. This book does claim to present many of the most compelling issues facing the people of the region today, in a straightforward way and with a consistent perspective that should be stimulating to anyone who cares about the economic and social problems caused by underdevelopment. This perspective could be called "popular political economy," and perhaps a few words are needed to explain this approach and how it relates to other common approaches to the regional reality.

We need critical perspectives and radical research in the Atlantic region, because without research which goes to the roots of economic and social power in the region, we can only be powerless to effect long-term, structural change. There are powerful reasons, however, most of them rooted in the region's dependence upon outside capital and the federal state, for the low visibility of such structural research.

In *K.C. Irving: The Art of the Industrialist* (1973), an interesting, if somewhat haphazard, journalistic account of New Brunswick's leading businessman, Russell Hunt and Robert Campbell tell a story that demonstrates the obstacles facing anyone undertaking such regional research. In the summer of 1971, the crew members of six ships connected to the Irving empire were try-ing to get their union certified as their bargaining agent. The workers on the ships believed that they were employed by an Irving-controlled company, and their union acted on this assumption in its application to the Canada Labour Relations Board.

As the board's hearings proceeded through the autumn, however, it became apparent that the corporate structure was so intricate that not only did the workers and their union not know who employed the seamen on the six ships, but many management employees of the company did not know either. The crew of the *Irving Ours Polaire*, for example, discovered that their vessel was owned jointly by three companies—Kent Lines, Universal Sales Limited, and J.D. Irving Limited—and in 1962 had been chartered by Irving Oil. If one followed the ownership chain up through the corporate maze, it became ap-parent that the employer, ultimately, was Irving. Legally, however, the matter was so complicated that the identity of the employer could not be ascertained. The workers on five of the six vessels could not organize or bargain collectively because they simply could not find out who their employer was. They knew that someone funded their pay cheques, knew they worked for some corporate giant, and knew that this entity, like most of southern New Brunswick's economy, must at least have some connection to K.C. Irving. However, no one could tell them, without a lengthy, expensive, and uncertain court case, just who it might be. Without this most rudimentary level of structural knowledge, they were powerless.

Everyone in the Atlantic region, with the exception of a very few powerful individuals, is in a position similar to these seamen, not just because of the obstacles placed in the way of collective bargaining, but because we simply do not know some of the most basic things we need to know about the social and economic structures which shape our lives. This is, of course, not just a regional problem, but in the regional context of underdevelopment and dependency, with an economy vulnerable to the whims of externally based capital and a distant federal state, a pervasive ignorance about who wields power and why is a serious obstacle to economic self-determination.

Whether offshore oil and gas deposits are explored, whether the forests are sprayed, whether our fish are harvested with freezer trawlers, whether our mines are open or closed—not only are we not consulted about these life and death matters, but we are rarely even given the background information others have used to make these decisions for us. Who wields economic and political power, and for what ends? These questions have been left almost completely unexplored in the Atlantic region. The media (much of it either Irving-con-trolled or dominated by other conservative interests) give us a steady drizzle of facts and opinions about the economy and society of the region but almost no tools to understand these facts and put them in historical perspective, and no way to form a critical perspective on self-serving editorial opinions.

The chapters within this book were written to redress this imbalance. Many were produced in response to the events of the day—a protest, a disaster, or the release of a Royal Commission. Apart from their common interest in exploring how power is distributed within the primary resource sector of the region, these chapters are not formally tied together. They are not in any way the product of an official "school," neither are they concentrated in a given area or resource sector. They range spatially across the Atlantic region, from Madawaska potato-growers in the west to oil workers on the Hibernia deposit in the east. They range topically from the impoverished fluorspar miners of Newfoundland to businessmen who make decisions affecting the whole region from Halifax's office towers.

Such a collection of writings, ranging across such broad areas and adopting a variety of perspectives and approaches, runs the risk of lacking coherence. Yet when we stand back and notice the underlying patterns these chapters reveal, we suddenly realize that they are, for all their variety, essentially about the same thing: how external and local capital and the state have reshaped the economy and society of the Atlantic region, particularly since 1945, in ways which have made its people economically dependent. They all argue, in other words, for the same basic idea: that there is a fundamental contradiction between capitalist development, as we have experienced it, and the interests of the majority of people in the Atlantic region.

Whether we are watching the North Atlantic fishermen trapped in a capitalist boom-and-bust cycle from which neither capital nor the federal state can rescue them; the landowners of Cape Breton trapped into taking environmental risks they neither chose nor accept; or potato growers caught in a vice of debt, rising costs, and restrictive contracts, we come up against the same patterns of development. Capitalism in the Atlantic region has failed to provide its people with economic well-being and has corrupted the region's environment. It has not granted fluorspar miners, Irish-moss harvesters, or inshore fishermen the right to participate in decisions that affect every aspect of their lives. To the limited extent that producers now have this right, they have it because they organized themselves to get it. Their struggles have been made immensely difficult by the paternalistic approach of the state and the unrestrained anti-labour strategies of capital.

For all their attention to very local cases and events, the chapters in this collection are all part of the story of the subordination of the region to capital, and of the deep economic, social, and cultural structures of dependence that have been imbedded within the Atlantic region since 1945. They all seek to uncover the hidden logic which has imbued the producers of the Atlantic region not with a sense of pride and position in their community but with a sense of tragic impasse. That hidden logic is to be found in the capitalist system.

It makes sense for critics of development in the region to focus on the primary sector—those industries which utilize raw or cultivated resources, such as fishing, farming, forestry, and mining—because this sector has a much more central position in the Atlantic region than it does in the more industrialized parts of the country.

According to the 1981 census, out of a regional labour force of 941,110 people, a total of 82,905 people were employed in the primary sector. This statistic, however, underestimates the numbers dependent upon primary resources, for much of what is called "secondary manufacturing" (which employs 148,400 people, according to the same source) is tied directly to the processing of primary resources. In Newfoundland, for example, while primary industries account for only 41.1 percent of employment in the goods-producing sector, 19.5 percent of employment in secondary industry was accounted for by fish processing, and 6.2 percent by pulp and paper; the fishing industry accounts for nearly half of the employment in the goods-producing sector of the province (Newfoundland, Royal Commission, 1986, 122).

Until the 1970s, a commonly accepted theory was that the region had failed to get beyond a wood, wind, and sail economy in the mid-nineteenth century mainly because it lacked the natural resources to do so (Saunders 1984). This interpretation is no longer given much weight, because of the discovery that the region underwent a process of rapid industrial development in the third quarter of the nineteenth century, one based on secondary industries such as sugar refining, steel, and textiles.

In response to this finding, scholars began to trace regional underdevelopment back to the processes through which this industrial base was brought under external control from 1890-1920, and to the catastrophe which overcame the economy in the 1920s. This crisis was triggered, it appears, by changes in tariffs, transportation policies prejudicial to the region, and the development of new energy sources rivalling the region's coal. What caused this collapse is still open to debate, but many writers (particularly those who emphasize the region's dependence on foreign or Canadian capital) argue that the process reflected the concentration and centralization of capital in central Canada. Added to this industrial decline was the crisis of traditional staple trades in the face of adverse international markets and new technologies (Acheson 1972, 1977; Alexander 1978; Forbes 1979). The historical period in which we are now living is, in an important sense, still reverberating with the sounds of this collapse of the 1920s, which not only wiped out many of the region's industrial achievements but weakened traditional staple trades such as fishing and forestry.

We hear the echoes of this collapse today in three areas. First, as far as capital is concerned, it was on the ruins of the region's first industrial economy that the names which now represent local capital—such as McCain, Sobey, Irving, and Jodrey—came to the fore, to fill the void left by the collapsing locally and externally controlled industries. These new capitalists attained their heights of power not, in the main, by developing productive industries but by expanding services and monopolizing trade. They did not accumulate capital by making here the manufactured goods the region had formerly imported (what is called a strategy of import substitution) but by exporting unprocessed or semiprocessed resources or by cornering the regional market in areas such as gas stations and grocery stores.

From these modest beginnings these capitalists expanded to the extent that, today, their empires are felt in every aspect of the region's economic life. Since the Second World War, every phase of their massive expansion has been underwritten by the development policies of the federal state. Their activities have been, in short, primarily parasitical rather than productive. They have not developed the region economically in terms of anything more than strict dependence on external capital and the federal state. Whenever their position is challenged, they are quick to cloak themselves in the mantle of "standing up for the region," but they are also quick to move away, invest abroad, and even undercut local producers by importing produce from other areas whenever these procedures suit their economic interests. The postwar influx of transnational capital, provided with free factories, grants, and loans by the state and with a labour force guaranteed to be paid less and, if necessary, "legally" deprived of its collective-bargaining rights, was rarely opposed by these dependent local businessmen. They have in fact often played a major role on the public bodies that brought these externally based corporations to the region.

Second, we sense the reverberations of the collapse of the region's industrial base in the policies of the state, both on the federal and provincial levels. "Development policy" has consistently had only one aim: to shore up whatever is left of the region's productive base on the basis of private ownership. Any idea, no matter how transparently unrealistic and short-sighted, will receive a respectful hearing from state planners—be this the brutal destruction of coastal communities in Newfoundland on the basis of a half-baked academic theory of "growth poles," or the investment of public monies in dubious publicity schemes supposedly designed to stimulate "entrepreneurship"—provided that it leaves control over investment in private hands. None of these programs can or will work, but to go beyond them would mean admitting that, for complex historical reasons, industrial capitalism in the region has collapsed as a realistic option. State planners and politicians face an almost impossible dilemma and respond with subsidies to producers of exotic sportscars or, more ominously, favours for the multinational arms industry. They air ideas of peopling Cape Breton Island with South Koreans and of creating zones in which laws protecting labour rights will be jettisoned. They will dabble in any utopianism, they will generate theory upon elegant theory (generally immune to any empirical test or public accountability, and applied in a haphazard, *ad hoc* manner), they will place the blame squarely on the presumed cultural defects of the region's population and the allegedly low quality of its work force, but they will not face the facts which have doomed every regional development policy since the Second World War to failure.

These facts suggest that industrial capitalism has been in acute crisis in the region since 1945. That this has not led to social upheaval is mainly a result of the role played by the state. In 1981 there were more public servants (99,855) in the region than producers in the primary sector (82,905). Estimates of Nova Scotia's 1985 gross domestic product (GDP) indicate that services contributed over three times as much to GDP as the primary sector; in fact, the contribution to GDP represented by social expenditures on public administration, health, and education was greater than that of the primary sector by a factor of 3.67, and greater than that of secondary manufacturing by a factor of 2.02. In Newfoundland, the picture is similar: the contribution to the provincial GDP represented by social expenditures on public administration, health, and education was greater than that of the primary sector by a factor of 2.70, and that of secondary manufacturing by a factor of 3.14. Services—most in the public sector—have long since overtaken the production of goods. A shrinking productive population is regulated and "served" by a vast number of bureaucrats, professionals, and service workers. Unemployment insurance, welfare, and short-term make-work projects complete the picture of popular dependence upon the state. State cutbacks—over which a powerless region has little influence—have a disproportionate impact on people whose other alternatives have been dispensed with. The resource sector, in this setting, functions as the insurance policy of many workers.

Recent growth in the regional economy has not, in short, constituted *development* in any real sense of the term. Postwar improvements in incomes were largely the result of increases in transfer payments of various kinds (notably unemployment insurance, old age pensions, and social assistance), rather than of any real expansion in stable and productive employment. Traditional industries (farming, fishing, forestry, coal and steel, shipbuilding) have declined as sources of employment, while few new, productive industries have been successfully established to take their place. The new jobs that have been created are predominantly in the service sector, with government being the most important element. Government is now the dominant actor in each provincial economy. The private sector is weak and is declining in its levels of capital investment. Much of so-called private investment is public money in the form of subsidies or tax write-offs. In sum, the pattern of development over the past few decades has been one of increasing dependence on foreign investment and federal government transfers, decline of traditional industries, and very weak private-sector growth.

Third, the direst impact of the long crisis of the regional economy has been its effect on workers and primary producers. Sympathetic outsiders frequently wonder why, given the weight of the evidence against the region's present path of development, the people of the region do not rise up and demand something else. They forget the dampening effects that out-migration and unemployment have on those who might protest. Economic decline weakens the workers' ability to fight back by undermining their bargaining position. It also inflicts them with the less tangible but very real cultural wounds of dependency: a cynical, "clientelist" attitude to politics; a sense of powerlessness in the face of paternalistic employers; and a pervasive despair over the prospects for change. Workers may respond to a sudden, sharp crisis of unemployment with militancy and radicalism, but they commonly respond to a protracted period of joblessness with fatalism, lethargy, and cynicism.

Workers and primary producers, especially in Newfoundland and Nova

Scotia, fought a ferocious struggle against capital in the 1920s and 1930s. They specifically demanded a break with the path of dependent development. Although popular agitation forced the state to soften some of the effects of the concentration and centralization of capital, ultimately the workers were defeated—in Nova Scotia by force of arms, and in Newfoundland by the imposition of a dictatorial commission government. In the wake of this defeat, and as the social consequences of underdevelopment have become more and more entrenched, popular mobilization has become far more difficult. Producers faced with the disappearance of their own jobs in economies with 20 percent official unemployment watch their step. If they organize, the multinationals will threaten to pull out. If they bargain over the price of their wood or their fish, the companies will turn for assistance to the normally compliant provincial governments and marketing boards or play off one set of producers against another.

Against these odds, fishermen, woodlot owners, farmers, and workers have won significant local victories. If they were to challenge the very path of development in the region, however, they would have to build far more powerful and cohesive political movements. Unless a strong force rooted in the working class, and uniting workers and primary producers, is able to force structural changes, the region's fate is sealed. There is no other significant social force interested in, or which could conceivably mount, such a structural challenge. Regional dependency arises out of deeply rooted structural forces, and not out of fleeting fluctuations in world trade or government programs. A mild response to structural dependency, one that does not confront these forces, will not and cannot achieve the momentum necessary for basic change. Throughout the western world, postwar workers have learned to live with capitalism through a compromise formula by which they have surrendered power within the workplace for collective-bargaining rights. In the Atlantic region, this compromise seriously limits the response to dependency and, in fact, helps guarantee its perpetuation, because it leaves workers' organizations without effective alternative strategies when their industries close down and their members start moving away.

Having said something about why resource questions are crucial and form a logical focus of research in the region, we would like to comment on what we have called "the political economy of the Atlantic region," for both components of this expression are subjects of much debate.

Political economy has been usefully summarized by Pat Marchak as the "study of power derived from or contingent on a system of property rights; the historical development of power relationships; and the cultural and social embodiments of them" (Marchak 1985, 673). It is an interdisciplinary perspective that combines insights into general rules of capitalist relations with the careful study of the history of a particular region in relationship to world capitalism. It is also a debate, frequently heated, over how social classes should be defined, how class affects regional underdevelopment, and the position of politics. In the dependent Atlantic region, where the notions of state-employed mainstream economists are quite frequently reflected in development policy, the debate within political economy over underdevelopment can make a difference for thousands of producers.

Thousands of Newfoundlanders were relocated on the basis of a thoroughly questionable and speculative theory of growth poles, and now, in response to equally dubious theories, the federal state appears to be ready to apply this relocation model to the region as a whole. Traditional life-support systems such as unemployment insurance compensation and industrial development programs may, if current prescriptions are followed, be unplugged in order to allow the market to dictate the patterns of investment and the nature of the labour market. This is an economic prescription for a regional resettlement program that will make the Newfoundland experience seem mild and humane by comparison. This view, of letting the market dictate, has over the past decade succeeded remarkably in migrating from the radical right-wing neoclassical fringe to the eclectic mainstream, and now, in fact, is actively shaping government policy.

Mainstream approaches to regional underdevelopment assume all countries were once underdeveloped, and that those which are presently underdeveloped have simply missed out on having an industrial revolution. These theories naturally lead to policies that will help this revolution to occur by removing internal obstacles such as poor education, cultural backwardness, lack of capital, inefficient governments, and so on. In the most extreme form of these theories, if wages are driven down and support programs are stopped, a point of equilibrium will be reached at which the region would once again become attractive to capital. Less extreme variants of mainstream economic theory see growth as determined by the attractiveness of the region to investors; this outlook lies behind the seemingly reckless expenditures of money to attract powerful multinationals to locate in the region.

Radical theories have taken a completely different tack, although their focus has varied over time. Marx initially thought that the capitalist revolution he saw first-hand in Britain would be duplicated on a national basis throughout the world on roughly the same model, as capital (driven by its own contradictions, mainly the tendency of the rate of profit to fall) would become ever more international. By the late nineteenth century, it was clear that this internationalization of capital would not lead to the emergence of a large number of autonomous capitalist states but, rather, a world in which developed countries pursued a policy of world conquest for control over markets, sources of raw materials, and safe places to invest capital. Still, theorists believed that once the colonies became independent and broke the political ties binding them to the developed world, they too would industrialize. By the late 1950s, this balanced industrial future seemed wildly optimistic, as systematic obstacles to development widened the gap between rich and poor countries. Theorists began to argue that the development of capitalism in the "metropolis" had occurred at the expense of its "satellites."

The system worked like a giant series of suction pumps, draining the satellites of their surpluses and concentrating the wealth in the metropolis.

By the 1980s, this "dependency theory" approach, as it came to be known, itself seemed to have limitations. It seemed to have lost sight of what goes on inside countries and regions—the struggles between classes, the effects of different national traditions, and the crucial realm of production in which not only commodities but social relations between people are made (Amin 1976, Blomström and Hettne 1984, Palma 1978). The dependency school, it is now generally conceded, became too mechanical in its approach, too narrowly focussed on the economy at the expense of a host of other historical forces, and too inclined to emphasize external factors. Yet the decline of the dependency school has not undermined the importance of many of its insights.

We now realize, to a greater extent than a decade ago, that we need to think of development not only as an economic but as a political, social, and cultural problem. Important recent work, for example, has made us realize that women in the region have borne the brunt of regional underdevelopment and, through their paid and unpaid labour, have made it possible for many primary producers to continue (Connelly and MacDonald 1983). Underdevelopment, we have discovered, represents a complex historical problem, not usefully approached through the neat equations and purely rational constructs of mainstream economic theory.

This radical approach lies behind the writing in this book, although not all our contributors would define their work in exactly the same way. Many prefer to put aside such general considerations and get on with the job of concrete analysis. This diversity of emphasis makes this book a good place to begin an exploration of central questions of regional dependency, but a bad place to end one. Interested readers are advised to read more broadly in the topic areas covered with the assistance of our recommendations for further reading.

The Atlantic region has a tradition of 80 years of critical analysis of regional underdevelopment, one of whose distinguishing features has been its connection to social struggle. Critical writing about political economy in the Atlantic region can be traced back to the pioneering work of Colin McKay who, with immense subtlety and sophistication, applied Marxist concepts of political economy to working-class culture and to resource questions in his writing in the *Eastern Labour News* (1909-13). Further critical work in political economy was carried out by Joe Wallace in the Halifax *Citizen* after World War I. In the 1970s the dependency framework was given its first regional elaboration in the pages of a socialist newspaper, the *East Coast Worker*, prior to its acceptance by many professional historians and sociologists. *Round One* was perhaps the most important popular development-education publication of this decade, but outstanding work was done in other media, such as the slide/tape show on Sydney Steel created by the Steel Research Group.

Yet, despite its popular, left-wing origins, regional political economy has increasingly become academic rather than popular in orientation. In fact, within radical political economy, those who attempt to put questions about property and political power in a more understandable way, or attempt to think about what practical steps could be taken on the basis of insights into dependency, have been heavily criticized for not being serious about theory and for being "populists." Political economy in Canada has tended to accept the premises of an increasingly narrow and anti-intellectual academic culture and has increasingly equated seriousness only with high theory.

Written by trade unionists as well as academics, social activists as well as social researchers and historians, these chapters reflect an opposite tendency, which holds that serious intellectual work implies and requires sustained political engagement. These chapters are written in the tradition of Colin McKay, the region's first radical political economist—as in his work, down-to-earth words for insights of considerable theoretical sophistication are used. These chapters refuse to acknowledge the conventional intellectual separation of economics and politics, and of nature and history. They illuminate dependency, not as an abstract theory of development but as a lived reality. Sociologist James Sacouman summarizes the spirit of this strain of regional political economy when he writes, "Paradoxically, that one great advantage we in the region have had is that we simply have not been able to afford the luxury of grand theorizing on a Canadian or worldwide scale. Our constituency, the real situation of urgency, and the plethora of stereotypes clouding our history have impelled Marxist intellectuals to take the historical-materialist dictum of concrete analysis more seriously" (Sacouman 1981, 138). From this perspective, and from the perspective which guides *New Maritimes*, it is wrong to see the political economist as someone who views empirical reality as so much "raw material" for an abstract model. What is needed, instead, is a method which gives us, finally, not abstractions but facts; not just an abstract model of "capitalist development on the periphery," we might say, but a concrete analysis of *this* society, whose underlying principles can be grasped only within a real historical process.

The greatest challenge ahead for regional political economy is not to develop ever-more-elaborate models of the structure of dependency or to accumulate more and more abundantly footnoted historical studies of the local rise and collapse of industry. Both of these are, of course, important, but they pale in significance beside the challenge of building some kind of practical alternative to the region's tragic impasse. This collection reflects well what regional political economy has accomplished: it has documented, really beyond question, the failure of postwar regional economic strategy; and it has shown the disastrous impact of this failure upon thousands of people, both in the resource sector and outside it. It also shows what now needs to be done: we need to think of a way to move off this bleak path of dependency and to build an alternative future for the region.

Further Reading:
Dependency and Resources

International Development Theory

Amin, Samir. *Unequal Development: An Essay on the Social Formations of Peripheral Capitalism* (New York, 1976).
Blomström, Magnus, and Hettne, Björn. *Development Theory in Transition: The Dependency Debate and Beyond: Third World Responses* (London, 1984).
Palma, Gabriel. "Dependency: A Formal Theory of Underdevelopment or a Methodology for the Analysis of Concrete Situations of Underdevelopment?" *World Development* 6 (1978): 881-924.

History

Acheson, T.W. "The National Policy and the Industrialization of the Maritimes, 1880-1910." *Acadiensis* 1, No. 2 (Spring 1972): 3-28.
————. "The Maritimes and 'Empire Canada.' " In D.J. Bercuson, ed., *Canada and the Burden of Unity* (Toronto, 1977), 87-114.
Alexander, David. "Economic Growth in the Atlantic Region, 1880 to 1940." *Acadiensis* 8, No. 1 (1978): 47-76.
Forbes, Ernest R. *Maritime Rights: The Maritime Rights Movement, 1919-1927, A Study in Canadian Regionalism* (Montreal, 1979).
Saunders, S.A. *The Economic History of the Maritime Provinces* (Fredericton, 1984).

Present Perspectives

Brym, Robert J., ed. *Regionalism in Canada* (Toronto, 1986).
Cannon, James B. "Explaining Regional Development in Atlantic Canada: A Review Essay." *Journal of Canadian Studies/Revue d'études canadiennes* 19, No. 3 (Autumn 1984): 65-86.
Connelly, Pat, and MacDonald, Martha. "Women's Work: Domestic and Wage Labour in a Nova Scotia Community." *Studies in Political Economy* No. 10 (Winter 1983): 45-72.
Frank, David. "The Nine Myths of Regional Disparity." *Canadian Dimension* 13, No. 2 (1978): 18-21.
Hunt, Russell, and Campbell, Robert. *K.C. Irving: The Art of the Industrialist* (Toronto, 1973).
Marchak, Patricia. "Canadian political economy." *Canadian Review of Sociology and Anthropology* 22, No. 5 (1985): 673-709.

Newfoundland, Royal Commission on Employment and Unemployment. *Building on Our Strengths* (St. John's, 1986).

Overton, James. "Uneven Regional Development in Canada: The Case of Newfoundland." *The Review of Radical Political Economics* 10, No. 3 (1978): 106-16.

Ridler, Neil B., ed. *Issues in Regional/Urban Development of Atlantic Canada* (Saint John, 1977).

Sacouman, R. James. "The 'Peripheral' Maritimes and Canada-Wide Marxist Political Economy." *Studies in Political Economy,* No. 6 (Autumn 1981): 135-50.

Savoie, Donald. *Regional Economic Development: Canada's Search for Solutions* (Toronto, 1986).

Veltmeyer, Henry. "The Capitalist Underdevelopment of Atlantic Canada." In Robert J. Brym and R. James Sacouman, eds., *Underdevelopment and Social Movements in Atlantic Canada* (Toronto, 1979), 17-35.

Part I

Agriculture

Introduction:
The New Corporate Clearances

We seem to be confronting two completely different worlds when we look at agriculture in the Atlantic Provinces. We see, on one side, the multinational and technologically sophisticated world of the McCains and the Sobeys, those textbook examples of capital's inherent tendencies towards concentration and centralization. On the other side we have the quietly languishing rural homesteads, so often abandoned to the elements or eking out a marginal existence in a world of ever-diminishing possibilities. The widespread abandonment of the region's farms and the diminution of its once numerous farming population provide the gloomy backdrop to the glittering factories and stores thrown up by agribusiness.

Is it merely a "backdrop"? Is this simply a case of "dualism"—on the one side, progress and technological innovation, and, on the other, "conservatism" and rural decay, or were there connections between the growth of large capital in agriculture (and, in the case of Sobeys, the service sector closely dependent on it) and the underdevelopment of this industry throughout the region? These four chapters, three focussing on the region's crucial potato industry, and one on a corporate empire which grew out of the merchandising of farm produce, argue that the links between capital accumulation and agrarian underdevelopment are compelling.

Tom Murphy argues that the consolidation and concentration of capital in the upper Saint John River Valley represent a wide-ranging capitalist transformation of agriculture that has meant the mechanization of some large farms in a dependent relationship with capital, but also the disappearance of 80 percent of New Brunswick's farms from 1951-81. Darrell McLaughlin and Marie Burge, from their vantage point as activists close to the National Farmers Union in New Brunswick and Prince Edward Island, argue that potato producers face an unequal exchange with capital—in New Brunswick because of the massive economic and political power of the processor, in Prince Edward Island because of the traditional influence of the potato shippers, and in both cases because of the active preference of the state for a business-dominated agricultural sector. Drawing on her longer and fully footnoted book on the Sobeys, Eleanor O'Donnell also underlines the role of the state, this time in feeding a vast, parasitical service empire that generates massive profits for its shareholders and directors but leaves farmers and workers in a position of dependence.

The underdevelopment of agriculture cannot be understood historically unless we put it in the context of distinct regional economic patterns, for although the forces changing regional agriculture are nation-wide, their impact has been regionally specific. Anthony Winson (1985), in a path-breaking study, argues that the underdevelopment of Maritime agriculture can be traced back to the predominant role of merchants pursuing tariff policies inimical to local industrial and agricultural development. He points out that regional agriculture suffered directly from the collapse of Maritime manufacturing in the period 1890-1920, because as industry contracted so did the farmers' markets. By 1940, Maritime farmers owned on the average about the same amount of land as Ontario farmers but farmed much less of it (59 percent of the average Ontario farm was in productive farmland, compared with 21 percent in Nova Scotia). While, in 1941, Ontario farms reported an average of $844 worth of machinery and equipment per farm, the same calculation gives us just $474 for the farms of P.E.I., $399 for those of New Brunswick, and just $332 for those of Nova Scotia. By 1950, over 50 percent of New Brunswick and Nova Scotia farms had an annual production valued at less than $250 per farm or were "part-time" operations; only about 20 percent of Ontario's farms were of this character.

This legacy of backwardness explains the rapidity of the clearances after the war. The farm labour force in Canada declined by some 21 percent from 1951-61 (only 15 percent in Ontario), but the decline for the Maritimes—45 percent—was over twice that of the country as a whole. In the Maritimes, more than in any other region of Canada, the mechanization of farms meant massive social dislocation. Between 1941 and 1981, in New Brunswick and Nova Scotia, respectively, 87 percent and 85 percent of all farms failed; P.E.I.'s rate of decline was only slightly less dramatic at 74 percent. Over the same period, the area of improved land went down by 50 percent in New Brunswick and Nova Scotia, while across the country as a whole it increased by about 18 percent. Even more serious than these indications of decline was a process of decapitalization which, accelerating after 1960, further widened the gap between the productive base of agriculture in the region as compared to others. Measured in constant 1981 dollars, the total value of capital had decreased by about 7 percent by 1971 in the Maritimes while, for the country as a whole, the value of all capital in agriculture had risen by 23 percent (Winson 1985, 431).

How do McCain in New Brunswick, or multinationals such as Canada Packers, Hostess Foods, and Stokeley Van Camp in Prince Edward Island and the Annapolis Valley, fit into this picture of rapid rural decline? The coming of agribusiness and the consolidation of farms were possible in the region only through the undermining of the masses of rural producers who had occupied both small and medium-sized farms. This swift transformation was the legacy of underdevelopment. Agribusiness could triumph so swiftly and so one-sidedly in Maritime agriculture because those who might have opposed it were on small and undercapitalized farms, enjoyed few local economic alternatives to dependence on corporations, and had been unable to achieve effective political organization. Business-oriented provincial governments, for their part, did everything they could to speed up the process of corporate takeover.

Agriculture seems to contradict one of the basic ideas of radical political economy: that capital tends to become more concentrated and centralized over time. Most farming today is still, at least formally, in the hands of small, family-oriented units. Massive, mechanized capitalist enterprises are unusual.

The family farm has survived longer than the artisan's workshop, according to some political economists, because it represents certain advantages to capital. Farmers bear the costs of supervising labour, the risks presented by the climate, and the burdens of subsisting in the long period between planting and harvesting. As one study summarized the position of New Brunswick potato farmers, "The farmer takes all the risks of production, storage and delivery. Before the season begins, he signs to deliver at the demand of the company and is liable to legal suit if he does not obey the company directives regarding fertilizer application, sprays, etc. If yield is poor, he is responsible for making up the difference. The company, on the other hand, is not even legally bound to take the potatoes which have been contracted" (Senopi 1980, 49). Some political economists argue that simple commodity production, exemplified by agriculture, represents a distinct form of exploitation within modern capitalism whereby simple commodity production is fully governed by the logic of capital without being transformed into wage labour (Chevalier 1982). Others think the persistence of the family farm stems from the difficulties of forcing farmers to sell out at times of crisis, and of coping with the political and social fall-out from any wholesale expropriation, but that these factors merely indicate that concentration and centralization in agriculture takes longer than it does in other sectors (Lianos 1984). There can be no denying the immense potency of the "family farm" as a political image, even when actual family farms are in their death throes.

These theoretical debates ultimately have a bearing on how extensively and how completely farming in the Maritimes will follow the McCain model. This model, as Tom Murphy points out, is one in which agriculture grows more and more akin to capitalist enterprise elsewhere. As one commentator graphically described the extent of capitalist penetration:

> Potatoes are grown on McCain land (Valley Farms Ltd.) enriched by McCain fertilizer (McCain Fertilizers Ltd.) using McCain seed (Foreston Seed Co. Ltd.). Harvesting is done with the McCain machinery (Thomas Equipment Ltd.) and the harvested potatoes are either stored in McCain facilities (Carleton Cold Storage Co. Ltd.), sent to McCain's plant for processing (McCain Foods Ltd.) or sold fresh. In the latter case, the potatoes are handled by McCain shippers (McCain Produce Co. Ltd.) which use McCain trucks (Day and Ross Ltd.) to move them to McCain storage facilities (Bayside Potatoport Ltd.) for export. The processed

potatoes can similarly be moved in McCain trucks (M. & D. Transfer Ltd.) for shipment abroad where one of McCain's sales distribution systems (McCain International Ltd.) handles the marketing (Senopi 1980, 34-35).

Is this the model all Maritime agriculture will follow in the future? The indications are mixed. Probably direct corporate landownership will proceed only to the extent that capital can use its ownership of land to keep commodity prices low. In a way, formal ownership of the land means little where virtually all production decisions, from what to plant to when to harvest, are in corporate hands. Even where potato farmers maintain some limited formal ownership over productive factors such as land, this legal ownership no longer entitles farmers to much, if any, control over their labour and poses few barriers to the exploitation of farmers by capital.

The patterns of capital accumulation and producers' dependence described in the chapters which follow are not confined to potatoes. Marie Burge has documented the ways in which business-oriented politicians have attempted to restrict entry to milk production through the selling of dairy quotas, which she has estimated would impose a start-up cost of about $50,000 for a beginning dairy farmer in P.E.I. (Burge 1984). Lorraine Begley has elsewhere demonstrated extensive corporate penetration of the P.E.I. hog-processing business, 85 percent of which was controlled in 1982 by footloose Canada Packers (Begley 1982). The region's links to the agricultural chemical industry have only just started to become an object for analysis and debate, but these clearly extend to a wide range of agricultural commodities (see Peabody 1982, Sharpe 1982).

The corporate clearances of the past 30 years have left a complicated situation in rural Atlantic Canada. It is important that the causes and theoretical implications of these immense changes be debated. As these forceful chapters point out, it is even more critical that these debates culminate in a new perspective on how the region might rationally manage its abundant agricultural wealth and transform an inherently unequal food system.

Potato Capitalism: McCain and Industrial Farming in New Brunswick

Tom Murphy

When most of us drive by the farms of the Maritimes, we have an image in our minds of what farming is like: It is a healthy, independent life. It is strong families keeping farms going through the generations. It is the freedom to plant whatever crops and raise whatever livestock offer the best hope for a good living. It is "the values of rural life," far removed from the sophistication and stress of the city. For two centuries, Maritime writers have reminded us of the virtues to be gained on a family farm. Make a farmer of a man, remarked Thomas Chandler Haliburton in his nineteenth-century classic, *Sam Slick*, and "you will have the satisfaction of seeing him an honest, an independent, and a respectable member of society; more honest than traders, more independent than professional men, and more respectable than either."

This vision, politicians assure us, is alive and well. The family farm is flourishing. A solid majority of farms in Canada and in the Maritimes are owned and operated by families. Social scientists might add: if there are fewer farms than there used to be, that is just because market forces have made agriculture more rational and efficient; the inefficient farmers have left and the productive ones have kept the family farm as a thriving concern. It is a nice story. Unfortunately, it is also wrong. The family farm, far from being alive and well in the Maritimes, is terminally ill.

Maybe, when you look at who owns the greatest number of farms, you can convince yourself that the family farm still survives, but you cannot when you look at the actual levels of production. In almost every commodity, a big and growing part of production now comes from a tiny percentage of farms firmly under the direct or indirect control of agribusiness. Maybe, when you look at the well-stocked supermarket shelves, and before you reach the cash register, you can persuade yourself that our production of food is a model of the free marketplace, but it is another story when you add up who has lost and who has won in the manipulation of the market. The winners are big business and the government, and the losers are the farmers driven from the land, the damaged environment, and the public.

Over the last three decades, capitalist agriculture has made huge strides towards taking over a wide range of farming activities in the Maritimes. This action has made almost everything we thought we knew about the "family

---

This chapter is based on an article first published in *New Maritimes* (February 1987).

farm" obsolete. Nowhere is this more true than in New Brunswick. The provincial statistics are startling. In New Brunswick in 1951, there were over 3 million acres of farmland in the hands of over 26,000 farmers. Thirty years later, 1 million acres remained in the hands of just over 4,000 farmers. If we go back to 1921, we find 36,655 farms in New Brunswick; there were 26,430 in 1951 but, by 1981, only 4,063 farms. In short, 80 percent of New Brunswick's farms disappeared between 1951 and 1981.

The strange case of the disappearing farms is just one aspect of a major revolution in New Brunswick agriculture. The phrase that best sums up this event is "capitalist transformation." Capitalism is a system in which some people have to sell their ability to work to other people. The traditional family farm was not "capitalist," because the individual farmer owned the land and tools, only rarely employed labourers, and marketed the farm's produce. However, since 1951, a capitalist revolution has completely transformed this traditional way of life. Farms have gone from the independent production of food to indirect or direct control by the forces of agribusiness. This transformation has not affected all the farms of the region at the same pace. There still are, in sectors such as dairy and beef farming, many traditional family farms. Here, milking machines and bulk cooling containers have made dairy farms bigger but haven't necessarily meant that the individual farm families have been marginalized. Elsewhere it is different, especially in the crucial potato sector.

The humble potato dominates the farms of the Maritimes. Although they contain only about 1.3 percent of Canada's cropland, the Maritime Provinces produce nearly one half of the country's potatoes. New Brunswick is second only to Prince Edward Island among the provinces in its dependence on potato production. Especially along the upper Saint John River, life revolves around the potato—and it is a way of life that has been completely transformed in the last 30 years.

The triumph of potato capitalism in New Brunswick can be seen most clearly if we first look at the potato farms as they existed up until the 1950s. In 1910, potato production was carried on in many different parts of New Brunswick. Outside the less agricultural counties bordering the Bay of Fundy (Charlotte, Kings, and St. John), potato production was distributed evenly among the province's major farming districts. However, by 1976 a staggering 77 percent of the province's potato acreage was concentrated into two relatively small areas of only a few parishes each: one centre is around Florenceville and the other borders Grand Falls.

Natural factors may explain this pattern, but only to a certain extent. What became New Brunswick's potato country was blessed with blocked, arable land and access to the Saint John River but, looking just at the quality and fertility of soil, and at weather patterns, the northern counties of Gloucester, Restigouche, and Northumberland were better endowed on these counts than the three counties of the upper Saint John River

Valley—Madawaska, Victoria, and Carleton—that came completely to dominate potato production. The politics of big business and the impact of external markets had more to do with this pattern than nature. As early as 1910, several of the large potato growers in the upper Saint John River Valley counties had formed shipping companies to market and move New Brunswick potatoes into the United States. In response to American market demands, land in potato production soared to all-time highs, as much as 78,000 acres. Then, after 1922, the American market collapsed when the U.S. government brought in tariff protection, and potato shippers looked for a new market—in Cuba.

There were two main groups of shippers: the Porter group, including Guy Porter of Bath, and four other shippers from Hartland, Bath, East Florenceville, and Woodstock; and the McCain group, headed by Andrew McCain of East Florenceville and four other shippers from Woodstock and Saint John. (The McCain Produce Company was incorporated in 1909.) As exposed in a detailed 1925 Royal Commission, these two groups gradually monopolized the potato trade through practices that ranged from the exploitative to the sordid. The Porter group was the stronger of the two factions. It succeeded by receiving kickbacks from the steamship companies, even on the potatoes shipped from the rival McCain clique. Intercepting telegrams destined for the other group and spying were common activities.

Yet, the sordid activities of the contesting groups were less damaging than the impact the two had when they managed to co-operate. One question on which they managed to come to an agreement was the price to be paid to the farmers for potatoes. These shippers prospered by gouging the farmer and consumer alike, paying New Brunswick farmers low prices for potatoes they could sell at exorbitant prices in Cuba. It was classic case of price-fixing. As the 1925 Royal Commission put it, the companies had entered "various agreements, arrangements, and combinations at different times, fixing a common price and preventing and lessening competition in and substantially controlling the transportation, purchase, sale and otherwise restraining or injuring trade or commerce in potatoes, to the detriment of or against the interest of the public." The federal government followed up on this clear finding with nothing whatsoever.

The unchecked monopolizing practices of these shippers concentrated potato production more and more in the upper Saint John River Valley counties, and the other counties of New Brunswick were gradually squeezed out of the picture. Yet, while the aggressive potato shippers slowly changed the geography of the potato industry, they did not yet plan a revolution in the industry itself. Most farms in the 1950s were still directly owned by farmers, with little or no debts to banks, and with the family providing most of the labour. The things the farming family needed for production, such as fertilizer and machinery, were bought, and the produce was sold through market channels.

If someone from 1851 had visited a New Brunswick farm in 1951, she would have noticed very little change over a century. She would have seen the cows being milked by hand and raised on home-produced feed. She would have seen the pigs and chickens foraging from the wastes and scraps of the barnyard, and heard the sound of lumber being cut and milled from the woodlot for farm buildings. If she had stopped to talk to the farmers, she would have discovered that the individual growers assumed considerable control over how the potatoes were produced and over the kinds of things needed to produce them. Deciding what quality and variety of seed should be grown was up to them alone. Potato farmers built and repaired much of their machinery, fertilized with manure from their own animals, and kept and traded their potato seed from year to year. The purchases they made were limited to things such as barrels, baskets, and, on larger farms, maybe a tractor. She would have been visiting a small, diversified domain made up of different grades of land—cropland, perhaps, on the better soils; pasture on the rockier and lower-grade land; and a good-sized woodlot—that would be only slightly more complicated than the farms of a century earlier.

In 1951, most farms were not one-crop operations. Potatoes were grown as a crop on over 20,000 farms in New Brunswick, but 93 percent of these farms grew less than 7.3 acres of potatoes. Only 3 percent of farms grew more than 12.3 acres of potatoes. Farms growing potatoes were still small, averaging just 130 acres in size, of which only one-third was improved land. Even in the upper Saint John River Valley counties, where potato production was most concentrated, the limit was 20-30 acres per farm. Very few farms had more. Potatoes naturally fit into a much more diversified agriculture.

In 1951 the six basic steps of potato production were much the same as they had been in 1851. Step 1, assembling seed, manure, storage containers, and other materials, was not difficult for 10 acres of potatoes. Step 2, field preparation, was the tougher job of ploughing, harrowing, spreading lime and manure, and picking rocks. (It is amazing to think that in 1921, when 78,000 acres of potatoes were grown, only one farm in 3,000 had a tractor, a ratio that had increased to only one farm in five by 1951.) Most farm families were able to handle this step, thanks to the fairly small potato acreages they were preparing. Steps 3 and 4, planting and cultivation/maintenance, meant the careful cutting of the tubers so an "eye" or sprout would be on each piece, and backbreaking weeding. Skipping ahead, step 6, storage and grading, presented few problems to most farmers. There were regulations governing the two chief kinds of potatoes produced—table stock and seed stock—but these were not strictly enforced.

Why had so little changed over the hundred years from 1851? The reason was the fifth critical step in the process: harvesting. In 1951 a strong and ambitious farmer might sow and cultivate 30 acres of potatoes without hiring somebody to work for him, but harvesting was another matter. To harvest even 5 acres of potatoes without hiring outside labour would have been a difficult task for all but the largest families, and 10 or more acres verged on the impossible. Farmers could hire part-time labour to help out. In Carleton and Victoria counties, school children were required to commence classes in mid-

August so they would be able to participate in the late-September harvest period. However, there were limits to how much labour could be obtained for the short period of potato harvesting—farmers who hired additional labour found that every other farmer in the area was looking for workers as well.

Harvesting posed the one big technological problem that prevented the potato industry from changing time-honoured ways of production. Agribusiness had made strides in monopolizing markets and shipping and had started its drive to make farmers dependent on insecticides and herbicides, but did not yet have a direct impact on potato farmers. Without mechanical harvesting, potato growing stayed within the limits of what the average farm family could manage. Manual harvesting kept the farms small, labour-intensive, and unspecialized—and it also kept them in the hands of independent farm families.

The opening of the first McCain plant to process potatoes into French fries, in January 1957, marked a decisive change in the stable world of New Brunswick potato producers. Since that time, McCain's growth has been phenomenal. In 25 years, from 1957-82, the company's work force grew from 30 to over 6,600 employees; from one New Brunswick potato plant to thirteen in seven different countries; from a product line of potatoes and peas to twelve varieties of frozen potato products, nineteen lines of vegetables, six varieties of frozen pizza, and eight types of juice. McCain has expanded from its single potato-processing plant to holdings in transportation, cold storage, fertilizer, machinery, beef feedlots, meat-processing plants, large-scale farms, wholesaling, and retailing. Its sales skyrocketed from $152,678 in 1957 to $47.7 million in 1971, and $695 million in 1981. McCain is now the largest producer of frozen French fries, and one of the three or four largest frozen-food processors, in the world. Its road to multinational prominence was paved by the federal and provincial governments. McCain has been the recipient of over $25 million in grants, bonds, guarantees, forgivable loans, and interest-free payable loans.

No aspect of potato production in the upper Saint John River Valley can be understood without recognizing McCain's control over the basic parts of farming: land, equipment and supplies, production, and marketing.

The relationship of farmers to the land has been changed completely, first by the inflation in farm values, and then by the severe economic crisis of the 1980s. Across all of New Brunswick the capital value per farm (in 1971 dollars) increased twelve-fold from 1941-81. Agribusiness increased production in the upper Saint John River Valley counties to produce huge "superfarms," and real-estate values became of prime significance. Higher farm prices were a two-edged sword: they benefited farmers who decided to cash in their chips after a lifetime of sweating in the fields, but meant that these retiring farmers were rarely replaced by young farmers just starting out. The high prices gave McCain immense power to buy land. When the time came for farmers to retire or sell out, the company was often the only buyer who could afford to purchase a large block of land at such inflated prices.

Ironically, when the value of farmland and buildings plummeted between 1981 and 1985, even more pressure was put on the producers, for farmers had been driven further and further into debt to the banks. In 1981 the value of New Brunswick's farmland and buildings (in constant 1981 dollars) was $440.6 million. In 1982 it was $380 million, and in 1985 it had fallen to $323.6 million, even less, in constant dollars, than it had been ten years earlier. At the same time, the total debt owed by New Brunswick farms reached dizzying heights, rising from $121.5 million in 1976 to $177.1 million in 1985.

These debt figures are even more shocking when one looks at the percentage of farm assets that are burdened by debt (the debt/asset ratio). For most small businesses, a debt/asset ratio of between .250 and .300 is the upper ceiling of the financial safety zone. In 1976 the debt/asset ratio of New Brunswick farms started out at .279, went through the ceiling in 1981 when it rose to .369, and reached the staggering height of .524 in 1985. In other words, 52 percent of New Brunswick farm holdings—buildings, land, equipment—is now mortgaged to a financial institution. Many farms are well above this average, some with all their assets burdened by debt.

McCain also exerts power over the land in a direct fashion. The company owns at least 15,000 acres in Carleton and Victoria counties, of which 6,000 acres are prime agricultural land. According to McCain's estimate, in 1976 the company grew 7 percent of New Brunswick's potatoes. McCain's farming subsidiary, Valley Farms Ltd., also cultivates peas, broccoli, beans, and assorted other vegetables for their frozen-product lines. Direct control of land gives McCain enormous influence over prices. McCain can draw on its own companies for inputs and, using hired labour and the most advanced production methods, can easily produce a ton of potatoes more cheaply than an average potato grower. This low production cost can then be used in negotiating with the independent farmers.

Year after year, McCain's contract price is lower than the farmer's cost of production but, because of McCain's special position in the market, farmers have to sell at that price or go out of business.

McCain also controls many of the things farmers need to grow potatoes, especially seed, fertilizer, and farm machinery, all of which can be obtained from McCain's subsidiary operations. In exchange for buying equipment from McCain-owned companies, McCain will arrange credit. A farmer wanting to buy one of the very expensive machines now required for potato harvesting might have a hard time convincing a loans officer from a chartered bank, but Thomas Equipment Ltd. will gladly extend credit, provided the farmer offers future potato crops as collateral. A potato grower who depends on a contract with McCain will think twice before purchasing a competitor's product. McCain is quite candid about the situation. "We have encouraged our contractors to buy fertilizer from one of our companies [McCain Fertilizers Ltd.] and farm machinery from Thomas Equipment, a subsidiary," Harrison McCain has remarked. "We will continue to do so because it is good business."

Corporate control over the supplies and equipment used in farming goes well beyond encouraging words to contractors. Individual farmers formerly controlled what kind of potatoes they planted but, with the advent of McCain Foods Ltd., this decision was no longer their own. The company laid down that Netted Gem potatoes were to be preferred over any other potato. According to Clause 9 of the 1980-81 McCain contract, if the grower did not comply with the specifications of the company's demand for potatoes, McCain reserved the right to buy suitable potatoes elsewhere, and any extra costs, expenses, or charges were to be paid in full by the grower in the fall of the next potato season with Netted Gem potatoes.

Probably the most dramatic change since 1951 has been in the area of potato production. Farmers formerly decided how best to grow their crops. Now, according to the McCain contract, growers are bound to "follow specifically and accept the instructions and advice of the Company with regard to the application of fertilizer for the growth of the said potatoes, and will also accept the direction of the Company as to the date of planting and the harvesting of said potatoes."

With the introduction of the mechanical harvester in the mid-1960s, the major obstacle to large-scale potato production was removed. Now 55 percent of potato farms have more than 33 acres of potatoes, and just 440 farmers cultivate over 52,000 acres, 97 percent of the province's potato acreage. Every step of the potato-growing process has been transformed. What had been an easy first step 30 years earlier—assembling the seed, lime, copper sulphate, and other supplies—had by 1981 been changed into a major, expensive operation. In the new system of chemical agriculture, farmers have to buy such insecticides as Di-Syston, Furadon, Pirimor, and Monitor, and specialized fungicides and herbicides such as Sencor, Dithane, and Reglone. The investment in seed alone can exceed $12,000 for a 100-acre potato plot. The variety, quantity, and health hazards of the materials being handled have put much of this work of assembling supplies outside the sphere of the family. Step 2, field preparation, has been transformed by powerful tractors capable of ploughing in 30-40 minutes the amount of land that would have taken a good day for a man and a team of horses to plough in 1951. The use of fertilizers has skyrocketed from 54 lb./acre in 1951 to 244 lb./acre in 1981.

Planting has been modernized through two- and four-row planters. Cultivation and maintenance are now dominated by chemicals, with applications made on the crop almost every week. As early as 1950 there was considerable interest in a chemical approach to agriculture. In 1951, for example, the New Brunswick Department of Agriculture established demonstration spray plots throughout the province to test the herbicides 2,4-D and 2,4,5-T, which were described as "non-poisonous, non-corrosive, and non-flammable." Many producers now contract to have their fields sprayed by airplane, although tractor-hauled ground sprayers are still the main method of chemical application. The bill for supplying chemicals for 100 acres exceeds $13,000. Fertilizer and lime bring the total to $29,000. Step 6, storage and grading, has changed beyond recognition. Farmers now have to meet rigid criteria for the size, specific gravity, and sugar content of their potatoes, and the processing sector, negligible in 1956, now accounts for well over one-third of the New Brunswick potato market.

If you want to see the new system at its most dramatic, visit the potato fields at harvest time. Probably no innovation has had a greater impact on potato production than the introduction of the harvester, which, outside a few holdout areas in Victoria County, now dominates most of the potato areas. The harvester commits the farmer to a completely new way of completing the production process. The conventional harvester requires a seven- or eight-person crew. The harvester's high expense creates a pressure to operate the machine at its highest capacity to save on fuel and labour costs. One harvester can, in an average three-week harvest period, reap between 150 and 195 acres of potatoes. For a farmer to justify the expense of a harvester and related equipment, he or she must plant at least 70 acres of potatoes. Harvesters mean bigger farms and a far greater degree of concentration on one product.

Besides control over land, supplies, and the production process, McCain, as the major market for potatoes, virtually sets the price it will pay to New Brunswick farmers. The Potato Marketing Board has done little to change this. The company's multinational stature helps it keep the prices paid for potatoes low. Tariff laws between Canada and the United States essentially permit the free movement of potatoes across the border so long as equal quantities move either way for processing. With this arrangement, McCain can guarantee a cheap supply—if Canadian farmers demand more money, McCain can always buy from the Americans. The summer of 1975 was a time of drought in New Brunswick, and there were local potato shortages. That year, McCain's preseason contract gave farmers $2.72 per hundredweight, and local growers outside this contract received $3.32, although the actual cost of producing a hundredweight of potatoes was $3.75. Why didn't a potato shortage force up these low prices? Because the federal Department of Agriculture gave McCain a licence to import potatoes and guaranteed that shortages at home could not be used to drive up the price of potatoes for provincial growers.

For farmers it has been a long, tough ride. In 1965, farmers received on average $2.20 per hundredweight; in 1974, $2.27. Over this ten-year period as a whole, average prices declined by one percent each year. Many years, such as those from 1966-71, were poor years, with prices well below $2.00. Although the total value of marketable potatoes increased from 1965-74 by an average of 0.6 percent per year, farm operating expenses and depreciation charges rose 5.6 percent per year. It is no wonder that by 1981, after a twentieth-century rerun of the Highland Clearances, there were only 740 potato farmers remaining in the province.

The crowning glory of the McCain system can be found in the company's contracts with potato producers. Under these contracts, the farmer's power to make decisions is simply taken away. The farmer no longer has any say in what variety of potato to plant, when to sow, when to reap, or how much fertilizer and how many chemicals to use. Horticultural practices, methods of storage—all the important factors having to do with the production of contracted potatoes—are dictated to him by the company. "There will be no tolerance for small size," says Clause 3 of the 1980-81 contract. It might have added that there will be no tolerance for the independence of the farmer either. As late as 1975 the McCain contract had a clause which stated McCain could refuse delivery of contracted potatoes without compensation to the farmer, even though the farmer was ready and willing to deliver them. The chartered banks added even more power to these contracts when they required, as collateral for loans, a producer's contract with the processor. "It's a tough contract, there isn't any question about it," Wallace McCain stated in a National Film Board interview, "and the contract, I agree, is one-sided."

The potato farmers of 1951 were independent producers. Now their position is completely changed. They may still own whatever potato land McCain has not seen fit to buy directly, they may still own some of their equipment, but the revolution in agriculture since the 1950s has deprived them of any influence over the labour process by which potatoes are produced and over the amount of money they receive for their labour. The gap between these farmers and industrial workers is diminishing all the time.

How exceptional is this pattern of swift, decisive transformation? What are its implications for the people of New Brunswick? Can anything be done about it?

The pattern in potatoes is not exceptional, it is just a dramatic and clear example of a much bigger process. Across New Brunswick, for example, the amount of hired labour increased nearly four times per reporting farm from 1951-81, and almost 20 percent of the province's farm sales in 1981 came from farms hiring more than five person-years. Mechanization has meant the abandonment of one-half million acres of improved land, leaving only the flattest and most machine-accessible to be farmed. The same patterns of capitalist transformation apply to other sectors in the province. Only 13 percent of hog producers control 85 percent of the province's production; in poultry, 99 percent of all meat-bird production was in the hands of just 7 percent of producers. In fact, poultry is an even more dramatic example than potatoes. In New Brunswick's modern facilities, one person over one year can maintain a flock of 20,000-25,000 laying hens—these facilities are more like factories than farms.

Across North America, the pattern is unmistakable. Seven out of every ten people engaged in farming in the past 30 years have left it. In Canada, three generations ago, about 40 percent of all Canadians lived or worked on a farm. Now 4 percent of the population grows food for the other 96 percent. The implications of this transition are enormous, for farmers and for society as a whole.

For many potato farmers, it means a tragic choice between abandoning land farmed by their families for generations or continuing to struggle on against corporate control and a crushing burden of debt. Those who choose to remain face total reliance on the strategies of agribusiness. Most of these strategies force the farmers to take the risks while the companies reap the rewards. Take, for example, McCain's ability to dictate what kind of potatoes farmers can grow. The Netted Gem is a variety which matures late, has only a moderate yield, requires additional chemical inputs, is highly susceptible to disease, and is intolerant of the wet and dry spell weather conditions so characteristic of New Brunswick summers. All in all, it is not a great bet. Yet this variety is increasingly becoming dominant. The only rationale for producing the Netted Gem is that it is the one most preferred by McCain for frozen French fries. In October 1982 a large proportion of the potato crop had to be buried because the tubers were deformed as a result of alternating wet and dry spells during the previous summer. The burden of this 1982 "potato disaster" was fully borne by the farmers.

For society, the implications of this revolution are equally startling. Our food security has shifted from the hands of many small producers to the hands of fewer and fewer enterprises; and it is the very nature of these enterprises to be geared to making profits in the short term over any long-term concern for the environment or social values.

Capitalist agriculture is heavily chemical and mechanical in orientation. Chemicals have been responsible, in part, for increases in productivity but may well carry severe consequences for human health. Certainly, they have a negative impact on the health of the soil. Fertilizers have delivered growth at the expense of soil structure, for chemical fertilizers, unlike natural enriching agents, do not contribute to soil humus. Heavy machinery, the other main ingredient in the growth of productivity, also creates severe ecological problems. The weight of the machinery compacts the soil, and the harvesters remove small rocks vital for soil structure. Continual deep ploughing contributes to sheet erosion. A 1980 study by the New Brunswick Department of Agriculture and Rural Development noted that soil loss, without conservation, has increased 5.2 times over the level of 1945. Sheet erosion has robbed as much as 20 tons of topsoil per acre every year from some New Brunswick farms and has already forced some land out of production.

Perhaps the most serious social cost is the hardest one to measure: the abandonment of an ideal of rural community. Ideally, family farming offers a workplace and home combined, an attractive environment in which to raise a family, participate in a community of producers, and develop skills in managing a complex system of people, technology, and natural resources. That ideal has been undermined by agribusiness, which wants businesslike farmers who lack the power to raise prices, and by governments, which want efficient production without expending large amounts from the public purse. The "family farm" lives on mainly as a phrase in the speeches of the very politicians who have done so much to make it a relic of the past. The family farm, by any usual definition, is terminally ill. Pledging allegiance to the concept fosters the illusion that farming is still in the hands of farmers.

Those who want to do something about the extraordinary transformation of our agriculture will need an ideal of rural life to aim at, but it can no longer be the family farm. There were many things, in fact, wrong with the traditional family farm. Stewardship of the land through sensitive and ecological practices often took second place to the reality of survival in the marketplace. Farmers—usually meaning the "male heads of household"—often survived by exploiting themselves, their spouses, and their families. There were few vacations. There was exposure to chemicals, the incredible dangers of heavy farm machinery, and the harshness and isolation of life at the mercy of the elements. Farm employees faced low wages and fell far behind workers in other industries. The traditional farm unit has not recognized the central role that women have played in its survival, and this chauvinism still persists.

Does this mean that we must give up on the role of the family in agriculture? No, it does not. In giving up the ideal of the family farm, we can start trying to think of other ways to preserve the family in farming. In any responsible and caring society, the family will continue to play a big role in the actual production of food and fibre. Group-farming arrangements, in which several families pool their resources and their labour to form a strong economic and social unit, can bring producers some of the benefits of the new technology without the powerlessness and exploitation such technology can represent elsewhere. In a co-operative venture there is greater access to credit and financial management, security in the case of illness or incapacity, and reduced physical risk. Several such experiments in co-operation have been conducted in Canada, notably on the Prairies.

Agribusiness, in its sweep through the potato industry of New Brunswick, sometimes appears unbeatable. It has at its heart a drive to accumulate more and more capital, take over more and more farmers and farmland, and fill more and more fields with monster machines and questionable chemicals. No challenge to it can afford to overlook its political and economic strength; it is so strong, in fact, that no alternative framework could long co-exist with it. If farmers are able to organize production in co-operative units and thus stabilize the family in farming, people with the skills, enthusiasm, and drive to resist McCain and its agribusiness agenda may be produced. Only that kind of organization and that kind of struggle will allow us to look to the future of agriculture, not with the sadness of lost dreams and abandoned farms, but with a measure of hope.

From Self-Reliance to Dependence to Struggle: Agribusiness and the Politics of Potatoes in New Brunswick

Darrell McLaughlin

On April 3, 1986, two meetings took place in Perth-Andover, New Brunswick. One meeting was quite large. Over 250 farmers crowded the school gym to talk about price-support programs for potatoes, a national marketing plan, and the stand New Brunswick had taken on these issues. These farmers were worried about the future of their farms and of their own place in an increasingly McCain-dominated potato industry. Although not all members of the National Farmers Union (NFU), they attended this NFU-organized meeting to see what could be done about the needs of the farm community. Hazen Myers, New Brunswick's Minister of Agriculture, was supposed to attend this large public forum but had backed out the day before.

The other meeting was quite different. A few shippers and representatives of the Seed Growers Association met discretely in a small motel with members of the New Brunswick Potato Agency. Three Conservative MLAs were in attendance. The purpose of this meeting was to work out the details of administering the newly announced potato-diversion program that had been put in the hands of the agency.

The next day, the Saint John *Telegraph Journal* published an upbeat story on this much smaller meeting under the headline, "New Brunswick Potato Farmers Get Help." The minister was applauded in quotes from members of the Potato Agency: "We are grateful for his many efforts to come up with this program," "The agency thanks the minister," and so on. The Irving-controlled Saint John daily did not even mention the much larger meeting of farmers that took place in the same town on the same day.

These two meetings, and how they were presented to the public, capture very nicely the real world of New Brunswick's potato farmers. It's a divided world. One group of farmers works at the grass roots. They aim at giving farmers the skill and confidence to understand their own experiences and to put these in a broader context. Out of this confidence, they reason, will come a movement strong enough to move governments and challenge the power of the corporations. The other group helps keep the government in control of the farmers. Farmers who support this strategy see the government as a neutral

---

This chapter is based on an article first published in *New Maritimes* (February 1987).

force and do not want to challenge the status quo.

Both meetings had one thing in common: everyone in the business, whether farmers, bureaucrats, or businessmen, knows that one cannot understand potatoes without understanding politics.

Anybody trying to understand the potato industry today must look at the change in state policies since the 1950s. Prior to the fifties, state policies could be described as relatively passive. In the years of that decade, New Brunswick farmers were largely self-reliant, and the provincial Department of Agriculture did little to discourage this. It prepared plans for farm implements that farmers could construct themselves, and even when it encouraged farmers to use chemical sprays, it did so by giving them plans for homemade, tractor-mounted weed sprayers.

Since then, in every phase of development, government policy has become more active in shaping the face of agriculture. In the late 1950s and the 1960s, the state began to worry about the large number of small, "inefficient" farms, the shortage of working capital, the deterioration of markets, and the lack of mechanization. Producers were warned that the success of the potato industry would be intimately connected to the success of the processing sector. By the 1970s, governments were well on their way to "rationalizing" agriculture. Although they continued to proclaim their support for the family farm, by the mid-seventies the concept of "viable-size family farms"—that is, big farms under the thumb of agribusiness—came into vogue.

In the 1980s, governments go even further. They no longer talk about farming but instead talk about one giant "agri-food system" in which farmers are to play only a small part. Land and capital, in this active state approach, are to grow bigger and bigger. The state, through the Farm Adjustment Board provincially and the Farm Credit Corporation federally, makes it possible for farmers to expand. As government agencies select those farmers who qualify for loans to buy land and machinery, they favour larger, business-minded production units. These farms have grown so big that, when it comes time for these large farms to change hands, no small farmer can possibly buy one.

State policy on research and technology follows the same "bigger is better" approach. The government has promoted the idea of the farmer as a consumer of supplies. It provides tests of chemical fertilizer rates, chemical pesticides trials, and variety evaluation. (The state has been zealously looking for a better processing potato.) Federal-provincial agreements emphasize technology transfer—larger potato planters, bigger harvests, more extensive grading facilities. So closely does the provincial government identify with agribusiness that when the Department of Agriculture holds its annual extension sessions, it is called a "trade show and seminar" and is jointly sponsored by agribusiness interests and government. All of these policies weed out producers who have smaller capital resources or are less aggressive.

Perhaps the most decisive state policy has been to feed millions of dollars from the public till into the agribusiness empires. The major recipient and beneficiary of government loans and grants in New Brunswick has been McCain, which has received $6.5 million in loan guarantees, $9 million in bond guarantees, $8 million in outright grants, $750,000 in interest-free loans, plus tax concessions, labour-training programs, and the general incentives open to all industrial companies.

This state support of big business will probably intensify in years to come. The federal government is presently proposing the introduction of "plant breeders' rights" which will allow companies to collect royalties for plant varieties they develop. McCain strongly supports this legislation. In contrast, over the past ten years, the NFU has persistently demanded a Canadian potato commission which would stabilize the potato industry for potato farmers and the community around them. McCain strongly opposes the legislation. Not surprisingly, the government has yet to introduce the appropriate legislation.

Governments cannot be considered neutral. They have repeatedly sided with the interests of the rich and powerful. If governments have done any good for potato farmers, it has been more by accident than design.

Of course, state policy is not always explicitly pro-business. If it were, there might be a significant farmers' revolt. In fact, to legitimize its policies, the state often involves itself in activities which seemingly support the organizing efforts of farmers. Core funding is provided to help start new organizations, and the government may even provide supporting staff and resources to assist in the operation of the new groups.

Here is the key to the easy relationship between the Seed Growers Association, the New Brunswick Potato Association, and the Shippers Association on the one hand, and the provincial government on the other. None of these groups is fully independent of the state. The New Brunswick Potato Agency, for example, in addition to ample financial support, enjoys official status thanks to legislation that forces all potato farmers to belong and pay levy to it. The government, in turn, recognizes the New Brunswick Potato Agency as the official representative of all New Brunswick potato farmers. The agency is unlikely to become a fierce critic of the policies of the very government which sustains it. It lacks any general analysis and remains locked into a narrow single-commodity focus. It has left the government free to do what it pleases and to dismiss the NFU as an unrepresentative organization. What the government has been pleased to do throughout the last 30 years is to hasten the industrialization of potato farming.

Why, outsiders and many farmers sometimes ask, don't the farmers of New Brunswick unite and do something about these problems? Why don't farmers organize, and make demands on the government?

Divisions passed on by history or fostered quite deliberately give us a good deal of the answer. New Brunswick farmers are divided by language, distance, ideology, and contrasting levels of knowledge and awareness; and competing economic interests separate large farmers from small farmers, contract growers from open-market growers, and seed producers from table-stock producers and processing-potato growers. Added to all these divisions are the disagreements that often arise through occasionally questionable business practices and routine political battles. The government fosters further division by funding any new farm organization, so that no one group can claim the unanimous loyalty of potato farmers.

Even a united farmers' movement would have a complicated battle to fight. Responsibility for agriculture is divided between the federal and provincial governments. It is extremely difficult for farmers, who must farm by day and organize by night, to arrive at a consensus on farm issues with producers everywhere in Canada, different provincial governments, and the federal government. The many layers of government bureaucracy buffer the efforts of farmers. In addition, the majority of farmers want only to farm and don't want to spend half their lives at meetings.

These are the obstacles, but what is the potential to overcome them? Historically, farmers have organized in three ways in response to economic crises. First, and especially in times of severe crisis, farmers have organized temporary groups to control the damage. In times of disastrously low prices, farmers have organized to get price stabilization, or aid of some kind. However, when the crisis has passed, so has the organization; only a small number of farmers have understood the value of continuous organization. By the time farmers face another crisis, many of the lessons previously learned have been forgotten.

Marketing co-ops have represented a second response by farmers to their problems. These co-ops have failed for a variety of reasons, the most common being a lack of communication skills among farmers themselves and the domination of individual over collective interests. Despite the co-op structure, farmers have continued to work as individuals on their own farms. Sometimes, for the sake of their own survival, individual farmers have abused the other members of the co-op. Managements have sometimes lacked the skills, but more often the understanding of what a co-op should be, and have attempted to apply corporate management principles, alienating members who have wanted to work collectively. Gradually this has led to the emergence of those who wish to use the group for personal gain.

A third force has been marketing boards. These have been the most disappointing. The state has long realized the value of an organization it could control and use to implement its policy of development. Provincial marketing boards have been its most effective tool to achieve this end, because they divide farmers by commodities and provincial boundaries.

Some farmers feel there are positive aspects to marketing boards, such as their inclusion of elected producers' members, but there is much debate over whether even this is really an advantage. Most farmers question the effectiveness of an organization that is under the jurisdiction of government, and the ability of such an organization to represent farmers' interests. Marketing boards are mainly oriented towards marketing and lack a general analysis on which to base their response to other issues that affect farmers.

The first New Brunswick Potato Marketing Board was introduced in the early 1950s. It was unsuccessful because of internal abuses and lacked producer support. The same board was resurrected in 1959-60 but could not shake off the memory of the earlier corruption. A third attempt was made by the government in 1967-69, but this organization was dissolved after massive protest by farmers. In 1975, following a statement by former federal Minister of Agriculture Eugene Whelan calling for potato farmers to put their house in order, another attempt was made both provincially and nationally under the "Potato Action Comittee." A province-wide vote rejected the marketing-board proposal, but a supplementary vote resulted in the establishment of the Western New Brunswick Potato Agency for producers of Carleton County. This board was later expanded to include the rest of the province, except Madawaska and Victoria counties.

In 1978 a second board was formed in Madawaska County and the Parish of Drummond, Victoria County. In 1979 a vote of Victoria County producers rejected the concept of a provincial marketing board, but in May 1980, the minister, Malcolm McLeod, imposed one board for the province—the New Brunswick Potato Agency.

Potato marketing boards in New Brunswick have been opposed in two quite different schools of thought. One group is opposed to boards because they want no changes. Interestingly, many from this group have been elected to the board of the New Brunswick Potato Agency itself, where they can make sure nothing happens. The other group, representing a very different school of thought, wants much more than the provincial government and McCain will allow.

With the establishment of the NFU in 1969, farmers launched a distinctive organization. Bringing together farmers critical of agribusiness and aware of the need for education and mobilization at the grass roots, the NFU resembled some of the earlier farmers' movements of the 1920s and 1930s.

Maritime farmers in the NFU have concentrated on resolving the potato marketing problem. Research quickly proved that marketing boards were based on false assumptions—the leading one being the idea that producers, government, corporations, and consumers all have the same interests at heart. In truth, the interests of government and industry are quite different from those of producers and consumers.

In 1975 the New Brunswick members of the NFU, in conjunction with the members in Prince Edward Island, developed a plan for marketing potatoes based on the experiences of farmers across Canada, refined this plan through discussion groups, and presented it to the Potato Action Committee. The NFU has continued to develop and refine the plan since that time. This plan emphasizes a national marketing structure, affording farmers an equal opportunity for delivery; the pooling of prices by varieties, classes, and grades; and supervision by a government-appointed commission directly answerable to Parliament. The NFU will negotiate with the commission on behalf of its members.

The NFU plan is different from other responses to the farm crisis because it recognizes the need for farmers to have a strong and effective national organization cutting across commodity lines and independent of government and industry. This organization must be free to make alliances with non-farm organizations to develop the political clout necessary to succeed.

No one knows if the NFU can succeed where others have failed. The obstacles are legion. Many farmers still believe, even in the face of overwhelming evidence to the contrary, that the New Brunswick Potato Agency will negotiate a plan which will meet their needs; they still hope state-sponsored efforts such as the Canadian Horticulture Task Force will come up with an effective national plan for potatoes. In addition, the small and medium-sized farmers, those who must sustain the NFU, may not be able to hold their positions as agribusiness takes over more and more aspects of potato production.

The NFU's fight against the government and agribusiness offers the only hope for small and medium-sized farmers. Real change depends on farmers working together to fight for the survival of farmers as a class. The future of potato farming is still open. It will take many more meetings, letters, and committed leaders before farmers can be assured of finding an honourable place therein.

The Political Education of Bud the Spud: Producers and Plebiscites on Prince Edward Island

Marie Burge

The song says that Bud the Spud is going down the highway smiling. Potato marketing on Prince Edward Island today raises the question, Who is smiling and why?

The ordinary producers who, by 1986, had received the cost of production for their product in only four out of the past fifteen years have little reason to smile, and provincial governments, rendered powerless over the past 30 years and unable to bring order to the Island potato industry, can produce at best a nervous facial tic. But potato dealer/shippers and processors might be mistaken for Cheshire cats. They are not only able to smile all the way to the bank, they also enjoy the satisfaction of the years of successful divide-and-conquer domination by which they have managed to protect their economic interests. The 1986 potato plebiscite brought out these perennial features of this crucial Island industry, but it also represented a distinct change. By a slim margin, the majority of the Island's potato producers voted to terminate the present potato-marketing plan and to disband the Potato Marketing Board. Farmers on small and medium-sized potato farms, backed by the National Farmers Union, defeated a status quo coalition of the Potato Marketing Board, the P.E.I. Potato Producers Association, the Potato Dealers Association, and the Federation of Agriculture. What lay behind this surprising result?

Plebiscites among farmers are nothing new on Prince Edward Island. On five occasions since the early 1950s, the Island's potato farmers have voted to express their views about the current marketing plan. Sometimes these expressions of their will have been taken seriously. Most often their vote has been ignored. If the plebiscite results coincided with the goals of the dominant dealer/shipper and processor sector, then they were acted upon. When they reflected an attempt to protect the interests of the growers, then they were considered "inconclusive."

This chapter was first published in a slightly different form in *New Maritimes* (February 1987).

The very nature of farm-products plebiscites creates a degree of confusion, and even cynicism, among ordinary farmers. Such plebiscites are caught up in a contradiction. On the one hand, the majority of farmers believe that a plebiscite represents a form of the democratic decision-making process, one in which they can participate. The procedures for voting often resemble those used in regular elections. Voters' lists are made up. Voting is by secret ballot. On one occasion, official Canadian election ballot boxes were used.

On the other hand, the reality is that these plebiscites are not much more than opinion polls. Government wants to know the "feeling" of the farmers but is not obliged to act on it.

Over a period of more than 30 years there has been one recurring conflict in each of the potato plebiscites. Large numbers of ordinary potato producers, on the one hand, question a marketing structure which consistently fails to protect their interests and which rarely provides them with enough to cover their cost of production. On the other hand, the small number of dealers, large growers, and processors prefer the wheeling and dealing of an antiquated free-enterprise system which has served them well.

The battleground is not that simple, however. For even though the system is equally kind to both the dealers and processors, these two groups have neither the same history nor the same level of control over producers.

The processing sector exerts tremendous economic and political control. Yet because only 18 percent of Island potatoes go to the processors, their sphere of influence is somewhat narrow. Most alert potato farmers understand the operations of processors, whose activities can be understood as an overt kind of oppression. The dealers however are harder to analyze—and probably harder to resist.

By and large, the potato industry on P.E.I. has historically been based on the production of seed potatoes for U.S. and offshore markets, and fresh table potatoes for central Canada. This is the domain of the dealers. In a given year, up to 65 percent of the potato crop goes through their hands. Many potato growers cannot even imagine a marketing system which would not be dominated by dealers. Many of them have grown up within an environment of dependence on these local trading entrepreneurs.

In the early days, potato dealers were often the "godfathers" to local farmers, providing them with seed, fertilizer, bags, sprays, and credit to plant and harvest the crop. In bad years, they may even have provided the grower with much-needed cash to ward off hunger and poverty during the difficult winter months.

This paternalist tradition helps explain why many farmers, even to this day, cling to a fruitless and destructive relationship with their local dealer and have not yet asked why the dealers' families seem to have had easier winters than they have. It is not uncommon for successful, present-day potato dealers to indicate that the same dependence on them by growers still exists. Dealers have often been heard to justify their existence with the claim that many potato farmers would not be able to put in a crop without their patronage. But in providing a debt-ridden farmer with credit and inputs for a crop, a dealer is able to negotiate for a quantity of the farmer's potatoes at a very low price.

Some dealers make small fortunes when a good year follows a bad one. In the spring of 1986, for example, a dealer who "helped" a young farmer put in his crop contracted with the grower for a number of trailer loads at 4¢ per lb. This represents a tidy profit. Dealers tend to do quite well in years of "over-supply," when low prices to the producers can be justified because of what is often called a "glut in the market." Dealers also have free rein to arrange whatever deals they can with their customary markets and are often able to negotiate above the "market price." There are no regulations to ensure that the returns from such deals are passed on to the farmer.

It would be a mistake to underestimate the agility of P.E.I. potato dealers. Though home-grown, they are not isolated innocents stumbling around snatching whatever pickings they happen to find in distant marketplaces. Among the old boys' club of roughly 80 licensed potato dealers in P.E.I. there is an incredible wealth of marketing knowledge. A mere 25 of them move about 80 percent of the total production destined for the seed and table market. Many of these dealers, with perhaps limited formal education or business training, have nevertheless been weaned on sophisticated international trade and are quite at home in the hard-nosed world of high finance. This small group exerts a great deal of power over many marketing decisions. Not only are they able to control a number of producers, either indirectly, through personal loyalty, or directly, through fear of reprisals, but they also exert an influence over government. In the 1986 plebiscite they were so powerful that they were able to persuade the Premier to change the rules for voter qualification in midstream, so that more of those who supported the dealers' interests would be included on the revised voters' list. Many of the potato dealers are also large growers. Among their associates are other large growers, to whom they give preferential treatment.

In 1981, there were approximately 600 potato-producing units (about half the 1971 number). A mere 54 producers (7 percent) produced nearly 40 percent of the potatoes. In the market—especially for table potatoes—there is a level of concentration close to monopoly. One broker, McKay and Hughes of Toronto, purchases 80 percent of all the P.E.I. table potatoes destined for the Toronto market. A few companies dominate the remaining sales (largely export seed). These include Canada Packers (with the largest share of the sales). Island Shipping and P.E.I. Produce.

Very few men thus dominate an industry that is crucial to the Island. Agriculture is among the highest contributors to the gross domestic product (GDP) of the Island, providing roughly $173 million annually to a GDP estimated at $1.2 billion in 1984. P.E.I., which produces 30 percent of the total Canadian potato harvest, is one of three provinces which produce potatoes over and above their own needs, and is responsible for about 58 percent of the Canadian potatoes destined for the export market. The potato industry employs about 4,000 people on the Island, 9 percent of the province's jobs.

Potatoes account for about 37 percent of farm cash income, a percentage which rises to close to 50 percent in years of cost-of-production prices.

A bad year has a highly noticeable impact on the P.E.I. economy. In 1986, for example, depressed potato prices resulted in serious losses to the provincial economy. It is estimated that if farmers had received the 6 cents/lb. cost-of-production instead of the 3 cents they did get, there would have been an extra $66 million in the Island economy.

The stakes in this game are high, and the odds are heavily loaded against the ordinary farmer. Under the present marketing plan, the ordinary farmer produces at a loss while the other sectors profit. For many farmers, this may mean losing the farm which has been in the family for generations, or it may mean having to work inhumanly hard both on and off the farm under incredible debt pressure.

The basic problems in the P.E.I. potato industry have changed little over the years. The apparent invincibility of the profiting sectors and the continual vulnerability of the potato farmers seem to remain constant. Various potato-grower groups and the state and its agencies have long attempted to break through this structure of control.

Between 1929 and 1932 the Potato Growers Association attempted to initiate a voluntary system which would have included pooling of prices. The dealers broke this initiative by offering higher prices to the growers than the association was offering. In 1934 the Legislature Agriculture Committee was urged by the Potato Growers Association to conduct a hearing. The association alleged that growers of certified seed potatoes were suffering big losses because of price cutting among the potato dealers. The Agriculture Committee did not get to the bottom of the charges but clearly established that the only way to eliminate the destructive competition would be to set up some form of one-desk selling. In the mid-1940s the Potato Growers Association established the Potato Marketing Board.

In the early 1950s the board acted as a single-desk selling agency. It guaranteed specific prices to the farmers for potatoes delivered to the board. The federal government paid the board the difference between the guaranteed price (plus handling charges) and the market price. In 1953 this system fell into disfavour. The uncontrolled importation of U.S. potatoes drove the prices down. The federal government had to come up with $2.4 million to pay the agreed difference. Prices to the farmers were lower than average. In a plebiscite, the potato producers voted to eliminate the compulsory one-desk buying-and-selling powers of the board. Although the Potato Marketing Board remained in existence, the removal of its powers put the dealers back into the driver's seat. In 1956, through provincial legislation, the present marketing plan was established. The Potato Marketing Board established under this legislation, though often presented as a producer board, has, in fact, strong dealer representation. Three of its nine members are nominated by the Potato Dealers Association and, consistently, many of the elected producers are also dealers.

The P.E.I. Potato Marketing Board, since the 1956 Act, has not been empowered to control the supply of potatoes produced or marketed, and it cannot set prices. The Act lacks provisions for amendment. The only way that price-setting and supply management can be introduced is by the rescinding of the Act and the dissolution of the marketing board established under it. This was precisely what the 1985 plebisicite aimed to do.

Both the constitution of the board and its inability to act in the interests of ordinary potato producers have been sore points during the past three decades. The Potato Marketing Board resisted all government attempts to change the basic marketing structure. For example, it successfuly resisted provincial government attempts to include potatoes under the 1969 Natural Products Marketing Act (NPMA). The unproclaimed Section 19 of the NPMA would have rescinded the 1956 Act and placed potatoes under the 1969 law. An ordinary meeting of the provincial Cabinet has the capacity to make this proclamation, but no government has yet had the political power or the courage to stand up against the interests represented by the marketing board.

In 1972 there was increased and volatile producer discontent over low potato prices. Under pressure from the NFU, Alex Campbell, the Premier of P.E.I. (and also Minister of Agriculture), called a plebiscite to determine the level of support for the NFU-proposed potato marketing commission. Sixty-four percent of producers indicated their approval. The passing of the Agricultural Products Marketing Act in 1973 (popularly called the NFU Act) enabled the establishment of marketing commissions and the right of farmers to appoint a bargaining agent. Later that same year, the provincial government insisted on a second plebiscite to establish the NFU as the official bargaining agent. An anti-NFU campaign was waged, and the union lost the vote. Once again the status quo was retained; the Potato Marketing Board was confirmed in control.

In 1980 the National Farm Products Marketing Council, under June Menzies, held hearings throughout Eastern Canada to judge the merits of a marketing plan proposed by the Eastern Canada Potato Producers Council (ECPPC). Although the proposed plan was quite weak, it was initially opposed by the P.E.I. Potato Marketing Board. After harsh criticism from potato producers about its presentation in the Charlottetown hearing, the board requested a second change and reversed its position in a presentation at the Montreal hearings. Another plebiscite was then called on P.E.I. in which 54 percent of potato producers supported the sixth draft of the ECPPC proposal. In spite of this expression of producers' opinions, in the fall of 1982, the provincial delegates to the ECPPC talks vetoed the seventh and final draft of the proposed plan. This sabotaged the lengthy and complicated process and brought the talks to a definite halt.

In early 1986, in the midst of extremely low potato prices, a new discontent grew among potato farmers. At a public meeting, the NFU was requested by producers to initiate the calling of a plebiscite asking for the termination of the present potato marketing plan and the disbanding of the marketing board.

The lines were quickly drawn. On one side, favouring the protection and maintenance of the status quo, were the Potato Marketing Board, the P.E.I. Potato Producers Association, the Potato Dealers Association, and the Federation of Agriculture. On the other side were the majority of the small and medium-sized potato farmers and the NFU. A massive publicity, canvassing, and advertising campaign was launched. The status quo group, using tactics similar to those witnessed in the 1973 plebiscite, accused the NFU of creating disorder and of trying to take control of the potato industry. Although 50.56 percent of the producers voted to disband the Potato Marketing Board, the vote was declared inconclusive, with the excuse that the 1956 Act requires a vote of 51 percent before the government is urged to take action.

Potato producers indicated in the 1986 plebiscite that they do not support the present marketing arrangement under the P.E.I. Potato Marketing Board. A watershed or just one more plebiscite? Certainly some powerful people on the Island are worried. The appointment of a Royal Commission to investigate potato marketing is a clear sign that the state is concerned about the level of discontent. Proposals for the structural reform of marketing are in the air, including a plan to include the supply management and pricing of potatoes under the National Farm Products Marketing Act.

Farmers know that no merely provincial solution is possible and that those with power over the industry will oppose any attempt to look for a marketing system that is national and could protect the interests of potato farmers. They also know that they will not gain control of their potatoes without a struggle with those who, for decades, have not only enjoyed the profit but have become accustomed to positions of unchallenged power in the Island community.

Leading the Way:
An Unauthorized Guide
to the Sobeys Empire

Eleanor O'Donnell

Big Business comes in two varieties in the Maritimes. Any multidivisional company not already controlled by a multinational or crown corporation is owned and jealously guarded by a small group of regional entrepreneurs. Most of these are family dynasties who are more than willing, as *Halifax* magazine put it in 1981, "to let the rest of the world believe the myth that few business opportunities exist in Canada's high-profile area of economic disparity. . . . Together they see to it that Ottawa's transfer payments are properly recycled through the local economy and that the largesse doesn't immediately flow back to whence it came." The Irvings and McCains of New Brunswick and the Jodreys and Sobeys of Nova Scotia are just some of the families who have become fabulously rich in one of the poorest parts of Canada.

The Sobeys are, first and foremost, middlemen. They provide a service—food distribution, for example—and they do it very well. They have also done very well by it. Profits from food distribution have financed the growth of a multimillion-dollar conglomerate, to which the Sobeys have given the appropriate name, Empire Company Limited. The *Financial Post* has called the family's corporate creation "an intricate network of powerful connections within the world's business elite." A stockbroker at Scotia Bond once told the Halifax *Chronicle-Herald* that the Sobey holdings extend into "just about every facet of life in the Atlantic provinces." The consolidated gross income of all Empire Company Limited holdings totalled about $600 million in 1982-83. Empire had an increase of earnings in 1983 of 34 percent. Sobeys is no longer simply a food chain—the majority of its assets are tied up in other fields, including drug stores, movie theatres, fast-food outlets, and shopping malls (see Figure 1). In 1983, Empire Company Limited's assets were divided as follows: food distribution, 39.7 percent; real estate, 36 percent; investments, 17.7 percent; and all other operations, 6.6 percent.

The Sobeys have come a long way from the small shop in Stellarton which John Sobey opened in 1906. John Sobey was a British Army sergeant stationed

---

This chapter is based on an article first published in *New Maritimes* (December 1984–January 1985). Both Frank Sobey and Henry Rhude have died since the original article was written.

in Bermuda in the late 1880s. Rather than return to England, he and his wife Eliza took up a land grant in the farming community of Lyons Brook, Pictou County. Frank Sobey was born in 1902, four years before his father opened his first shop. In 1920, Frank persuaded his father to try something completely new: a fresh-produce counter in their small grocery and butcher shop.

Figure 1. The Sobeys Empire, 1982–83: Corporate Structure

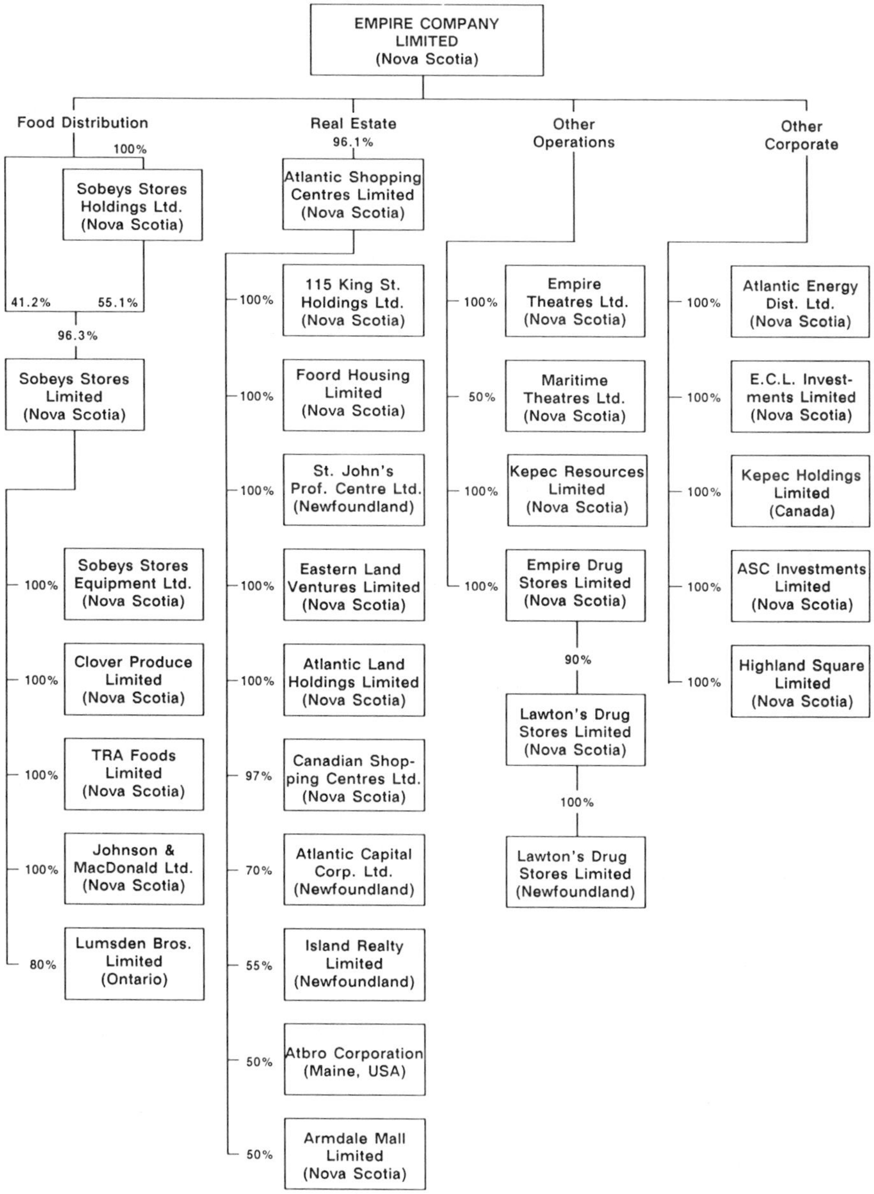

Source: From an Empire Company Limited prospectus.

Frank was right: that's what the customers wanted. More stores and local takeovers ensued. Wartime rationing assured the merchants a steady supply of customers. In 1946, Sobeys Stores Limited was incorporated. By then, the family owned fourteen stores, a bakery and a wholesale warehouse, and was ready to embark on its next major venture—Nova Scotia's first supermarkets.

"Frank was always a trader," says his old friend and the former publisher of the New Glasgow *Evening News*, Harry Sutherland. "He had a real knack for making a buck." Frank's brother Harold observed the way money could be made: "On one occasion, Frank bought lambs for $3 each, sold meat, and the following year sold the pelts—for $3 apiece." Frank knew how to navigate the often stormy waters of business. "Frank knew when to cut losses," according to an associate. "He's shrewd enough to make the tough decisions when necessary." Between 1946 and 1953, this meant opening nine modern supermarkets and expanding warehouse facilities—but also shutting down seven smaller outlets.

Frank Sobey became a living testimonial to the Protestant work ethic. He was the local boy who made good. The *Financial Post* would describe his lifestyle as "down-to-earth, if not frugal," and *Halifax* magazine added that the family as a whole was "averse to fads and frills." The story of the man who stopped his formal education at Grade 8 but continued to learn from a subscription to the *Financial Post*, who started with his father's small food business and built it into a company now worth $500-600 million, seemed to prove that hard work and enterprise could bring success, even in the Maritimes.

This reputation for hard work and enterprise helped to keep Frank Sobey in the mayor's seat in Stellarton for 22 years. Eric Dennis conveys the sense of Sobey's career as Mayor of Stellarton when he writes, "He never had to run an election for the mayor's seat. The good townspeople just didn't put anyone up against him. . . . His more than two decades on the job included the grim Depression years when money to operate a municipality was hard to come by."

Sobey had a knack for getting the most out of the provincial government. Later, he would recall a deal he made in financing the municipal payroll by getting local men onto the staff of a special provincial sewer and paving project. A little worried about the propriety of the deal, Sobey was reassured by the minister responsible: "Frank, if this ever gets in the papers, you're through. But as long as it is going along as it is now and there's nothing said about it, continue."

Then as now, the watchword was discretion. Sobey and the other principal in the "Pictou County Mafia," industrialist R.B. Cameron—whose sister Irene married Frank's brother Harold—emerged from these years as the powerful, discrete men who were to shape far more than the town affairs of Stellarton.

However, there was always a lot more to the Frank Sobey story than shrewd bargaining, foresight, and the making of purely local connections.

Sobeys would not have grown to its present proportions without the help of multinationals. First there was the bank. Unlike thousands of Nova Scotian businessmen who faced loan refusals and foreclosures through the Depression years, Sobey could count on a reliable credit supply thanks to the intervention with the Bank of Nova Scotia of bank director H.L. Enman (a mutually profitable association which eventually saw Enman appointed to the Board of Directors of Industrial Estates Limited [IEL]).

Perhaps most important, there was Garfield Weston. In 1968, Sobeys sold a 40 percent interest in its stores to Loblaws, controlled by Weston, owner of the largest food empire in Canada and one of the largest in the world. The deal allowed Sobey to diversify into many other areas, to make an Empire of what would have otherwise remained a mere grocery chain.

Thirteen years later, in 1981, the Sobeys bought these shares back from Weston, in a move that was consistently misrepresented in the regional press as an instance of local entrepreneurs standing up for the Maritimes. Quite the contrary: the real story of the Weston-Sobeys relationship, as manifested in this whole purchase/buy-back series of events, is its part in the emergence of vast conglomerates to control large proportions of the international food industry.

The scale of this development is staggering. Several years ago, Canadians learned that four grocery chains controlled 44 percent of all markets in the country, and nearly three-quarters of the market in the Atlantic Provinces. (As long ago as 1976, a background report for the Royal Commission on Corporate Concentration found that just under 6 percent of all corporations in the Canadian economy accounted for over 90 percent of all the assets of the country and 86 percent of sales.) The level of corporate concentration in Canada's food industry was more than twice that of the United States.

The independent grocer has become a figure of the past. Sobeys now controls the Atlantic produce division of Canada Packers and holds a major interest in National Sea Products. The expanding convenience-store market is to a large extent supplied through the various wholesaling branches of the empire—Johnson and MacDonald, Clover, and TRA Foods. Through its interest in the giant Provigo food chain in Quebec, Sobeys also has an interest in the Provi-Soir convenience stores in that province.

A very small number of food buyers, wholesalers, and processors control virtually the entire market in Canada. Their very size and corporate structure affect the determination of prices, because the buyers are also their own best customers. Canada Packers or Clover Produce (Sobeys) buy potatoes from the farmer; Clover sells wholesale to the Sobeys store. Each time an item changes hands and passes from one company name to another, the magic word "value-added" is spoken, and the price goes up.

The price advantage that bigness allows is phenomenal. For consumers, a price difference of two to three cents is just that. However, when stores deal in millions of dollars each week, the pennies add up. A good example can be found in the Provigo chain in Quebec (Sobeys investment: $41 million). This chain was found guilty of taking unfair advantage of a system of rebates, efficiency allowances, and lower prices for milk. The chain was able to reap $20 million from such practices. It was fined about $1,000. Apart from such shady transactions, food chains benefit simply by virtue of the elimination of competition. One recent study has established that Canadian consumers pay an estimated 40 cents per dollar more because of lack of competition.

The buying practices of the huge chains tend to reinforce their position. Five buying groups controlled 85 percent of retail food sales through 14,000 stores across Canada in 1982. According to the *Financial Report on Business*, they favour the major food processors such as Nabisco or Canada Packers, and high-volume, high-profit merchandise.

Although Sobeys has a reputation for buying locally grown food, what it actually sells differs little from the commodities in any other supermarket. If, for example, Sobeys can make more profit by importing green beans from Quebec or the United States, it will. While local Maritime farmers grew tons of green beans in the summer of 1983, Sobeys, for all its talk of being the "Home Store," let these beans rot while it carried Quebec beans in its stores. Like farmers the world over, Maritimers find their traditions of self-sufficiency being undermined as local production is geared more to the world market than to local requirements.

As Sobeys has come to diversify more and more, with investments in oil and gas, real estate, insurance, pay-TV, amusement centres, and car rentals, its food business occupies a smaller and smaller proportion of its interests. Just under 40 percent of Sobeys' total assets are represented by its food operations. "The quality of management," says *Halifax* magazine, "is more important to them than the nature of the industry." For the farmer or corner grocer of days gone by, food distribution or production was simply a way of making a living, but in the age of multinational corporations, these activities have become principally means of making profit. The effects of this change are devastating—on the quality of food available, on the working conditions of employees, and on the countries reliant upon single-export crops for their foreign exchange.

One of the major results of the emerging structure of power in the food industry of the Maritimes has been the rise of a coterie of business associates to immense influence in decisions affecting the lives of thousands of people in the region. Nowhere is this more clearly symbolized than in the gleaming Halifax offices of the law firm of Stewart, MacKeen and Covert. The floor plan of this powerful Halifax firm is suggestive of the distribution of power in the region. In the middle office is Frank Covert, senior partner in the firm. Covert—who once bragged that in the course of his career he had "come into contact with all of the men in Nova Scotia who have, in my lifetime, done great things in the business and political worlds"—served as a legal advisor to the Sobeys. He was also chairman of the restructuring committee of National Sea; the successful bidders for National Sea Products were the Sobey and Jodrey group. In the office next to Covert's is Henry Rhude. Rhude was chief legal advisor to the Sobeys for years and sits on the boards of all the important Sobeys companies. He used to be the chairman of National Sea and is Chief Executive Officer of Central Trust. In the office on the other side of Covert's could be found William Mingo, a director of food companies of great interest to the Sobeys as well—Avon Foods Limited and Ben's Bread (both controlled by Jodrey enterprises).

The present reality of the Sobeys' business world is captured more by a quiet, plush law office, the heart of the Empire, than by the image of Frank's humble beginnings in a Pictou County store that the Sobeys are so fond of projecting. "A person can get where he wants to go," Sobey told the Halifax *Chronicle-Herald*'s *Nova Scotian*, "if he is prepared to spend time thinking and scheming and reading all he can about the kind of business in which he is involved." It worked, unquestionably, for Sobey, but those days are gone. One man, no matter how obsessed with getting ahead, can aspire to little more in the contemporary conglomerate than to be a cog in a vast, impersonal machine. Maritime in name, multinational in reality, Sobeys may have emerged from Nova Scotia, but it now belongs to the world of international business, the world of the obsessive consumption by the big of the small.

If the idea of Sobeys as the daring creation of a single-minded entrepreneur is a little simple, so is the idea that Sobeys represents the triumph of free enterprise. In 1983, Frank Sobey was heard to say, "Supply and demand in the market place is the only thing that will really make things work properly. Government shouldn't try to interfere." The Sobeys have always talked in this tough, conservative way but, in fact, the Sobeys empire could not have attained its present position without public help. It is useful to invoke supply and demand, and useful to condemn the state, but it is essential to get government help in the form of subsidies and handouts, and even to shape the government's development policies.

The close relationship between the Empire and the state can be seen at all three levels of government. Probably the clearest case at the municipal level is provided by the urban renewal of downtown Halifax.

Who owns Nova Scotia? "If you look at the board of directors of Halifax Developments Ltd.," which built Scotia Square, said a leading Halifax businessman in 1970, "you get almost all the big ones." Halifax Developments Limited (HDL) was created in the 1960s to develop a vacant lot in downtown Halifax. That lot would turn into Scotia Square. HDL is now 75 percent controlled by the Sobey and Jodrey families.

HDL's Scotia Square development was in the same league as other multimillion-dollar developments such as Place Ville Marie in Montreal or the Toronto Dominion Centre in Toronto but, unlike the others, Scotia Square depended much more on subsidies from various levels of government than on private enterprise.

Poor people once lived on the site of Scotia Square: by the 1960s, the area had long been declared unfit for human habitation. "It was something out of

Dickens," recalls one metro resident. The seventeen acres were described in a 1952 submission to Halifax City Council: "Cockroach, bedbug and rat infested houses are common for many dwellers in the slum areas of our city." In one group of 291 buildings, 41 percent had no minimum sanitation, the reports said, and in another, "972 persons are crowded into 783 rooms." There was naturally a lot of public support for urban renewal. The poor in the neighbourhood were dispersed and the buildings razed at public expense.

Much of the land belonged to former mayor Leonard A. Kitz, soon to become a member of HDL. Because government would pay 75 percent of the costs of surveys for slum clearance projects under the National Housing Act, developers had received a state subsidy even before construction began. By 1965, Mayor Charles Vaughan was ready to issue what he called "the challenge of development," and local businessmen set to work. According to Halifax author Elizabeth Pacey, Major-General K.C. Appleyard strolled down to the Halifax Club one afternoon and formed a new development company. The list of directors was impressive: Roy A. Jodrey of Hantsport, a director of no fewer than 56 companies; J.C. MacKeen, director of 21 companies, including the Royal Bank and Nova Scotia Light and Power; Harold P. Connor of National Sea Products; Colonel S.C. Oland, head of the Oland brewing family; A. Russell Harrington of Nova Scotia Light and Power; J.H. Mowbray Jones of Bowater Mersey Paper Company in Liverpool; Leonard A. Kitz; Malcolm H.D. McAlpine, president of one of the largest construction firms in the world, of the same name; and last, but by no means least, Frank Sobey of Stellarton.

When these men arrived at the Halifax City Council Chamber to announce their plan, they had almost no concrete details, but they had something more important—commanding political power. Although the Scotia Square proposal required $17 million in public money—more than other, competing proposals—City Council rushed to approve it. The results can be seen today in downtown Halifax.

What is more difficult to see is the balance sheet of winners and losers. The biggest losers were those who stood to benefit from social housing. The Central Mortgage and Housing Corporation (CMHC, whose principal mandate is housing) provided 25 percent of the cost of the Cogswell interchange of roads leading to Scotia Square, as well as other roadways. Robert Collier, an authority on urban development, argues that without the CMHC the project could not have gone ahead. Although social housing was the original purpose for so many subsidies, housing for working people was lost in the shuffle. Even the city of Halifax probably lost. A 1976 study which examined the actual dollar costs and benefits of Scotia Square estimated that the city had gained $2,678,317 in increased revenues as a result of downtown development, but had paid out $3,056,003 for additional services. Left out of this estimate were the huge costs borne by other levels of government.

The biggest winners were the developers, particularly the Jodrey and Sobey interests. They had taken very few risks. As writer James Lorimer points out in his book *The Developers*, the moneyed families of Canada—the Sobeys, Woodwards, Eatons, and Richardsons—became involved in real estate development only after other entrepreneurs had demonstrated how fabulously profitable this business was. Each step along the path was guided by the friendly hand of the government, and that path led to immense riches for the investors. At the end of its 1979 fiscal year, HDL had assets of $55 million. It was able to parlay this financial strength into control over a financial institution, Nova Scotia Savings and Loan (NSSL), with assets of about $400 million. According to the terms of a 1980 agreement, HDL, through purchase of 15 percent of the shares of NSSL, would have five of its directors on the NSSL board, while NSSL directors would all be eligible for the HDL board. The Sobey/Jodrey group was able to purchase over $2 million worth of shares with an initial cash outlay of just over a quarter of the full cost. In an economic system in which getting loans is a matter of business survival, it bought a large say in how the region is developed in future.

The marriage between the Sobeys and the government produced many more offspring besides Scotia Square and HDL. On the provincial level, the most important was Industrial Estates Limited (IEL).

Established by Robert Stanfield's government in 1957, IEL was a response to the problem of regional underdevelopment. The new crown corporation was charged with stimulating economic growth. Frank Sobey headed it for the first 13 years of its existence. The *Atlantic Advocate* described IEL in 1965:

> Nova Scotia is riding the happiest economic wave in its history as Industrial Estates Limited, commonly called I.E.L., like a ship laden with good tidings, brings home cargo after cargo of new industries. With president Frank H. Sobey at the helm, I.E.L. has bucked storms of despair and survived the doldrums of apathy in its efforts to inspire new industries to locate in this Atlantic coast peninsula. The healthy industrial climate that now envelops the province through the efforts of I.E.L. has relieved and, in some cases, dispelled the fear of economic illness. . . .

The government would give private enterprise money to start up, acting as a generous public benefactor for the free-enterprise system. Once launched with government help, the new businesses would prosper and grow. It was like magic. Even better, Frank Sobey was administering the cure for free!

Right at the centre of this development, said the *Atlantic Advocate,* was Sobey:

> Frank Sobey, like the other members of I.E.L.'s twelve-man board of directors, receives no salary for his time-consuming work in promoting industry for this province. . . . It has been said the generous amount of time devoted to I.E.L. by Frank Sobey often is at the expense of his own

business—Sobeys Stores Limited. However, as well as being chairman of his grocery chain and president of I.E.L., he is also chairman of United Steel Corporation and Deuterium of Canada Limited. He is a director of nearly twenty other companies whose total assets exceed three and a quarter billion dollars. . . .

Frank Sobey's selfless and tireless efforts on behalf of Nova Scotia have been amply praised. But there is another point of view about his IEL cure for the Nova Scotia economy. "All Frank Sobey did was get contracts for all his friends," remembers one bitter opponent. The multiple directorships of IEL board members, their secret transactions, and their apparent indifference to the public's demands for disclosure have been persistent controversies. "They used to say one of them paid more taxes on his home in Armdale," remembers Eileen Stubbs, former mayor of Dartmouth, "than he did on all his properties in the Burnside Industrial Park."

IEL's way of doing business practically guaranteed charges of conflict of interest. If you were a qualified manufacturer, IEL would build a plant for you on a site you chose, lease it back to you on a long-term basis, give you an option to buy at book value any time you chose to do so, provide financing of up to 80 percent of the cost of installed machinery and equipment, provide loans of up to 50 percent of the cost of land, plant, and machinery, and limit the tax rate to 1 percent of the assessed value of the land.

IEL tended to help well-established multinationals rather than the small struggling local companies that may have genuinely needed the assistance. The Moirs chocolate factory was moved from Halifax to Dartmouth thanks to IEL, for example. Moirs belongs to one of the biggest multinationals in existence, Standard Brands. IEL also gave assistance to Oland Breweries, which is owned by the giant Labatts conglomerate. "They were funny companies that IEL helped," remarks Eileen Stubbs. Some of them were in the province for only a very short time. These were the "runaway shops," footloose industries in pursuit of friendly governments and low wages. One such shop was the General Instruments electronics assembly plant in Sydney. While the city's homeowners paid taxes at a 3.5 percent rate, General Instruments paid 1 percent, received $75,000 in free water and power services, a million-dollar plant at nominal rents, and an interest-free loan of $2.9 million. Wages were set at 85 cents per hour in 1965. In 1974, General Instruments announced its departure for the more favourable climate of Mexico, where the going wage was 55 cents per hour. Twelve hundred Nova Scotia women lost their jobs.

In came the companies—from the United States, England, France, and Sweden. Some stayed, but many left. Conspicuous failures, such as Clairtone, suggested that IEL was less than prudent with public money. Transactions among members of the board of IEL were embarrassing. As documented by economist Roy George in a book on the subject, "Egan, an IEL director, had had a large interest in Paceships, a builder of pleasure boats at Mahone Bay, which IEL took over in 1962. J.C. MacKeen, chairman of the IEL board, became a director of Clairtone while an IEL deal with Clairtone was under negotiation. Sobey, President of IEL, was a director of Tibbetts Paints, another IEL client.'' Secrecy was Sobey's watchword while at the helm of IEL, and millions of public dollars were spent without systematic public accountability.

Michelin Tires was Sobey's biggest catch. Backed by the impressive "Pictou County Mafia," a powerful business campaign persuaded the provincial Cabinet to restrict the powers of the Labour Relations Board, change the conditions for certification of unions, and, subsequently, to alter the Trade Union Act. Just after the "Michelin Regulation" was imposed that changed the rules for craft unions, the Sobeys were able to stave off unionization campaigns in their own company. The Sobeys were among the discreet, unacknowledged architects of the sweeping anti-labour changes in Nova Scotia in the 1970s—including the later "Michelin Bill." All were designed to accommodate the needs of the huge French multinational.

The hand of the Sobeys empire can be seen at the federal level as well. In 1984 the Halifax *Chronicle-Herald* mounted an impressive propaganda campaign against any restructuring of the fishery that would involve a federal crown corporation. The newspaper warned that a crown corporation would mean "collectivization on the Soviet or Chinese model." The alternative was private enterprise. Frank Sobey agreed. In a letter to the editor, printed beside a portrait, he denounced a crown corporation in the fishery as a "disaster" for Nova Scotia. In the same edition, son Donald Sobey announced that the Sobeys empire had become involved in a private bid for National Sea Products, because "we want to see free enterprise work, we want to see it remain in Nova Scotia hands."

Once more the empire and its allies pulled off a stunning financial coup. They kept National Sea Products in Nova Scotia hands—that is, in the hands of the Sobeys, the Jodreys, the Morrows, and other interests (47 percent), and in the hands of the Bank of Nova Scotia (14 percent). Nineteen percent of the shares were considered "common float," and 20 percent ownership went to the federal government. In this "private" solution, 20 percent public ownership had to be tolerated, especially since, at $90 million, the federal government's input was over four times that of the private investors! The provincial government's contribution of $25 million towards eliminating the $34 million debt apparently did not warrant any equity at all.

Sobeys had saved the day; private, local ownership had defeated the socialist hordes; National Sea Products was to remain in "Nova Scotia hands"; but those hands in fact are becoming less Nova Scotian all the time, with oil wells in Alberta, investments in the international textile industry, New England supermarkets, and a $25 million stake in a fish-processing plant in Uruguay.

The Sobeys empire, in its many dimensions, has taken on the industrial development of Nova Scotia. As head of Industrial Estates Limited, Frank

Sobey spent over $200 million in public funds. From IEL to HDL to National Sea Products, the empire has fed from the hand of the state, but Frank Sobey persists in regarding most governments as "far too socialistic." William Sobey suggests cutting back on unemployment insurance benefits as a way of helping the economy. The myth of the Horatio Alger story, the small-town boy who made good by dint of hard work and competitiveness, dies hard. It is still useful when it comes time to attack crown corporations or social welfare. However, the facts cannot be denied: the immensely profitable Sobeys Empire would not exist had it not been supported repeatedly and generously by public funds. Horatio Alger, it turns out, had a rich uncle all along.

While the Sobeys empire transformed the economy of the Maritimes, it helped change the images Maritimers have of themselves and their region. This far-reaching cultural change has had a profoundly conservative impact. The Sobeys empire has made a pitch to Maritimers on the basis of their shared "cultural values" and at the same time has used these values to perpetuate its hold on Maritime society. We belong here, Sobeys tells us in its advertisements, we belong to you. The catch is that we also belong to them.

The Sobey family has been carefully packaged so that it can represent what are perceived as the stalwart, traditional values of the Maritimes. Frank Sobey still went to work in his eighties in Stellarton; his wife Irene used to help out on busy nights at the cash register in the Stellarton store; the modesty and discretion of the entire family: these details are carefully reported. Sobey is the quiet hero, a devoted public servant. "Just how much Frank Sobey is worth he doesn't say—and he probably doesn't know, or particularly care," writes one admirer. "His happiness doesn't come from counting it up but from the satisfaction of discovering one more opportunity to test his entrepreneurial wits, grasping it, turning the acquisition into another winner and, in the process, serving his family, community, province and nation." Frank Sobey was given an honorary doctorate from Dalhousie and inducted into the Business Hall of Fame. Donald Sobey became a distinguished governor of Dalhousie University. William Sobey was named a director of the prestigious Dalhousie Medical Research Foundation and the World Wildlife Fund. The Dalhousie Art Gallery expressed deep gratitude for the Sobeys' "special statement of public responsibility" for arranging the temporary loan of family-owned paintings. The National Sea Products affair is described as "one of the most daring moves" in the history of business in the Atlantic Provinces. Ceremonies, awards, laudatory speeches, glowing articles—all these messages repeat the same idea. The Sobeys are solid Maritimers, they really care about the region, and they really care about you.

What's at work here is a kind of paternalism. We see far more in the Sobey corporate identity than just a big impersonal conglomerate that happens to be a local product. We are led to trust in Sobeys, to believe that the Sobeys really care about us, to want people like the Sobeys to be guardians of our economic security. The 1984 debate over the restructuring of the fishery was fought out in just these terms—we were told to see this rather sordid affair as a moral crusade, with our Maritime captains of industry fighting for "us" against the faceless bureaucrats of Ottawa.

Before we laugh at the simplicity with which the local newspapers presented this mythical view, or jump to correct all the factual mistakes it incoporated, we ought to remember one important fact: it worked. People bought it. The paternalism of the Sobeys empire is a potent ideology, because it addresses real regional issues. It speaks to the sense that Maritimers have of a distinct identity and distinct interests, and proceeds to turn this sense to the most conservative of possible uses. "Friendly, That's Us," goes the advertising slogan of the Sobeys; "Proud to be Maritimers." In an intangible but very real way, Sobeys has made our idea of ourselves and our regional identity into company property.

Just how far this image can go can be seen in a booklet aptly titled "Nova Scotia's Profit Formula," issued by IEL when Frank Sobey was the boss. The pamphlet outlined all the advantages of locating in Nova Scotia—guarantees of tax holidays, free plant locations, workers who would work at a fraction of the cost of workers elsewhere. "Labour, government and management seem to get along unusually well in Nova Scotia," the pamphlet enthused, "businessmen, union leaders and government officials are working together." This happy state of affairs, from IEL's point of view, had something to do with the culture of the local workers. "Virtually every plant manager I talked to gave the Nova Scotian worker very high marks for mastering assignments rapidly, and once mastering them performing a full day's work for a full day's pay. This may sound old fashioned these days, but evidently Nova Scotian workers still cling to many old-time values. It's part of the intrinsic charm of the place. . . ."

Intrinsic charm, the shrewd investor was advised, could pay a good dividend. However, there is a further reason for this in the Sobeys/IEL scheme of things: part of the "intrinsic charm" of the Maritimes, in their view, was that workers were not organized in strong trade unions and were not apt to demand the going rate for their labour. The stick of anti-unionism accompanies the carrot of regional pride.

Few firms in the Maritimes have resisted trade unionism as militantly as those owned by the Sobeys. In 1980 the Sobeys had about 70 stores in the Atlantic Provinces and the Gaspé; only 7 had unions. (Some of their major competitors, in contrast, had complete union shops.) Organizing a union in Saint John, for example, started in 1968, with six stores. After a three-month strike in the wintertime, the company gave in but closed three stores, putting one-third of the 125 original employees out on the street.

In 1980, employees of Sobeys in Dalhousie, N.B., asked the Retail, Wholesale and Department Store Workers' Union to help unionize their store. They reported they were earning an average of $180 a week, while unionized employees doing the same work at a competing store were paid $301. By

August, union and management were negotiating, but still had not agreed on whether the grocery store manager and one of the cashiers should be defined as staff or management. They referred the dispute to the Labour Relations Board.

In October the board told Sobeys and the union to negotiate the status of the two employees. On November 12, union and management met again, but meanwhile the company had given large pay hikes to employees in non-union stores. Sobeys also informed the grocery manager and the cashier that they had no choice but to be management. One month later, on December 11, the employees voted to strike. The strike began the next day. The cashier and the grocery manager were fired.

On January 9, 1981, the Labour Relations Board told both union and management to return to negotiations. Negotiations continued until January 28, when Sobeys asked that two more employees—the produce manager and the meat manager—be excluded from the bargaining unit. Talks ceased. About five weeks later, Sobeys closed the store down permanently, even though it was then the only supermarket in the downtown area.

"They didn't like unions, they tried to break us, and we ended up going on strike! And they ended up locking the door on us!" remembers one worker in the store. She had been promised to be on full-time work and warned that, because of her union activities, she would long remain a part-time employee. "I don't think they realized we'd stick to it, because we went out on a Friday morning, they thought it was a big joke. They all came out, most of them, and they're looking at us in the window, and they're laughing because it's the wintertime and it's cold and they're saying, 'Well, we can run this place.' They brought a meat manager and cashier in from Campbellton and a supervisor and a young girl from Quebec. . . . I still have my letter saying why they'd have to close the store, because it was not a 'viable' operation. And it said, very politely, that if we ever needed any help with anything or were ever looking for another job, please contact Sobeys. So they're always very polite."

George Vair, who works for the Retail, Wholesale, and Department Store Workers' Union, adds that Sobeys works through a subtle form of paternalism. "They do it very, very subtly. It's a constant campaign to short-cut the union. Sobeys don't want a lot of arbitrations and fighting. They're smart enough to realize that this only builds strength within the union. . . . When they opened a new store here in Saint John, they hired all full-time employees from outside the province. They got paid more than the union contract. And then when they hired new employees, these ones were told in no uncertain terms that this store isn't unionized, and should it become unionized, then the company would have to think about less staff. Or, in one of the stores, there were profit-sharing plans and pension. The non-union employees got them and the union ones didn't. The good side of Sobeys always has an edge to it. I don't see them as any less fair, and even, in some cases, even more fair than, say, Dominion, or some of the others. If an employee has a particular problem, they'd probably bend over farther to assist. But it's just this: don't get organized. Sobeys wants it to be what Sobeys *gives* them, they don't want the employees to decide on their own what they want. . . . Like, maybe they'd even give somebody a couple of days off with pay, if they wanted to get a moose licence or something. In a non-union store, they would remind him, 'Now, if there was a union here, we couldn't do that because then we'd have to do it for everybody.' It's just things like that. It's really a thought-out, continuous campaign."

The "intrinsic charm" of the Maritimes is preserved through this kind of paternalism—but, now and again, the gloves come off. The vice-president of Sobeys Stores, D.B. Eddy, became so proficient at resisting trade unions that he established his own consulting business to help curb union sentiment. According to the union, at the time of the Newcastle strike, Eddy lectured his employees "as if they were naughty school children."

Farmers are caught in the same web of paternalism. The Sobeys have an image, carefully cultivated, of being only a slightly bigger version of the hardworking, dependable Maritime farmer. Reflecting on how he learned about business, Frank Sobey told the *Financial Post:* "I learned you had to know all the costs that went into a product, then price it a little higher, so, like the farmer, you would have seed for the next year and the year after." To the ever-receptive *Chronicle-Herald* he remarked: "I think I learned more sound business practices as a boy and young man dealing with farmers than I could have learned any other place."

It is a comforting image, but it does not explain the structural crisis of Canadian agriculture. It does not explain why a giant empire can flourish where so many ordinary farmers are being driven into bankruptcy.

Brewster Kneen, a farmer in Pictou County, Nova Scotia observes that the problem is not really Sobeys—it is the whole structure of the system. "Very early on with Northumberland Co-op, I got acquainted with the head meat merchandizer for Sobeys. I have to say that after five years, we as farmers couldn't ask for a better person to deal with. . . . If Northumberland Co-op was willing to organize sheep farmers, then Sobeys was delighted to deal with us. . . . People from outside would have a hard time understanding how a supplier with such a miniscule commodity—lamb—could in fact get along with such a giant. Because of their particular buying policy and an interest in the welfare of local producers, farmers here have received the best prices in Canada for their lamb. But at the same time, we have to look at the larger context. The first load of lamb that I recall marketing was sold to Sobeys for $2.00, and now four years later our current prices are still the same. Meanwhile, our hydro and machinery costs have at least doubled, not to mention interest rates. Now that's not Sobey's fault, that is the entire marketing system for the red meat industry."

Now that Maritimers have become the subjects of this invisible empire, this paternalism will have an impact far beyond the farms and supermarkets of the region. The response of the Sobeys empire to the restructuring of the fishery was simply a bigger version of the same mode of operations that has long governed Sobeys Stores. Like the Sobeys workers, we will all find ourselves being lectured on the evils of outside agitators, and taught to admire the fatherlike entrepreneur and, like trusting children, to accept the leadership of this invisible empire, "leading the way" for the people of the region.

There may be an alternative. If enough people learned that production for profit in agriculture is destructive of human communities the world over, they would be less easily persuaded that the Sobeys are heroes. If people reflected on the huge mark-ups in grocery stores and the perilous position of Maritime farmers, they'd start demanding a more rational system for farmers and consumers. If enough people realized the damage the Sobeys empire has done to the workers in the region, Empire Company Limited could be forced to recognize the rights of trade unions to exist.

In the end, mythology can't cover over all the realities people see around them every day. It can't completely remove the evidence that the system by which Sobeys has profited so well is undemocratic and irrational.

The Sobeys have indeed been "leading the way," but is this really where we want to go?

Further Reading: Agriculture

History

Conrad, Margaret. "Apple Blossom Time in the Annapolis Valley, 1880-1957." *Acadiensis* 9, No. 2 (Spring 1980): 14-39.

Jannsen, W. "Agriculture in Transition." In V. Smitheram et al., eds., *The Garden Transformed: Prince Edward Island, 1945-1980* (Charlottetown, 1982), pp. 115-129.

Sinclair, Peter R. "From Peasants to Corporations: The Development of Capitalist Agriculture in Canada's Maritime Provinces." In John A. Fry, ed., *Contradictions in Canadian Society* (Toronto, 1984), pp. 276-291.

Winson, Anthony. "The uneven development of Canadian agriculture: farming in the Maritimes and Ontario." *Canadian Journal of Sociology* 10, No. 4 (Fall 1985): 411-38.

Theory

Chevalier, Jacques. "There Is Nothing Simple About Simple Commodity Production." *Studies in Political Economy,* No. 7 (Winter 1982): 89-124.

Hedley, Max J. "Independent commodity production and the dynamics of tradition." *Canadian Review of Sociology and Anthropology* 13, No. 4 (November 1976): 413-21.

Lianos, Theodore P. "Concentration and Centralization of Capital in Agriculture." *Studies in Political Economy,* No. 14 (Summer 1984): 99-116.

Present Perspectives

Begley, Lorraine. "Canada Packers—The Citizenship of Selfishness." *New Maritimes* (December 1982): 5-6.

Burge, Irene, and Phelan, Reg. "Slaughterhouse Jive." *New Maritimes* (March 1985): 7-8.

Burge, Marie. "Shooting Pool with the P.E.I. Milk Marketing Board." *New Maritimes* (April 1984): 9-10.

MacLean, Eleanor O'Donnell. *Leading the Way: An Unauthorized Guide to the Sobey Empire* (Halifax, 1985).

McLaren, K. "Farmers, Feds and Fries: Potato Farming in the St. John Valley." *Round One*, No. 7 (March 1977).

Peabody, George. *Sustainable Agriculture* (Halifax: Ecology Action Centre, 1982).

Senopi Consultants. *Report on the Situation of New Brunswick Potato*

Farmers for the National Farmers Union (Petit Rocher: mimeo, 1980).

Sharpe, Jean. "A Time to Weigh the Costs—Pesticides in P.E.I." *New Maritimes* (November 1983): 7-8.

Part II

Fishing

Introduction:
"The Tragedy of the Commons"
or the Common Tragedies of Capital?

Picture a pasture open to all, a commons that every herdsman is entitled to use. The rational herdsman concludes that the only sensible course for him or her to pursue is to add another animal to his herd, and another, and another. It is to be expected that each herdsman will try to keep as many cattle as possible on the common pasture, and therein lies the "tragedy of the commons." Each person is locked into a system that compels him to increase his herd without limit in a world that is, unfortunately, limited. Freedom in a commons brings ruin to all. Ruin is the destination towards which all the herdsmen would rush, each pursuing his own best interest in a society that believes in the freedom of the commons (Baden and Hardin 1977).

The "tragedy of the commons" has been a recurring motif in the politics of the North Atlantic fishery. It has been used as much by policymakers regulating the fishery as by academics interpreting its history. For many interpreters and policymakers, it is the very nature of this resource—probably the most important sector of any in shaping the history and culture of the Atlantic region—that has created the unique contours of the fishing industry. What other "private enterprise" industry, they ask, relies on common property which migrates blithely across the lines drawn by sovereign nation-states, government departments, and groups of fishermen? Open access to a common-property resource led to what the industry's greatest historian, Harold Innis, called the "inherently divisive" nature of the fishery. Nations, rival mercantile groups, and often-divided groups of inshore and offshore fishermen competed for the same resource. Ultimately, Innis argued, the divisiveness of the fishery weighed heavily against the region's ability to adapt and adjust to the industrial realities of the twentieth century (Innis 1978).

Another peculiarity of the present-day fishery is the high visibility of the federal government. What other privately owned industry has been governed so directly and so comprehensively by the federal government, acting through the Department of Fisheries and Oceans? Again, most interpretations of the fishery stress that this state policy is rooted in the state's fear that profits would be diminished, stocks depleted, and the economic rent (the difference between total harvesting cost and sustainable revenue) dissipated if things were simply allowed to take their own course. Too many herdsmen destroy the commons; too many harvesters imperil a common-access fishery. Access must, accordingly, be limited and planned by the state. These imperatives have, it is argued, moulded the unique patterns found today in the North Atlantic fishery.

The nature of the resource base is obviously important, and no interpretation could realistically overlook it. Partly because of the open access of the resource, the fishery has indeed been immensely divisive throughout its history, as rival governments, capitalists, and fishermen struggle to maximize their economic rewards. This competitive pressure has diminished fish stocks and, although the region continues to rely very heavily on the fishery, fishing has proved disappointing as an engine of economic growth. Situated close to one of the greatest renewable sources of food energy in the world, the fishing industry, our oldest resource industry and the lifeline of coastal communities in all four provinces, has, for some reason, been plagued by poverty, instability, and conflict. For many, the responsibility for this failure lies in the flawed character of the resource itself.

The chapters in Part II argue that this interpretation is at best only half right. Rick Williams, in two chapters on the state's response to the recent crisis of the fishery, suggests that corporate strategies and a capitalist state's reluctance to go to the roots of the industry's crisis lie at the heart of the problem. Bernie Conway suggests that one critical factor is the abdication of the provincial government from any effective role in the P.E.I. industry. Mary Boyd, looking at the P.E.I. Irish moss industry—not, strictly speaking, "fishing," but included in this section because its participants are closely bound to the fishing industry—suggests that the struggles over this marine resource have had more to do with multinational price wars than with the resource itself.

As these chapters suggest, the peculiar character of the resource gives us only half the fishery equation. The other half is the structure of economic and political power, a structure which has, throughout the history of the fishery, brought the interests of capital and the state into direct contradiction with the goal of preserving fish stocks and the communities dependent upon them. The tragedy of the fishery is a complex series of tragedies rooted in the basic contradiction between the individual producers' interests in conserving the resource on which their future depends, and capital's inherent tendency to overexploit the resource in the interest of its profits and further expansion.

The history of capitalism in the North Atlantic fishery falls into two periods. The first, from 1500 to about 1880, was the period of "mercantilism," when the basic structure of today's fishing industry took shape. Control over the region's most important fisheries lay in the hands of European merchants, and the region's salt cod trade came to occupy an important position in such markets as Spain, Portugal, Italy, Greece, Brazil, and the Caribbean (Ryan 1986). Two externally based merchant groups stand out in the mercantile period. Both had strategies to guarantee their profits by monopolizing the resource. The Westcountrymen, from the western extremity of England, played a decisive role in the settlement and economy of Newfoundland. At least initially, they discouraged settlement in order to avoid competition in the cod fishery from a resident population on the New-foundland coast. The Jerseymen, from the Channel Islands, operated a very different inshore fishery in a number of establishments on the Gulf of St. Lawrence. They encouraged settlement, but maintained their control over access to the fish through the "truck system." In this system, the merchant minimized competition from independent producers by providing the gear and provisions for the year's fishery, all on credit against repayment in fish at the end of the season. "The merchant took over the individual fisherman's risk of a season's capital outlay . . . [and] the fisherman in return guaranteed to sell his catch to the merchant" (Ommer 1981, 111). Thanks to the truck system, in no other staple trade was access to the resource so immediately open, and in no other way was it so tightly monopolized by merchants' capital.

The consequences of the truck system for regional development were grave. Found in many parts of the region, from the Gaspé to Newfoundland, the truck system varied according to whether the merchant house exercised complete or only partial domination over the fishermen (Samson 1984). Although it succeeded in saving merchants from the overcompetition implied by the "tragedy of the commons," it also meant that the profits from the fishery benefited only the foreign-controlled industry, and not the people of the dependent fishing communities, who survived largely without roads, schools, or medical facilities. "In other words," writes historian Rosemary Ommer, "in the merchant's solution to his problem of making a profit out of the fishery lay the roots of regional under-development. Either the merchant business or the region could grow, but not both, since the merchant's solution required the removal of backward and final demand staple linkages if he were to maintain control of the resource" (Ommer 1985, 127).

The industrialism that replaced this old mercantile pattern after 1880 did so in a very halting and uneven manner—so much so that remnants of the truck system could still be found in mid-twentieth-century Newfoundland. In some parts of the Maritimes, especially Nova Scotia, the transition occurred in the nineteenth century. From the 1880s to 1900 the truck system fell in many communities, as capital poured in to take advantage of the region's abundant lobster resource, with the inevitable result that capitalist-oriented lobster "clearcutting" started to undermine the stocks. Despite this "progress," industrialization of the Nova Scotia fishing industry lagged far behind that of New England, depended on cheap labour and cheap raw materials, and left the social costs associated with training and with maintaining meagre living standards on the shoulders of the fishing family (Barrett 1979, 132). The merchants had controlled access to the fishery through the truck system, but industrial capital concentrated its control in processing, transportation, and marketing.

The Second World War transformed the fishing industry even further by intensifying the drive to industrialization. The most startling development of the 1940s was the restructuring and consolidation of Canadian capital into one vast monopoly, National Sea Products, which became the largest organization on the Atlantic coast of North America engaged in the production and processing of fish. *Modernization* became the key word of the 1950s and 1960s. In Newfoundland, the federal government presided over a steady postwar decline in salt-fish production (Alexander 1976), while whole communities were uprooted in a provincial resettlement program intended to rationalize social services and create "growth poles." State policy came to embrace a strategy of heavy investment in draggers, trawling gear, cold-storage plants, and an experimental inshore boat design, the longliner (Barrett 1984, 79).

Like any corporation, National Sea Products expanded in response to rising market values. Although fish landings dropped from 1959-61, market values soared between 1960 and 1963, prompting a massive expansion, including construction of the largest fish-processing plant in North America in 1964 (Barrett 1984, 86). Bolstered by lavish subsidies and driven by the promise of high profits, National Sea pursued a policy of frenzied overexpansion and increased specialization. Although most species of groundfish were in decline from 1969 onward, National Sea embarked on expansion into Newfoundland, with a large new plant and a new vessel design for trawlers. The state paid for National Sea's rapid expansion, while the company achieved multinational status with its American and Bermudian holdings. The inevitable crises in fish stocks (also partially caused by the activities of foreign trawlers) led, not to serious reappraisals of fishing strategy, but to further government bail-outs. Since 1960 the industry has followed an apparent six to seven year cycle of boom and bust (Macdonald 1984). The 1981 groundfish crisis, which prompted the state interventions studied in two of the chapters which follow, was merely the latest, albeit an unusually severe, instalment in the tumultuous history of capital in this sector.

Did the character of the resource determine the nature of the industry that was built on it? Only to a limited extent, argue those who have studied one fascinating counterexample, that of Iceland. While the Newfoundland government adopted an economic model of heavy, land-based industrialization and hesitated to break the hold of the merchants, and while Ottawa restricted itself to a minor role, in Iceland an interventionist state moved in the early twentieth century to build a strong fishing industry. The result is that, drawing on much the same resource as the Atlantic region, the Icelandic fishery (paralleled by that of Norway) has been able to sustain one of the highest standards of living in the world.

The key to so much of the history of the fishing industry is the federal state. In Newfoundland, which was independent of Canada until 1949, the island's government missed the chance to develop a diversified economy on the basis of the staple. In the Maritimes, the federal state intervened to protect stocks but not to structure the industry.

The federal state now plays an immensely powerful role in the industry. The declaration of the 200-mile limit in 1977, the active management of fish stocks and the issuing of licences, the setting of policies regarding freezer trawlers and the allocation of access to such resources as the northern cod stocks—in all these spheres, the state plays a uniquely direct role in the industry. Yet it does not, finally, manage patterns of investment, and these are a vital contributing factor to the industry's destructive cycles of expansion and collapse. "To manage only one half of the industry is a rather futile exercise," remarks L.G. Barrett. "Until public ownership is asserted over the production and marketing sectors of the industry, the age-old problems associated with fragmentation, consignment selling, and low prices will continue to impoverish producers and workers alike. Until that form of control is exercised, capital will continue to blackmail the state for greater quotas or extensions of resource boundaries. Pressures will continually re-emerge for re-evaluations of fishery policy, particularly when factions of capital can garner the support of provincial states" (Barrett 1984, 97). Fortunately, since the war, these factions of capital have been opposed by vigorous unions which, especially in the case of Newfoundland, have proven themselves quite capable of presenting alternative perspectives on the fishery (Inglis 1985).

Do we face in the North Atlantic fishery the tragedy of the commons, or do we not in fact face one of the very common tragedies of capital in the region, the contradiction between ecologically and socially responsible resource management and the corporate pursuit of profits?

One insightful anthropological investigation into the ways in which a fishing community actually manages access to the fishing resource points out that we cannot simply assume, as the "tragedy of the commons" perspective invites us to do, that local producers will exhaust resources in a competitive and destructive dash for the spoils. Local fishing communities have evolved systems of informal property rights that reduce competition among those holding rights of access to the resource—a collective form of management at the opposite pole of the economists' simplistic and abstract model of self-interested individuals maximizing utilities and damning the social and ecological consequences (Davis 1984). It would only be by generalizing from this unwritten but real form of community control to a model of co-management in which the state and primary producers participated equally, and by drastically limiting if not eliminating the role of capital, that the region's fishing industry might be relieved of its disastrous, seven-year cycles of expansion and collapse.

The stakes for the region are high. According to the Kirby Report, 84,558 people in the region resided in full-time fishermen's households—46,911 in Newfoundland, 8,080 in New Brunswick, 5,142 in P.E.I., and 24,324 in Nova Scotia. An additional 58,663 people resided in part-time fishermen's households—35,984 in Newfoundland, 9,386 in New Brunswick, 3,072 in P.E.I., and 10,220 in Nova Scotia. The Report estimates that there are 1,300 small fishing communities in the region, and at least one-third of the active labour force in these communities is engaged in fishing or fish-processing work (Canada, Task Force on Atlantic Fisheries, 1983, 64 and 23). The industry is particularly crucial for women, who make up a high percentage of workers in fish packing, where they often work under poor conditions at low rates of pay. Since the recent "restructuring" required no basic change in the way capital and the state go fishing, it is likely that all these producers, workers, and communities will continue to suffer from the industry's established record of boom and bust.

The fishery is a complex of species, interests, classes, and technologies. It will never be entirely predictable. The question remains, however, whether it can ever be freed from capital's cycles of expansion and collapse. It is to these aspects of the structure of the fishery, rather than just to the intrinsic nature of the resource base, that we should look for answers to the key question: Why is a coastal region that has so long attracted the fishing fleets of the world unable to make its own fishing industry secure and prosperous?

The Poor Man's Machiavelli: Michael Kirby and the Atlantic Fisheries

Rick Williams

Niccolo Machiavelli was a brilliant Italian political writer who hung around princes and despots in the sixteenth century and advised them on how to manipulate the people to gain their devious ends. Michael Kirby might well be his twentieth-century reincarnation.

Kirby first came to national attention in 1981 when he was Pierre Trudeau's chief advisor on federal-provincial relations. In the heat of the battle over the Constitution, a memo was leaked in which Kirby coolly and cynically proposed that the differences among the provinces be exploited to make them look infantile and quarrelsome. The feds would then have public support to ignore the provinces and act unilaterally on the Charter of Rights and patriation of the Constitution. Kirby had led off the report with a suitable quotation from Machiavelli. The press had a field day, making much of Kirby's connection with the ruthless Italian schemer.

Later, Michael Kirby had another hour upon the stage, this time as the principal author of *Navigating Troubled Waters: A New Policy for the Atlantic Fisheries.* This was the report of the Task Force on Atlantic Fisheries that Kirby had chaired, and which had been working since early 1982 to develop a complete and largely new policy framework in response to the major economic crisis gripping the entire east coast fishery.

Kirby looked like a winner. The response to the report was largely positive, and if a few dissident voices were heard here and there, the press seemed fully prepared to depict Kirby as the potential saviour of the industry, the wise and judicious technocrat who had risen above factional squabbles to solve the problems confronting all sectors of the fishery. Nobody seemed to notice that, near the beginning of the summary version of the report, Kirby had quoted Machiavelli once again: "The great majority of mankind are satisfied with appearances, as though they were realities, and are often more influenced by the things that seem than by those that are." The apparent intention of this reference is to express a view which recurs again and again throughout the report: We are being rational, we are looking at the facts, dealing with the realities, impartially and objectively. Everyone else is expressing their ignorance and/or their narrow interests.

More than anything else in the report, the background information, the

This chapter is based on an article first published in *New Maritimes* (March 1983).

thoroughness, or the recommendations themselves, this arrogant confidence in the unbiased expertise of the policymaker—as expressed, of course, by the policymaker himself—stands out. Kirby is a master of a very old, very Machiavellian trick. According to his report, all participants in the fisheries debates are "ideological." All of them "use exaggeration and slogans that obscure issues and discourage rational debate." All of them, that is, except Kirby himself. By some miracle Kirby the Rational rose above such petty partisanship and exaggerations.

As a policy framework which purports to take into account the interests of all sectors of the industry and, indeed, of the society of the Maritimes and Newfoundland as a whole, the Kirby Report is very likely a shell game, a masterful illusion. Both in itself, and in the politics of its implementation, it has succeeded in creating the appearance of reform, accountability to the whole community, and structural change, without addressing the reality of corporate dominance and the powerlessness and marginality of the great majority of workers and primary producers in the industry. The Kirby Report represents a major disappointment, if not a setback, for the following reasons:

1. The report aims to further accelerate monopoly control. It proposes no significant changes in the corporate structure of the industry or in the overall direction of development.

2. The report proposes no major change in governments' role in the industry as guardians of the broad public interest. There are vague references to equity participation and proposals for investments in marketing efforts and infrastructure (transport, wharf facilities, etc.), but no real increase in governments' capacity to own, regulate, or control the corporate sector and the flow of capital.

3. The major recommendations affecting inshore fishermen, while making important references to the needs for improved incomes and collective bargaining rights, do little concretely to address the vulnerability and dependence of fishermen and their communities relative to the corporate sector. In certain key areas, the report proposes to seriously weaken and divide inshore fishermen while drawing them into a more highly integrated and "rationalized," corporate-controlled fishery. The highly publicized concessions on bargaining rights and unemployment insurance (UI) compensation regulations thus appear to be tack-ons, largely unrelated to the main themes of the report.

In January 1977, Canada set in place the 200-mile Fisheries Protective Zone. This was heralded as an historic turning point for the badly underdeveloped east-coast fishery. The 200-mile zone would for the time first make effective conservation and resource management practical possibilities. It would also remove the foreign fleets that were strip mining the fish stocks and keeping Canadian inshore and offshore fishermen in the poorhouse. Now the fish would be all ours and, presumably, since we had expelled our competitors, so would the markets to sell them.

For a few years it looked like the dream was coming true. Catches and earnings increased dramatically, and millions of investment dollars flowed into the industry from 1977-81. There was much dynamism in the corporate sector as new plants were opened, as new vessels were purchased, and as smaller companies were taken over by the giants. With this boom in the fishery came new stresses and strains. The larger companies constantly pressed for a greater share of the fish stocks to feed their massive investments in big draggers and new plants. Inshore fishermen in turn became more organized and effective in fighting to protect their precarious livings. In Newfoundland the fishermen's union emerged as a power in the politics of the industry, and in the Maritimes the Maritime Fishermen's Union got a solid start in New Brunswick, and has since developed a real presence in Prince Edward Island and Nova Scotia.

The federal Minister of Fisheries throughout the period, Romeo LeBlanc, played a curious and perhaps critical role in resisting the pressures of the larger companies in the policy sphere. LeBlanc seemed to maintain an alternative vision of a more balanced fishery which would provide maximal employment and social benefits in the rural fishing communities of the region. Under his regime, licences were frozen for new company draggers, the large vessels were restricted in the Gulf of St. Lawrence, and fishermen's organizations were encouraged.

By 1981, high interest rates and recessionary conditions had brought the mini-boom to a dramatic conclusion. Markets had stagnated and fishermen's incomes at all levels were seriously jeopardized. Most serious of all was the crisis in the corporate sector. Three out of the big four processors in the region—H.B. Nickerson's Ltd. in Nova Scotia and Fisheries Products Ltd. and the Lake Group in Newfoundland—were rumoured to be in severe financial straits, if not bankruptcy. Only National Sea Products Ltd., ostensibly owned by Nickerson's, was surviving intact. Since these companies provided the lion's share of the processing and marketing for the industry as a whole, their imminent collapse was clearly a major threat to the economy of the region.

The companies were calling for massive injections of government money to get them through this crisis, and it became clear that the feds were going to have to put up some pretty hefty sums (rumour had set the figure at $1 billion for the bail-out and the new investment needed). Having come to their rescue twice before in the previous decade, the government was reluctant this time to just turn over the money and let the companies carry on as before.

It was in this context that the Kirby Task Force was formed and given a mandate. If the federal government had wanted to continue to prop up the companies, they could have simply handed over the funds. The fact that they didn't suggests that LeBlanc and others were successful in convincing the Cabinet that all or most of the companies were not competent to carry the major responsibility for rebuilding the industry, and that major government intervention aimed at restructuring the entire fishery was called for. To many observers, the Task Force initiative seemed like it might possibly be one of those unusual historic events from which lasting and positive change could emerge. Hope springs eternal.

The terms of reference for the Task Force specifically enjoined it to "proceed on an urgent basis" in light of the severity of the crisis. It was to "inquire into and report upon the current conditions and future directions of the Atlantic Coast fisheries" with regard to three problem areas: industry and corporate structure, government policy and regulations, and the social context of the Atlantic fishery. The Task Force was to report to an ad hoc Committee of Ministers, which included the new Fisheries Minister, Pierre DeBané; Romeo LeBlanc; Gerald Regan; and the new economic development super-minister, Don Johnson. It was to produce a blueprint for "how to achieve and maintain a viable Atlantic fishing industry, with due consideration for the overall economic and social development of the Atlantic provinces." It was to present worked-up policy options concerning corporate structure, "degrees of private sector versus public sector involvement," and several other problem areas. In short, Kirby had a mandate to radically alter the whole basis of development in the fishing industry, which in turn would have a massive effect upon the regional economy. It was an historic opportunity, a watershed—and he blew it.

A lot of people were very impressed with the personnel of the Task Force and the speed with which it was set up. Kirby would chair the committee, whose other members included Peter J. Nicholson, a vice-president of H.B. Nickerson's Ltd.; Victor Rabinovitch, a senior Canadian Labour Congress staff member; Art May, a widely respected fisheries bureaucrat; and Father Des McGrath, a long-standing leader of fishermen's organizations in Newfoundland and a co-founder with Richard Cashin of the Newfoundland Fishermen Food and Allied Workers Union. The Task Force held literally hundreds of meetings with fishermen's organizations and local groups, with processors and advisory bodies and individual spokespersons. Fishermen particularly were impressed with the thoroughness, preparation, attentiveness, and obvious hard work of the Task Force representatives.

Three very important independent research studies were also commissioned by the Task Force. One was a survey of incomes and expenditures of over 1,000 fishermen which has produced the best data to date on this key problem area. A second examined the revenues and costs of 100 fish plants, and a third analyzed marketing conditions for groundfish (cod, haddock, redfish, and other bottom-feeding species) and herring.

The report was originally due in late summer, but the Task Force extended its work into the fall. The report had evidently been written by November, but its publication was repeatedly postponed. "Informed sources" reported that the Cabinet was split on the recommendations dealing with the financial crisis of the companies. When the report was finally released on February

17th, Pierre DeBané simultaneously announced that all of its 57 recommendations had been accepted by the government except one having to do with authority over licensing and a few others on marketing. He then explained that the issue of financial aid to the companies was also on hold pending further study and decisions by another ad hoc ministerial committee. Kirby had not provided the answers they wanted, and so this major element in the overall process—perhaps the most important element—was left unresolved.

The Kirby Report is quite candid and provides useful information on the corporate structure of the industry. It points out that:

> Among other Canadian food industries only one, poultry processing, is more concentrated than fish processing. The marketing of Atlantic Canadian groundfish and herring is even more concentrated than the processing sector. This concentration has increased over the past decade. In 1978 the four largest firms . . . produced 63% of all Atlantic Canadian groundfish and marketed 70%. These firms marketed 90% of frozen fillets and 85% of blocks. . . . National Sea Products, with sales of $314 million in 1981, is the largest seafood organization in the countries of the North Atlantic (p. 52).

In another section of the report, Kirby graphically expresses what many see as the basic inadequacy of the corporate structure in the region:

> A combination of an historically weak financial structure, severe losses in 1980 and 1981, and excessive borrowing to finance expansion and to cover losses has left the processing sector in an exceptionally weak financial position. Although the problem is industry-wide, it is most severe amongst the offshore groundfish processors, in particular the large companies with extensive operations in Newfoundland. Unless financial assistance is made available, a number of major companies will go bankrupt (p. 121).

For over a decade, critics have been attacking the development strategy employed by government and the corporate sector because the rapid shift to large-scale harvesting and processing facilities seemed likely to overburden the industry with "foreign" debt. Like all primary industries, the fishery is subject to cycles of boom and bust, and too much debt load would force overexploitation of the fish stocks just to maintain the necessary cash flow. This is the real reason why "quality" is such a big issue.

Although fishermen and perhaps even Cabinet ministers were looking for a possible reversal of these long-standing and clearly inadequate industry structures, Kirby has provided a very weak and hesitant response. The report specifically recommends that government not establish "a new general program of financial assistance for either fishermen or processors." The private money markets will remain the principal source of investment capital.

There is provision, as mentioned, for some form of emergency intervention:

> The Task Force is engaged in negotiations that are expected to lead to a restructuring of those offshore processing companies that are virtually insolvent at the present time. The restructuring of the assets of these companies into a viable company (or companies) may only be able to be achieved with an infusion of government funds, most likely by way of government equity. But this assistance should be a one-time effort only, after which the resulting business should stand on its own (p. 123).

The main message here is between the lines. First of all, Kirby himself has recommended no government takeover, and his bias is clearly in favour of continued private-sector dominance in the industry, including opening the door for the re-entry of direct foreign investment under specific conditions.

More important, this most crucial area of Kirby's blueprint is being negotiated with the provincial governments, the companies, and the banks. Whereas all the other aspects of the policy were in effect decreed after broad consultation, and supposedly all fit together, this element is to be negotiated with the very people whose limited competence and narrow interests have generated the massive problems documented by the report.

The Kirby Task Force split into two planning processes—one for workers and fishermen, and a separate, much more secretive one for the companies and the banks. This second policy debate—with options ranging all the way from nationalization to letting the three biggies go bankrupt—had all the makings of the major ideological battle that Kirby has taken such great pains to avoid.

To give Kirby his due, he recognizes the need for unions and urges Nova Scotia and Prince Edward Island to allow collective bargaining rights to inshore fishermen. Moreover, the research done for the Task Force has generated excellent new information. The Task Force concludes, for example, taking all income sources into account, that almost one-third of the households of full-time fishermen have total incomes below Canada's official rural poverty line, and estimates that 40 percent of the households of part-time fishermen have total incomes below the rural poverty line.

But apart from overdue recognition of collective bargaining rights, the report's three other strategies for improving incomes—reduction in the number of both full-time and part-time fishermen, changes in such transfer programs as UI, and improving earnings through upgrading the quality of fish—conceal threats to the long-term interests of inshore fishermen. Changes from a system of licensing of boats and gear to one of licensing individual inshore fishermen by the species they fish regardless of gear type would, according to Kirby, result in higher quality products, more efficient use of technologies, less cut-throat competition for stocks, and more effective stock management. However, such quota licences would be a "quasi-property right," and any fisherman could sell his or her quota, or could buy quota from others. This raises the spectre of a "rationalization" of the inshore fishery as drastic as that which has virtually decimated agriculture, with no guarantee of higher earnings for the fishermen who remain. (A safer alternative would be to separate the issue of the quota licence from property rights and market pressures, and simply to develop a mechanism for determining the optimal number of fishermen in a given area for a given species.) Similarly, while Kirby's recommendations for unemployment insurance changes seem favourable for fishermen, his long-term goal is to make unemployment insurance unnecessary through improved earnings and bonus payments for quality. Again, one smells a rat, since virtually all full-time fishermen can get their stamps for unemployment insurance, while the benefits of a bonus system or price subsidy based on quality would be unequally distributed and place greater pressure on those on the bottom rungs of the ladder. Finally, although schemes for improving fish quality are unobjectionable, the report contains no clear analysis of how this would affect the fishermen's costs.

No one should be deceived by the appearance of "scientific" neutrality the new Machiavelli has given these conservative recommendations. Ducking the issue of a major government role in winning new markets or rebuilding the processing sector, the Kirby Task Force, for all its good research and limited reforms, returns strategies for the fisheries to reliance on unregulated market forces and monopoly capitalist structures.

The public ownership option to these strategies has major drawbacks and itself offers no guarantee of a better deal for plant workers and fishermen. However, it does offer a greater opportunity for stabilization, rational planning, and adequate resource management. It might well provide a far more solid ground on which workers and primary producers could struggle for security, adequate incomes, and a say over their lives.

The Restructuring That Wasn't:
The Scandal at National Sea

Rick Williams

A few years ago I received an invitation to have lunch with the publisher and editor of the Toronto *Globe and Mail*. They were on a fact-finding tour of the Maritimes preparatory to establishing their new identity as Canada's national newspaper. In particular, they were developing editorial policy on the fishing industry and, said the local *Globe* reporter who set it up, wanted to pick my brains about the inshore sector.

The lunch was both free and enlightening. Declining the mandatory martini in order to maintain maximum clarity, I launched into an analysis of the problems and potential of the inshore fishery. I described the industry as being in transition from traditional semi-subsistence production to modern, integrated production and marketing structures dominated by a few large companies. I argued that greed and poor planning on the part of the companies, supported by federal and provincial governments, had destabilized and threatened to destroy the inshore sector. The inshore fishery, I pressed home, was essential to the fishing industry and to regional society overall.

Just as I was hitting my stride, one of the *Globe* heavies cut me off. I was wrong, he explained very condescendingly. He and his colleague had met with the Nickersons (at H.B. Nickerson & Sons Ltd.), the Morrows (at National Sea Products Ltd.), the provincial Minister of Fisheries, and federal officials, and they knew where it was really at. There were too many fishermen, their methods were backward, and they were seriously limiting the profitability of the big companies because government policies were biased in their favour. He asked me rhetorically whether I proposed to sacrifice the development of a modern industry just to perpetuate a romantic way of life.

It was not a question of romantic versus realistic, I insisted, rising to the red herring, because the massive corporate expansion model was not going to work. The companies had financed their growth, not through gradual reinvestment of surpluses from successful operations but through heavy borrowing. The industry was still chronically underdeveloped as capitalist industries go, and the margins were too low to sustain such dramatic increases in capital costs. Fishing had always been a boom-and-bust industry. Sometimes the fish didn't show up to be caught, for reasons only the fish could know. Stocks could be seriously depleted through overfishing. Markets were extremely

This chapter is based on an article first published in *New Martimes* (April 1984).

unstable. In any given year the industry was vulnerable to changes in currency exchange rates, price competition with chicken and beef products, and the comings and goings of competitor countries in the major U.S. market. The in-shore industry, I concluded, was much better geared to these realities in terms of capitalization methods, appropriate technologies, and the ability to adjust to changes in fish stocks and markets. The offshore industry was a whale in a china shop.

This was my best stuff, delivered with flair, conviction, and appropriate mumbo jumbo. At the least, I expected some respect. Instead, two Upper Canadian noses went up in the air, sniffed, and abruptly changed the subject. As I remember it, the brief remainder of the lunch was occupied with in-depth analysis of the Leafs' playoff chances. Nice to meet you, Mr. Williams, very interesting. Now screw off.

So, this is the way editorial policy gets set by "Canada's national newspaper." A couple of senior people come and meet other senior people. Dissident voices are edited out or ignored, and a lot of liquor is slung around to cement the bonding of regional elites. The *Globe* says, "the East is strong," and important people on the boards of banks and stockbrokers' firms conclude, presumably, that the East is in fact strong.

Less than four years later the Nickersons, the Morrows, and the other big fish companies were all bankrupt. There is general recognition that they expanded too fast, invested too heavily, and borrowed too much.

Meanwhile, I was waiting in vain for a call from Richard Doyle, Editor, and Roy Megarry, Publisher, to say "You were right, Rick, we should have listened," or maybe another lunch so I could give them the goods on oil and gas.

Before we can do anything about the real problems in the fishing industry or the regional economy, we have to get ourselves into better touch with reality. The trouble with understanding reality, as the computer programmers say, is "garbage in: garbage out." If all the information we get is wrong, those of us who don't have access to better facts and ideas have to work with what we've got, and with the predictable results. To change reality, we have to learn from our collective experience; but if our experience is interpreted for us by incompetents or court jesters, we learn false lessons.

The mainstream media in the Atlantic region, including the *Globe*, combines good, objective reporting of facts with wild, wishful thinking about what they really mean. Bankrupt for new understandings, the people who control the economy keep trying all the things that have never worked before, each time on a grander, more ridiculous scale. The response from the media peanut gallery, almost invariably, is wild applause. The emperor's new clothes are not just admired by the media, they are stitched together with loving attention to detail.

In an article entitled "The Nickerson Empire," in June 1979, the *Atlantic Advocate* hailed the emergence of H.B. Nickerson Ltd. as "one of the biggest conglomerates in eastern Canada." According to the *Atlantic Advocate*, "The Nickerson organization recognizes the responsibilities of its corporate citizenship in Atlantic Canada, is cognizant of its role in developing and protecting the fishery resource and its responsibility for developing new markets and new products."

After extensively describing how wonderfully big the Nickerson empire is, the article provided Jerry Nickerson with a platform for promoting his own self-interest as the interest of every person in the region and every fish in the North Atlantic:

> The private sector should assume responsibility toward achieving the greatest economic benefits reasonably possible from the fishery and also discharge its responsibilities to those for whom the fishery is a way of life. . . . Ottawa should encourage [i.e., provide lots of money for] investment in commercial fishing vessels, encourage private Canadian ownership and operation of handling, processing, freezing and cold storage facilities, as well as encourage more private enterprise in foreign marketing.

The *Atlantic Advocate* article epitomizes the regional media's treatment of fundamental economic issues: The future is bright. We must trust our own local business elite. They have our interests at heart. Government is a necessary evil which should obey the direction of the far more knowledgeable, competent, and efficient private sector. Public enterprise will surely fail.

As a consequence of this profound bias in the interpretation of our collective experience, people in the Maritimes and Newfoundland have not been led to question the policies and power plays which have been jeopardizing their economic futures. Although even an amateur like myself could see fundamental problems in the structure of the fishing industry, and government reports were full of foreboding, all the public got was the good news. The Maritimes—Fantasyland of the East.

In 1977 the federal government set up the 200-mile protective zone, effectively establishing a monopoly for Canadian fish companies over the richest fishing grounds in the world. A lot of money had already been flowing into the industry in anticipation of a boom.

The largest, most modern fish company was National Sea Products Ltd., controlled by the Morrow family, which owned only a minority of its shares. In 1976 a struggle for control involving the great capitalist families of Nova Scotia began—the Morrows, Smiths, and Connors in one group (all traditional fish entrepreneurs); the Jodreys (agriculture and pulp and power in the Valley); and the Sobeys (groceries in Pictou County). Everyone was shocked when, in late 1977, it was the H.B. Nickerson group from North Sydney which won outright control. Gerry Regan, then premier, described it as a "horse swallowing an elephant."

In the light of the 1984 crisis, we know how the Nickersons had pulled off the coup. It wasn't their own money that bought control—it was hundreds of millions from the Bank of Nova Scotia. The banks wanted into the industry, and the Nickersons had convinced them that they were the boys to best run it with their money. And run it they did. Their only strategy was: Invest! Invest! After the Nickerson's takeover, investment by National Sea in trawlers increased from $2 million in 1978, to $12.7 million in 1979, and $18.3 million in 1980. Investments in land, buildings, and machinery went from $4 million in 1977, to $21 million in 1979, and $10.6 million in 1980. Long-term debt increased from zero in 1977 to $17 million in 1980. Net income fell from a $10.6 million surplus in 1978 to a $1 million dollar loss in 1980. In three short years, National Sea went from borderline profitability to gross over-capitalization and near insolvency.

The management rationalization for the massive failure of Nickerson/National Sea in 1982 is that the recession and high interest rates caught them at a bad time. They also blame the federal government for not allowing them to build even more large vessels, and for restructuring trawler operations in the Gulf, where fish stocks were already badly depleted.

The simple reality is that the Nickerson/National team was guilty of stupendous mismanagement and bad planning, and the banks even more so, for giving them all that money to play with. Recession is cyclical and inevitable in a capitalist economy, and high interest rates, as one aspect of that cycle, are just one section of the economy gaining at the expense of others. (What the banks lost in the fishing industry they gained in the mortgage market.) To blame such conditions is to say more about your own incompetence in failing to foresee them than about the economy itself.

Once Nickerson/National Sea had gotten themselves into this debt squeeze, their only way to stay afloat was to maximize production just to hold onto the cash to keep the banks at bay. The result was a strip mining of the fish stocks, producing as much as possible and pushing product onto the market as quickly as could be managed.

This was the opposite of wise planning. Most fish products from the region were being sold as frozen fish blocks to institutional markets (schools, hospitals, and prisons). Stuck with these high-volume, low market-value products, Canadian fish companies received a reputation for poor quality. Canadian fish failed to capture a strong place in the restaurant and fresh-fish market where the image of quality could be established, and the companies found themselves on a treadmill, needing to catch and market more and more fish just to maintain income.

This was bad for fish stocks, and it hurt inshore fishermen and plant workers. Prices to inshore fishermen, who depended on the big companies, were depressed. Wages were held down as well.

By 1982 the Big Five companies in the Atlantic region (Nickerson and National in Nova Scotia; and Fisheries Products Ltd., the Lake Group, and John Penny & Sons Ltd. in Newfoundland) were all bankrupt or close to it. Among them, they accounted for over 50 percent of the processing of fish in the region, and caught 75 percent of the fish they processed with their own vessels. Their crisis was therefore a crisis in the entire industry.

When the fish companies had a similar crisis in the late 1970s, the federal government bailed them out with millions of dollars of subsidies on ground-fish prices. This time the feds said there would be no more good money chasing bad. Headed by Michael Kirby, a task force was set up to recommend to the government major changes in the strucutre of the industry and new ways to use government money to deal with the crisis.

It is much clearer now than it was when the Kirby Report was published in 1983 that the best intentions of the government to bring real change have been largely defeated, at least in the Maritimes. The biggest issue was ducked by the report. Kirby promised further negotiations on restructuring of the companies, but without any guarantee of a stronger government role. Although it was clear from the beginning that the feds would eventually step in to keep the companies afloat, the issue to be decided was whether it would be another giveaway, or whether some real structural change and greater accountability would be purchased with the people's money.

A deal was worked out in Newfoundland first. The three bankrupt companies and some Nickerson/National assets would be put together into one new company. The federal government would invest $75 million to purchase equity and 60 percent control, while the provincial government would convert $31.5 million debt to equity with 25 percent control, and the Bank of Nova Scotia would exchange $44.1 million debt for 12 percent control. The board of the new company would have five federal representatives, three provincial appointees, one from the bank and one from the employees (that is, the Newfoundland Fishermen, Food, and Allied Workers Union).

There was a lot of rhetoric about returning to private ownership as soon as possible, but the reality was a government takeover. There was also rhetoric about a "social contract" to restrain wage demands in return for a greater say for the union at the management level. In short, the Newfoundland deal looked like a new kind of capitalism in the Atlantic region. There was a clear recognition that the private sector had failed, that state control was necessary, and that the industry might be run on a less than profit-making basis in order to maintain a viable regional economy.

In Nova Scotia, things didn't go as smoothly. A deal similar to Newfoundland's was announced in early October. A consortium was to be formed by the federal government, the Nova Scotia government, and the Bank of Nova Scotia. This new company would have total control of the bankrupt H.B. Nickerson & Sons Ltd., and therefore majority control of National Sea Products Ltd. All of Nickerson's viable fishing assets would be amalgamated into National Sea, and the federal government would invest $80 million of new capital. The province and the bank were both converting debt to equity—some $55 million from the former and $75 million from the bank. The new capital would give the consortium 75 percent control of National Sea. Again, a half-hearted government takeover with control fragmented four ways among the feds, the bank, the province and minority shareholders (the Morrows, Jodreys, Sobeys, etc.). However, the agreement was announced in Port Hawkesbury with the province in accord.

From the time of the October announcement, there evolved a complicated and somewhat hysterical struggle to prevent the *de facto* nationalization of the Nickerson/National Sea empire. The weak link in the agreement was the province. At the time of the announcement, Premier Buchanan had pointed out that, in case anyone didn't know already, "We're not socialists. We believe in the private enterprise system, and that given a chance it can work."

When the pressure mounted against the deal from the small to medium-sized fish companies, and was amplified by the media, Buchanan lost his nerve. Finally, when a group of local businessmen, headed by David Hennigar from the Jodrey group, came out of the woodwork with a ludicrous offer to take control with a measley $10 million investment, Buchanan backed out of the federal agreement.

Between December and February, there was a stand-off. The minority shareholders still had titular control of a bankrupt National Sea. They therefore set up a committee of the board to receive offers. The federal government, the only actor with real money to spend, did not have majority control without provincial and Bank of Nova Scotia co-operation, and the bank, by calling in its loans, could foreclose at any time. It had to be persuaded to delay until a deal could be worked out.

In an atmosphere of high tension, a deal for continued private control was announced in the first week of February. To make a long and complicated story short, the federal government would invest $90 million and would get 20 percent control of the equity of the new National Sea Products Ltd. The Province of Nova Scotia would invest $52 million in return for no equity. The private sector company would put up $20 million new investment and get 47 percent control. There would be a public float of new shares worth $15 million which would spread remaining control over the private sector.

The federal contribution of $90 million would be made up of $10 million immediate cash, $70 million to the Bank of Nova Scotia over five years to pay off the Nickerson's debt, and another $10 million to cover interest charges on the remaining bank debt. The valuable fishing assets of H.B. Nickerson & Sons would be contributed to National Sea as well.

The provincial government was owed $52 million by Nickerson/National Sea. It will convert $25 million to equity (on a non-voting basis), with the rest remaining an interest-free loan for five years. In addition, the new company would have the option to convert the provincial equity back to debt if it wished to avoid dividend payments.

The Toronto Dominion Bank took over the Bank of Nova Scotia's position, assuming $75 million of the debt. It will hold this in the form of a cute little item called the "difficulty preferred share" for which Revenue Canada will require no payment of taxes on the dividends—another substantial public subsidy.

By any standards, the crisis in the Nova Scotia fishing industry had been "resolved" by an outrageous scandal. The banks had been bailed out. The Nickersons received $3 million cash for their National Sea shares, so they were OK. The people of Nova Scotia, whose government was already $5 billion in debt, had handed over $50 million more to the private sector with no equity position. The people of Canada had handed over $90 million with no meaningful control over the use of this investment. No changes in the overall direction of the company were announced. There had been, in a word, no "restructuring."

Why did this happen? To understand it, we must return to the media. If any kind of "objective" analysis of the performance of the private sector in the fishing industry had been made widely known, the bankers and the corporate managers, instead of calling the shots on restructuring, would have been hiding in the furthermost reaches of the Princess mine. But when the agreement was announced in October, and the hysterical attack on government control began, the media went to work. The so-called "independents," the small to medium-sized fish plants, didn't know what they wanted. Some called for letting Nickerson/National go bankrupt. Others insisted on a return to private enterprise, even though competition with the huge company had put many of them out of business. The content mattered little—the main point was to enthusiastically endorse private enterprise and condemn government control.

Ernest Cadegan, the head of the association of independents, said 200 privately owned plants would be in jeopardy, and the October agreement represented the "destruction of the industry." Wayne Thorburne, owner of a large offshore herring seiner and director of the Southwest Seiners Association, said the province would be "selling out" the fishing industry if it accepted the federal plan. He was quoted in the *Chronicle-Herald* as saying that, "If some form of take-over happens, you may as well call it curtains because it will be all over."

Roger Smith, operator of three plants in Shelburne and Yarmouth counties, said, "The processors have seen a planned federal takeover of the fishing industry coming for years. They're trying to cram it down our throats. There is going to be no more free enterprise. They think they're our saviours and they are going to do what they want to do regardless of what anybody else thinks. . . . the people in control are socialists in the way they think." Darrell Nickerson, president of the Bear Point, Shag Harbour, Woods Harbour Fishermen's Association, said, "Any government control over Nova Scotia fishing companies would spell an enormous disaster for the coastline. You can't compete with a Crown Corporation, or whatever you want to call it. They'll knock off the small independent plants which have long been the back-bone of our fishing industry."

Scores of such statements were reproduced in the media as expressions of the views of "fishermen" or "the fishing industry." The problem is not that these points of view were conveyed, but how they were conveyed. Expressions of narrow self-interest, parroted, unquestioned assumptions about "free enterprise" versus government, profoundly ignorant statements about the roles of different sectors of the industry—all were presented without any critical context. One or two fishermen were taken as representative of all fishermen. The differences between a Wayne Thorburne, likely a very wealthy man, and an inshore guy in Pictou County who has to sell to National Sea Products, were ignored. There was no debate over values, principles, or historical interpretations. The devastating incompetence of private sector management was never even identified as a factor.

Of course the head of the hysteria department has been the *Chronicle-Herald/Mail-Star:* "Most government adventures in areas traditionally reserved to private enterprise have been characterized by incompetence and extravagance, and would often as not result in bankruptcy but for enormous and wasteful infusions of more public money." The papers went on in their January 3, 1984, editorial to blame the Nickerson/National Sea crisis on federal policy and too much federal money. After the February agreement, however, they applauded the two governments for these "enormous and wasteful infusions of more public money" because, of course, private ownership would result: "As for apprehensions about public control of National Sea Products, these are unfounded under the arrangements. . . . Both governments certainly take a minority equity position which, however, appears essentially to be debt accommodation and postponement."

The Halifax-Dartmouth *Daily News* went even further: "A mere $25 million in new money and a roll-over of another $25 million which National Sea Products owes to the province, has saved the company from the hands of the federal government and the nationalization that many thought would be the death knell for the Nova Scotia fishery. For a company with a debt of $220 million and, until now, equity of $40 million, the accepted plan of financier David Hennigar is a major coup."

Rather quietly behind all this furor, a major change had occured. A key actor in the private-sector coup at National Sea was David Hennigar of Scotia Investments Ltd., representative of the Jodrey empire, which controls Minas Basin Pulp and Paper, Canadian Keyes Fibre Ltd., Avon Foods Ltd., Bedford Village Properties Ltd., and eighteen other companies in Nova Scotia.

Scotia Investments Ltd., had now become the dominant partner in both National Sea Products Ltd. and Halifax Developments Ltd., two companies which bring together the ruling families of Nova Scotia. The Jodreys seemed to be dominant. The Sobeys were there, together with Harold Connor and H.B. Rhude from the old National Sea board. There was also Russell Harrington who, together with Rhude and Connor, was on the board of Central and Eastern Trust, a major regional finance institution.

J.J. Jodrey, chairman of the Jodrey empire, is on the board of the Bank of Nova Scotia. Frank Covert—a member of the Stewart, MacKeen and Covert law firm together with J.W. Mingo (also on the board of National Sea Products and Minas Basin Pulp and Power) and, previously, the late H.B. Rhude—is President of Ben's Ltd. and Maritime Paper Ltd. (a Jodrey satellite) and is on the board of Canadian Keyes Fibre, Maritime Steel, National Sea Products, Scotia Investments, and the Royal Bank.

Frank Covert headed the subcommittee of the National Sea board that received proposals for the takeover by the Jodreys and the Sobeys. He negotiated with the Royal Bank with regard to the $75 million debt owed by National Sea.

A few things are clear. There is a ruling class, in the classic sense, in Nova Scotia, and it really came together on the National Sea deal. The federal government, particularly Fisheries Minister DeBané and the cynical Michael Kirby, were completely outclassed on the deal. The provincial government merely did as it was told.

The National Sea scandal deserves much greater study because of the unusual visibility of the ruling class in its relations with the state and with central Canadian capital through the banks. There was clearly a strong ideological element in the whole issue of keeping regional control of a strategic industry and preventing the expansion of public ownership in such a sector. In relation to the real game going on at this level, the issue as presented by the media seems entirely beside the point. It brings to mind Plato's allegory of the cave—the idea that what we take to be reality is just shadows on the wall of a cave where we are held by our ignorance and confusion. The real, important action takes place outside in the sunshine, but the shadows on the wall, no matter how ridiculous and nonsensical their message, seem to hold our attention.

It was true in 1980 and is still true today: the corporate structure just won't work in the fishing industry. Millions were invested in the wrong kinds of technology and infrastructure. The corporate structure can't produce the quality the markets demand, and it can't adapt to either environmental or economic realities.

Nationalization, in and of itself, would not have been *the* solution to the structural problems of the fisheries, but it would have meant that, finally, the industry had bitten the bullet and started to dismantle the monster it had created. Massive costs would have had to be borne in the short run to find stability and "profitability" in the long run. Those costs would have had to be spread over the whole industry and the society, not forced onto the poorest sectors.

Instead, we have a new private-sector ownership, this time a more powerful and competent one, which will fight hard to make the Nickerson/National Sea empire profitable. It may even succeed, but at what cost? Fish plants have already closed in Halifax and Pictou. There will be wage roll-backs. There will be pushes for greater "efficiency" and "productivity" in the plants, meaning more output for less wages, more accidents, more sickness, more misery for the largely female work force. There will be lower prices for fishermen. There will be greater pressure on the fish stocks as the company strives to make money off its ridiculously overdeveloped dragger fleet. Inshore fishermen will have to fight continually to reduce dragger effort, and government managers will be caught in never-ending battles, with plant closings and layoffs used by the companies as blackmail.

In short, this is not restructuring, it is destruction. Inshore fishermen are going to be plunged back into a desperate struggle for the survival of their livelihoods. However, this time around, not as many will be confused about the identity of their real enemy, or about the only long-term goal worth fighting for: an industry that actually supports the people of the region and gives them the means to live here, as they have fought to do for generations.

Underdeveloping the P.E.I. Fishery

Bernie Conway

The Prince Edward Island fishery is a complicated combination of jurisdictions, species, licences, and people. It is all the more intricate because it must be seen not in isolation, but as a segment of the Gulf of St. Lawrence fishery, and of the Northwest Atlantic fishery of which that is a part.

Yet no matter how complex the P.E.I. fishery is, one thing is simple. Without a say in the price of fish, forced to bear increases in costs and to take what they are given for their product, fishermen on the Island are little more than pawns in the fishery on which they depend but which is not run for their benefit.

There are approximately 1,700 commercial-licensed fishermen on P.E.I. Of these, roughly 1,300 are lobster fishermen. The other 400 are active in the groundfish, scallop, tuna, aquaculture, and Irish moss (shore or rake) fisheries. Especially in recent years, it takes two good species to keep a fisherman alive—lobster and herring, for example, or lobster and tuna—and many Island fishermen hold more than one licence. Some, unfortunately, have to make do with just one.

The P.E.I. fishery is broken into three districts: 7b, from Tignish to North Lake, has 633 fishermen; 7b1, from Souris to Victoria, 393 fishermen; and 8, Victoria to Sea Cow Pond, 262 fishermen. Districts 7b and 7b1 fish lobster in the spring (May and June) and District 8 fishes lobster in the fall (August 10/October 10).

The prices paid for fish reflect the different buyers in each district. In 7b and 8, the United Maritime Fishermen (UMF) and National Sea Products Ltd. are the major buyers, while in District 7b1, the buyers are smaller firms which tend to share their markets. In 7b1, the prices for lobsters last year were $2.25 for canners and $2.75 for markets. In 7b, National Sea and UMF paid base prices of $1.08 for canners and $2.25 for markets; and, in District 8, where National Sea is the major buyer, it paid $1.55 and $1.80.

These figures are crucial because lobster accounts for close to 70 percent of total income for Island fishermen. Other shellfish (scallops, clams, and oysters) account for 12 percent. Pelagics—tuna, mackerel, and, herring—make up 8 percent, and groundfish account for the rest, about 10 percent.

How does the state fit into this picture? Beyond denying the fishermen the

---

This chapter was first published in a different form in *New Maritimes* (April 1984).

right of collective bargaining, the provincial government has played a tiny and ineffectual role in the Island fishery. The provincial fisheries budget of $700,000 (after salaries) means very few improvements in the lives of ordinary fishermen. Most of it goes into the provincial propaganda exercise of subsidies. Fibreglass holding tanks, for example, had cost $300 each before the province introduced a $300 subsidy on them. The price then jumped to $600. Boat subsidies work the same way. If a fisherman is buying a boat and has a $10,000 subsidy, the price of the boat goes up $10,000.

One of the most insidious provincial programs is one called Near and Off-shore Fleet Development, which provides 35 percent of capital costs for a boat to a maximum of $60,000. The province has helped purchase two boats under this program, an expenditure representing 17 percent of the after-salaries fisheries budget, spent on just two favoured fishermen.

The P.E.I. government also contributes to the Island fishery through advisory committees on different species. These consist of hand-picked hacks who are transported to Charlottetown every couple of months to state their agreement with whatever the government was going to do anyway. The federal Department of Fisheries and Oceans (DFO) makes use of such committees as well. The hand-picked people who participate differ in at least one respect from those on the provincial advisory committees. They receive one or two trips to the mainland at government expense in addition to their trips to Charlottetown. Such committees supposedly propose policies, but the DFO sets the guidelines, and even when fishermen do make such policy decisions, they can be overruled by a group of departmental bureaucrats.

The DFO, like the province, is tied more closely to businessmen than to fishermen. There is typically an interchange of middle-level executives between the two, and the result seems to be a group of frustrated civil servants in the Department of Fisheries, most of whom view fishermen with contempt.

Also involved in the Island fishery is a third arm of government, the P.E.I. Fishermen's Association (PEIFA). This group, which claims to speak for 1,000 fishermen, is actually funded by government. Beyond periodic, weak-kneed threats, it is unable to do anything for fishermen other than to encourage the businessmen's mentality that, if you didn't succeed, then you didn't work hard enough. A sense of the association's political perspective can be had from the details of its conventions. At one recent convention in Summerside, a banquet was sponsored by the DFO and one of the guest speakers was James McGrath who, as Minister of Fisheries in the Clark government, shares responsibility for destroying cod in the Gulf of St. Lawrence. The association's orientation is very local. It fosters the view that "all fishermen are enemies except those in my region," and even these are considered potential threats. Together, the fishermen's association and the Department of Fisheries do joint projects, promote the idea that decisions regarding the business of the fishery are best left up to businessmen, and encourage fishermen to be submissive. Many well-intentioned fishermen have belonged to the association but, because of its dismal record, many also have left.

The Maritime Fishermen's Union (MFU), on the other hand, believes there are powerful elements in society that keep fishermen from any say in their industry. The MFU is viewed as a threat by the DFO, the provincial government, and the fishermen's association. They look on MFU members as though they were from a different planet, and try to portray the union through the media as a group whose only real ambition is to go on strike. To a certain extent, this propaganda drive has been successful. In a 1983 plebiscite on collective-bargaining rights for fishermen, business and government won. As had been hoped, fishermen were left in a state of confusion, blaming each other for the troubles of the industry.

Without some fundamental reform, the situation of the fishermen will remain the same. Without the right to bargain the price of fish, they will continue to purchase their inputs retail and sell their products wholesale. This is untenable and unequal, and it will not be tolerated forever.

Of Pride and Prices: Miminegash, Moss, and the Multinationals

Mary Boyd

Irish moss is one of the most important and versatile marine resources in the Maritimes. Found in the coastal waters of all the region's provinces, the two main concentrations of this seaweed grow between Yarmouth and the Pubnicos in southwestern Nova Scotia, and in west Prince County, Prince Edward Island. Irish moss has been so important for West Prince residents that Miminegash, the home of the two main multinational plants which buy the raw seaweed from moss harvesters, has been dubbed "The Irish Moss Capital of the World."

The biological term for Irish moss is *Chrondrus crispus.* When this seaweed is put through an extraction process it produces a gum called carrageen, which acts as a gelling agent for a variety of products ranging from medical and pharmaceutical goods to cosmetics, toothpaste, and foods such as ice cream, chocolate milk, bread, and instant breakfasts.

"The Moss" is harvested in two ways: (1) Boat owners go out to the moss beds, which are found in fairly shallow waters off the coast, and detach large quantities with a rake; when their boats are filled, they either deliver it directly to the company in its wet form or take it home and spread it in their yards where it is dried by the sun. (2) Some of the moss which is detached by the rakes floats to the surface and is tossed onto the shore during storms and high tides. Most of this is gathered by women, who also have the choice of selling the moss in its wet form or drying it in their yards. It is estimated that 70 percent of Irish moss harvesters in West Prince, P.E.I., are women.

An extensive study of the industry commissioned by the Social Action Commission of the (Roman Catholic) Diocese of Charlottetown in 1977 estimated that 750 families in the Maritimes depended on Irish moss as their primary source of income. The study, called *Global Village/Global Pillage*, also revealed that between 1,000 and 1,500 families depended on Irish moss as a secondary source of income, while another 200-300 families were seasonally employed in buying, drying, and shipping the product.

Despite the commercial value of carrageen, the price paid to Irish moss harvesters has always been extremely low and subject to much fluctuation.

In 1974 a sort of boom was created by the arrival in the industry of the P.E.I. Marine Plants Co-operative. Prior to the appearance of the Co-op,

---

This chapter is based on an article first published in *New Maritimes* (April 1983).

moss buying in Miminegash was controlled by three firms — Marine Colloids of Rockland, Maine; Genu Products Canada, Ltd., a Canadian subsidiary of the Hercules Corporation of Wilmington, Delaware (which has an extraction plant in Copenhagen, Denmark); and the now defunct P.E.I. Seaweeds, Ltd., owned by Litex Industry of Glostrup, Denmark. The buying spree sparked by the appearance of the Co-op, however, resulted in moss stockpiling by the multinationals. This led to problems of overharvesting, and in 1975 and 1976 the P.E.I. harvest volume was down 60 percent and earnings fell 71 percent from $3.1 million to $0.9 million.

Another short-lived boom was experienced in 1979, when wet moss prices increased to 6 cents/lb. and dry moss to 30 cents/lb. By 1980, the price of dry moss had fallen to 22 cents/lb. and in 1981 it dropped again—to 20 cents/lb. (5.85 cents/lb. for wet).

There were two main reasons why prices dropped so rapidly. The Co-operative had lost its market to the world's second largest Irish moss company, C.E.C.A., located in France. When its other customer, Stauffer Chemicals, also closed their doors to the Co-op in 1980, it was forced out of business. Secondly, in 1979, Marine Colloids thought it had found a substitute for Irish moss in moss farms set up in the Philippines, and they stopped buying West Prince moss altogether. The remaining company, Genu Products, also began to cash in on cheaper moss produced by low-paid farmers in Chile and the Philippines, and slowed down its purchasing.

A great deal of the funding for Marine Colloids' and Genu's experimentation with developing moss farms in the Philippines came from the National Research Council of Canada. The amount is estimated to be in the area of $6 million, despite the fact that both companies had clearly stated their goal of eliminating Maritime harvesters.

The steady decline in prices, together with the steady increase in the cost of living, weighed heavily on the minds of West Prince harvesters as they approached the opening of the 1982 Irish moss season. Two groups—the Miminegash Women in Support of Fishing and the West Prince Irish Moss Harvesters Organization—became involved in searching for alternatives to the multinationals. Both groups pressed for the revival of a defunct extraction plant which had been under construction in Anglo, near Tignish.

With the impending announcement of the 1982 moss price, it was the Miminegash Women in Support of Fishing who really took the bull by the horns and began mobilizing harvesters for better prices.

The release in 1977 of the Social Action Commission's *Global Village/Global Pillage*, it was generally thought, had contributed to improved moss prices in the late 1970s. With this in mind, the Miminegash Women contacted the commission, and in a series of study sessions in the spring of 1982, they researched together the real reasons for low Irish moss prices.

The Women in Support of Fishing developed three hypotheses from this process: that Irish moss is controlled by big companies, that government supports the companies over harvesters, and that there is a lack of harvester involvement in solving their own problems. Together with the Social Action Commission, they then developed an extensive questionnaire about the industry, which they planned to test with West Prince harvesters.

Then in June, 1982, claiming high interest rates and a world market glut, the company announced the 1982 price—17 cents/lb. for dry moss and 5¼ cents for wet. The Women in Support of Fishing immediately called a general meeting of moss harvesters for June 9th at the Miminegash Fire Hall. More than a hundred harvesters turned out. Each was given a copy of a questionnaire to answer. The questions themselves reflected the conclusions of the women's enquiry into the industry, and by the time the business meeting began it was evident that harvesters were more than disgruntled with the 1982 offer. The boat owners voted 27-18 in favour of withholding moss until the price improved.

The next morning more than 200 harvesters were picketing for higher prices. A steering committee of harvesters was formed out of a coalition of the Maritime Fishermen's Union, Women in Support of Fishing, and the West Prince Irish Moss Harvesters Organization, as well as representatives of the fishing ports where moss is harvested.

Research undertaken by the Social Action Commission, meanwhile, showed that there was no glut on the international Irish moss market at all. Rather, a fierce price war involving Marine Colloids, C.E.C.A., and Genu—numbers one, two and three, respectively, in the industry—was taking place. In an attempt to expand its part of the American market, Genu had cut its price for carrageen in the United States by 16 cents/lb.

In fact, general world trends were towards higher prices for *Chondrus crispus*. In Brittany, France, harvesters were getting the equivalent of 26 cents/lb. for dry moss and 7¾ cents/lb. for wet. As close to P.E.I. as Yarmouth, N.S., prices were 30 cents/lb. for dry moss and 6-6¾ cents for wet, for moss of approximately the same quality.

Armed with this evidence, West Prince harvesters held back the sale of their moss. On June 11, two days after the vote at the Fire Hall, the Genu manager agreed in a meeting to raise the price for moss raked in boats to 20 cents/lb. After much prodding, he promised to cable Copenhagen to relate harvester demands of 30 cents/lb. (dry) and 7 cents/lb. (wet). Two days later he informed harvesters that 20 cents/lb. would be paid for all dry moss.

The harvesters held firm. Many meetings followed. The steering committee and its allies met with Premier Lee and astounded him by refusing to ask for a subsidy which they saw as a benefit only to the multinational. An offer of 22 cents/lb. from Genu's main competitor, Marine Colloids, was rejected.

The Minister of Social Services gave permission to harvesters, who by now had not received any income for several weeks, to ask the regional Social Services centre for emergency food as well as medical and heating supplies.

Finally, after withholding their product for 25 days, the harvesters won a settlement—a bottom-line price of 24 cents/lb. for dry moss and 6 cents/lb. for wet. This was still low in comparison to southwestern Nova Scotia, but it was an important and inspiring victory. The struggle was over, and there was no more company talk about a glut on the market. Genu and Marine Colloids couldn't get enough West Prince moss, and the harvesters had one of their best years in some time.

Fishermen have paid tribute to the Miminegash Women in Support of Fishing for giving backbone and spark to this whole effort. The strength of these women's inner conviction undermined the multinationals' strategy that the harvesters would have to sell their moss in order to get UIC stamps for the winter. By saying, "To hell with UIC," and by making it known to all that the cheques they received for the hard work of harvesting moss were not much more than social-assistance payments anyway, the women surmounted this strategy of the companies, mobilized the harvesters, and gained a victory.

Further Reading: Fishing

History

Alexander, David. "The political economy of fishing in Newfoundland." *Journal of Canadian Studies* 11, No. 1 (February 1976): 32-40.

Barrett, L.G. "Underdevelopment and Social Movements in the Nova Scotia Fishing Industry to 1938." In Robert J. Brym and R. James Sacouman, eds., *Underdevelopment and Social Movements in Atlantic Canada* (Toronto, 1979), pp. 127-60.

———. "Capital and the state in Atlantic Canada. The structural context of fishery policy between 1939 and 1977." In Cynthia Lamson and Arthur J. Hanson, eds., *Atlantic Fisheries and Coastal Communities: Fisheries Decision-Making Case Studies* (Halifax, 1984), pp. 77-131.

Inglis, Gordon. *More Than Just a Union: The Story of the NFFAWU* (St. John's, 1985).

Innis, H.A. *The Cod Fisheries* (Toronto, revised edition, 1978).

Ommer, Rosemary. " 'All the Fish of the Post': Resource Property Rights and Development in a Nineteenth-Century Inshore Fishery." *Acadiensis* 10, No. 2 (Spring 1981): 107-23.

———. "What's Wrong with Canadian Fish?" *Journal of Canadian Studies/ Revue d'études canadiennes* 20, No. 3 (Autumn 1985): 122-42.

Ryan, Shannon. *Fish Out of Water: The Newfoundland Saltfish Trade, 1814-1914* (St. John's, 1986).

Samson, Roch. *Fishermen and Merchants in 19th Century Gaspé: The Fishermen-Dealers of William Hyman and Sons* (Ottawa: Parks Canada, 1984).

Sinclair, Peter. *From Traps to Draggers: Domestic Commodity Production in Northwest Newfoundland, 1850-1982* (St. John's, 1985).

Present Perspectives

Barrett, L.G., and A. Davis. "Floundering in Troubled Waters: The Political Economy of the Atlantic Fishery and the Task Force on Atlantic Fisheries." *Journal of Canadian Studies* 19, No. 1 (1984): 125-37.

Canada, Task Force on Atlantic Fisheries. *Navigating Troubled Waters: A New Policy for the Atlantic Fisheries* (Ottawa, 1983).

Carter, Roger. *Something's Fishy: Public Policy and Private Corporations in the Newfoundland Fishery* (St. John's, 1982).

Connelly, Pat, and Martha MacDonald. "Women's Work: Domestic and Wage Labour in a Nova Scotia Community." *Studies in Political Economy,* No. 10 (Winter 1983): 45-72.

Davis, Anthony. "Property Rights and Access Management in the Small Boat

Fishery: A Case Study from Southwest Nova Scotia." In Lamson, Cynthia, and Hanson, Arthur J., eds. *Atlantic Fisheries and Coastal Communities: Fisheries Decision-Making Case Studies* (Halifax, 1984), pp. 133-64.

Fishery Research Group. *The Social Impact of Technological Change in Newfoundland's Deepsea Fishery* (St. John's, 1986).

Hardin, Garrett. "The Tragedy of the Commons." In John Baden and Garrett J. Hardin, eds., *Managing the Commons* (San Francisco, 1977), pp. 16-30.

MacDonald, R.D.S. "Canadian Fisheries Policy and the Development of Atlantic Coast Groundfisheries Management." In Lamson, Cynthia, and Hanson, Arthur J., eds., *Atlantic Fisheries and Coastal Communities: Fisheries Decision-Making Case Studies* (Halifax, 1984), pp. 15-75.

McFarland, Joan. "Changing Modes of Social Control in a New Brunswick Fish Packing Town." *Studies in Political Economy,* No. 4 (Autumn 1980): 99-113.

Patton, Donald J. *Industrial Development and the Atlantic Fishery* (Ottawa, 1981).

Part III

Forestry

Introduction: From Towering Pines to the Multinationals' Pulpstand

Of all the primary industries, forestry has recently generated the most sustained and intensive debate over management and public access. For most people in the region, forestry issues are encountered in the midst of impassioned debates over herbicides and pesticides (anaylzed in the chapters by Christopher Majka, Bruce Livesey, and Aaron Schneider), in which the rival scientific claims of pulp and paper companies, provincial governments, and critical environmentalists are paraded before uncomprehending justices, a predictably pro-industry media, and a divided public. These debates have convincingly shown that there are reserves of popular resistance in the region which can be tapped by a hardworking and talented political leadership.

At the same time, these environmental debates have often missed something: a sense of the region's historically rooted social and political structures. Without a sense of why capital must treat the forests in ways which threaten the people dependent upon them, we can hardly understand why the forests of the region have deteriorated so rapidly over the past century, or the state policies which have enthusiastically underwritten such exploitation.

Consider Elizabeth May's account of her leadership of the Cape Breton Landowners Against the Spray (May 1982). Most readers will come away from her autobiographical treatment of this struggle over the spraying of budworm larvae with an image of the pulp and paper companies as big, sleepy, corporate dinosaurs, roused from their sound sleep by the shouts of environmentalists. As for the state, it is a neutral force, capable of "seeing reason" after the petitions flow in and the "people's elected representatives" set to work. The limitations of this benign view of both capital and the state were fully exposed in the 1982-83 Herbicides Trials, in which fifteen plaintiffs took Nova Scotia Forest Industries (NSFI) to court in an effort to stop the company from using a mixture of 2,4-D and 2,4,5-T against broad-leaved plants in forest plots across Cape Breton and in Antigonish County. This struggle showed not only how high the system stacks the cards against popular participation in resource decisions, but also the economic logic which would keep the companies spraying even if the scientific evidence for the effectiveness of the spray was weak.

Environmental debates cannot be understood in isolation. To understand events such as these, we must put them in the historical context of the conversion of the region's once diversified and towering forests into today's more homogeneous and stunted corporate pulpstand. This is the "new forest"

95

analyzed by Julia McMahon in her chapter.

It all goes back, McMahon notes, to the early nineteenth century, for the "new forest" of today is merely the latest in a succession of regimes imposed upon the forests and dependent communities to maximize the profits of external capital. By the mid-nineteenth century, lumbering had already changed the face of the forest. The most accessible trees had been the first to go: the pine trees within about three miles from streams large enough to float timber down in the spring. By mid-century the areas in New Brunswick that had been the richest 50 years before were the most heavily culled (Wynn 1981, 152). Much the same pattern of response to British and West-Indian demand can be found in Nova Scotia, although the province never became so completely dependent on the one staple (Johnson 1986, Part 5; Robertson 1984). In contrast, the island of Newfoundland's 23,000 square miles of forest were only intermittently exploited as an open-access resource until the second half of the nineteenth century and, even by the end of the 1890s, one found only a small forest industry based on sawmilling (Hiller 1982, 42).

The twentieth century completed the process set in motion a century before. Lumbering was pushed into inaccessible areas thanks to the railway and portable sawmills (Nova Scotian mill owners successfully looted Newfoundland's Humber Valley forests, for example), but the most striking change was the rise of the pulp industry.

This transformation began in a small way during the third quarter of the nineteenth century and gathered steam in the first three decades of the twentieth century. In Newfoundland, vast tracts of forest land came under the control of the Harmsworths, who controlled a London publishing empire and newspapers such as the *Daily Mail, Daily Mirror,* and *Evening News.* These businessmen worried that paper supplies would dry up in an increasingly controlled world market, and especially if war engulfed Europe. To them, Newfoundland's timber represented a precious reserve. To the provincial government, the Harmsworths and their Anglo-Newfoundland Development Company represented capital and the prospect of industrial development. In 1905, they obtained "what amounted to a perpetual lease on extremely favourable terms of 2,300 square miles of timber lands, and a good source of water power linked by rail to the head of Red Indian Lake and to shipping facilities at Lewisporte" (Hiller 1982, 57). This effectively shut out the sawmilling industry from the better stands of timber in the interior and confined it to a three-mile coastal reserve; it also "prevented the government from periodically reviewing the direct financial return from the industry, which has remained abnormally low" (Hiller 1982, 68).

Although Nova Scotia and New Brunswick did not mark the transition to the pulpwood forest quite as dramatically as Newfoundland, by the 1950s the balance had decisively shifted in favour of pulp in both provinces. In 1917 the Fraser Companies, formerly preoccupied with lumber, entered the pulp business and erected a pulp mill at Edmundston, and in 1929 the Mersey Paper

Company mill began its operations in Queens County, Nova Scotia. After the Second World War, the Nova Scotia government aggressively recruited foreign capital to the pulp and paper industry, and it signed an agreement with Swedish-controlled NSFI in 1958, leasing up to 1.7 million acres; this was followed by agreements with Bowater and Scott Maritimes in 1962 and 1965 respectively (Orton 1983, 3). Since the Second World War, the forest-management policy of the provincial government has been oriented towards providing cheap feed stock to the pulp and paper mills controlled by multinational companies. Pulpwood, which before 1961 made up about 30 percent of the annual harvest cut from Nova Scotia's woods, now accounts for about 80 percent of the harvest (Orton 1983, 1).

The strategy of concentrating on the production of pulp for multinationals is open to many questions. Some are straightforwardly economic. International pulp and paper markets are notoriously volatile, and the whole history of the industry since the 1920s has been one of boom and bust. As one environmentalist has pointed out, should the technology of pulp and paper change and permit the utilization of tropical crops grown annually instead of every 50 years, the restructuring of the region's forests to suit the needs of multinational capital will suddenly seem to have been a remarkably short-sighted strategy (Peabody, 4).

Even without such a technological change, the economic position of small-woodlot owners has long been an unenviable one. In New Brunswick, some 35,000 small-woodlot owners face a controlled market for their wood (six major companies owned ten pulp mills and two-thirds of the sawmilling industry in 1984), and have managed, through their marketing organizations, to soften but not to eliminate the drastic effects of an unstable market for their product. In Nova Scotia, small-woodlot owners, who own about 75 percent of the province's forested land, must now confront the recent recommendations of the Nova Scotia *Royal Commission Report on Forestry* (1984). This report, Aaron Schneider's chapter notes, foreshadows uniform control over the management of private woodlands. Under this system, industries supplying pesticides, fertilizers, and seedlings would secure a viable market, while small-woodlot owners would be required to adopt capital-intensive technology to survive in a highly competitive market. Not only would the small producer lose his independence and his ability to readjust to changed international markets, but his economic returns would continue to be extremely low. The primary beneficiaries of this project would be the foreign-owned corporations.

The economic questions raised by the position of the woodlot owners in a forest industry "rationalized" to suit multinational capital are directly related to the broader ecological questions raised by the deterioration of the region's forests. Not only do provincial management strategies place little priority on the living standards of wood producers, but they also blindly accept the premises of the new industrial forest and its indiscriminate use of chemicals and clearcutting.

and clearcutting.

The aerial spraying of chemical insecticides to stop spruce budworms from eating the foliage of balsam fir, white spruce, and red spruce—the three tree species most widely used for pulpwood production—has been a policy of the New Brunswick government for the past four decades. Over these decades the spruce-budworm infestation spread from a small part of the province to cover virtually the entire forested area. Although New Brunswick has graduated from its earlier love of DDT, it still relies upon fenitrothion, whose ominous implications for health and safety are only starting to be understood. The regional experience with herbicides, some of which later earned world disrepute under the name of "Agent Orange," has scarcely been happier. In the absence of scientific evidence for their effectiveness in increasing forest yields, the continued use of herbicides can only be explained in terms of the benefits reaped by the chemical companies.

Clearcutting is another management technique that has raised questions about the long-term impact of the new political economy of the postwar forest industries, even in minds otherwise attuned to the corporate mainstream (see Johnson 1986, 355-56). Clearcutting is a method in which all marketable trees on a given site are cut down and removed, leaving tops, branches, and other slash behind. It has the advantage of being the cheapest way of harvesting in the short term. It has the disadvantage of removing nutrients, eroding the soil, and threatening wildlife. The reforestation of clearcuts by spruce and balsam fir offers a particularly inviting environment for the spruce budworm, which thrives best in conifer plantations rather than in mixed stands or in stands of softwoods of unequal age. Clearcutting and chemicals are always tied together in the corporate management of the forest.

None of these phenomena—the poverty of woodlot owners, the poisoning of animals and workers by herbicides and pesticides, or the conversion of the region's forests into a massive pulp plantation—can be understood apart from the requirements of transnational capital. The fate of the forests in a dependent region such as Atlantic Canada is decided by the demands of daily newspapers in Washington and London, not by any principle of co-existing with the forests and all the other species sheltered by them. The harsh irony is that the new corporate forest has and will continue to undermine the delicate mechanisms of the region's forests without providing security to local living standards or the prospect of indigenous industrial development.

The consequences for the forests of this extreme form of regional dependency promise to be dire. As one environmentalist has put it: "A forest that continues to specialize in the growth of softwoods—particularly the single age stands of softwood that result from clearcut harvesting policies—will continue to be a forest that is sick, subject to chronic insect infestations, an unstable environment for its inhabitants, and an uncertain economic base for the communities that depend on it" (Peabody, 16).

The New Forest in Nova Scotia

Julia McMahon

Over three hundred years ago, the first settlers in Nova Scotia found a strong and vital forest, rich in valuable pines, spruces, and other woods. The forests were pushed back for farms, felled for fuel and shelter, and harvested for trade and shipbuilding. They were a life-giving resource upon which the young communities constructed their economy.

Today, when driving along the province's highways, one sees mile after mile of toothpick trees and deserted farms, interrupted only by the uneven strip developments that cling to the road. With ever-increasing speed, people and forests are disappearing from the rural landscape.

The history of the forests points out the strange logic of forest exploitation. The depletion of this resource proceeded in stages, as successive wood industries consumed the wood they needed for their own production. In this process, the quality and diversity of the forest was diminished. The first stage, the exporting of masts and squared timber, was over by the early 1880s, but the shipbuilding and sawmilling industries that utilized less valuable timber continued to export to Britain and her colonies in the West Indies. These industries outlived the squared timber trade, only to meet the same fate 40 years later. With the advent of a national transportation system and of competition from other "frontier" products, Nova Scotia sawmillers were forced to turn on their forests with a vengeance or go out of business. Against such determined efforts, the forests could not compete. The province's virgin forests were gone long before the turn of the last century.

In the same style, the early twentieth-century growth of a small wood-pulp industry and the development of an intensive multinational industry in the 1960s have appeared as logical developments in the ongoing use of the forest. In the present, most sophisticated phase of the forest industry, the multinational pulp and paper mills have convinced us that the forests of Nova Scotia are worthless unless they are in their hands. Meeting the needs of the pulp and paper industry has meant growing corporate control of the resource and the use of highly mechanized woodcutting technology to move a large and constant supply of pulpwood from the forest site to the mill. For Nova Scotia, this has meant the minimization of woods employment, the rapid elimination of the small private producer, the depopulation of the rural area, and the loss, for the province, of resource revenues. In the long term, Nova Scotians will

This chapter is adapted from an article first published in *Round One*, No. 6 (October 1975).

have to face the consequences of an intensified devaluation of and loss of control over the resource.

The survival of the farm unit in most of Nova Scotia has been based on the integration of agriculture, fishing, and woodcutting with intermittent periods of wage employment. Specialization was possible only in the rare instances where agricultural land was rich and fertile.

On the small Nova Scotia farm, the woodlot met many subsistence needs. It supplied fuel, building supplies, game, maple sugar, wild foods, and medicinal herbs, and in times of trouble it provided a cash crop.

When the pulp and paper industry moved in to take advantage of a ready source of raw materials, it provided a large additional market for pulpwood to the woodlot owner. However, the beneficial effects of these new pulpwood markets were soon outweighed by the growing domination of the pulp companies over the whole rural sector.

The last quarter century has been marked by this increasing dominance. The large-capacity mills have made increasingly heavier demands on forest resources. They have demanded higher productivity and relatively lower prices per cord. The richly diversified woodlot has been reduced to a one-dimensional pulpwood production yard. Woodlot owners, already confronted with the disastrous decline of the rest of the rural economy, now face a rapid and unremitting squeeze on their position as producers and sellers of wood.

In Nova Scotia, two pulp mills in the eastern part of the province, Scott Maritimes Ltd. and Nova Scotia Forest Industries (NSFI), are predominant in production, employment, and intensity of forest use. Both are modern, large-capacity mills, whose large work forces give them an important position in the provincial economy.

The first large-capacity pulp mill, Nova Scotia Pulp Ltd., was built by a Swedish multinational, Stora Kopparbergs Bergslags AB, in the early 1960s. Stora's interest in Nova Scotia began when the completion of the Canso Causeway created an ice-free, deepwater port, with access to a vast hinterland of forest resources. Stora initially built a $46 million subsidiary that was designed to produce 130,000 tons of sulphite pulp. The mill employed 350 people and opened a major new market for private wood producers in eastern Nova Scotia.

In 1969, Stora negotiated an $86 million expansion with the provincial and federal governments to extend the sulphite operation and add on one of two promised newsprint lines. In 1975, at full production, the mill could produce 175,000 tons of sulphite pulp and 160,000 tons of newsprint yearly for export (90 percent going to the United States). At the time of the expansion, Stora integrated the actual production processes into the parent company, creating a new division of Stora called Nova Scotia Forest Industries, and leaving the subsidiary, Nova Scotia Pulp Ltd., as a holding company for the assets.

Government pursuit of more multinational investment to force industrial growth and create industrial jobs has become standard policy since the arrival of Stora. Such "planning" is driven by a political necessity to create jobs. Already faced with a lack of domestic capital, and unwilling to undertake such investments itself, government puts the resource up for sale to the multinational corporations. In this trade-off, government fails to consider the nature or the long-term security of the jobs that have been created. It fails to consider what other jobs and livelihoods have been eliminated or what other alternatives are made impossible by the presence of the multinational.

Stora can claim to have created over 2,000 jobs in eastern Nova Scotia. The importance of these jobs and therefore of Stora to the provincial economy is not disputed. In 1975, of the approximately 800 jobs at the mill, 400 were in administration and in the woodlands department. Only about 400 production jobs had been created. These jobs were relatively well paid and were unionized. The bulk of the employment was in the woods, where more than 1,000 jobs had been provided. Except for the 200 workers who worked for the company, private woodcutters were not unionized. The majority were employed by smaller private companies working in small operations throughout the crown land leases. Woodcutters faced low wages, seasonal work, poor working conditions, and minimal long-term security. Faced with the pressures of maintaining its wood supply, the corporation did not concentrate on improving wages and working conditions. Instead, Stora's policy of mechanizing its woods operations suggests a clear trend to eliminate as much of the woods employment as possible.

The woodlot owner is in no more favourable a position now. Although not accustomed to thinking of themselves as employees of the corporation, woodlot owners have no other market for their pulpwood and are consequently being forced out of production by the minimal price they receive for privately produced pulpwood. The declining number of jobs in the woods and the plight of the woodlot owners are the other side of Stora's job-creation record.

Direct government financial investment in Stora has been substantial. At the time of the initial construction, it involved a free 100-acre mill site, a long-term loan for a water supply piped from the mainland side of the strait, exemption from almost all local taxes, and prolonged low electricity rates. The major incentive, a mammoth 50-year crown lease, granted control of 1,300,000 acres of government timberland in the seven eastern counties of the province. The corporation's payment to the provincial government was a token $1.00 per cord cut, with a production limit set at 150,000 cords per year.

At the time of the expansion in the late 1960s, the company demanded large subsidies, threatening to leave unless government invested heavily in its growth. The result was a $30 million long-term loan from the Cape Breton Development Corporation (Devco), a $5 million outright grant from the Area Development Agency, assistance with interest payments from both Devco and the provincial government on the $30 million loan, and a renegotiation of the crown lease. Another 200,000 acres were added to the leasehold, bringing the total acreage to 1,500,000 acres. Stora also demanded and received greatly increased intensive-cutting rights and more overall control of the forest. Its harvesting quota was more than doubled, to 330,000 cords per year, on a 15 percent increase in timberland.

Stora's 50-year lease of 1,500,000 acres amounted to one-third of the total land area of the seven eastern counties of Nova Scotia. No exact figures are available for the changing patterns of land ownership in these counties but, throughout the province as a whole, the shift from small to large forest land-holdings has been dramatic. Small owners have seen their share of the woodlands shrink from 75 percent to less than 50 percent since the late 1950s. Through direct ownership or long-term government leases, the corporations now control more than half of the province's woodlands.

On this vast leasehold, Stora has adopted a policy of industrial forestry. It has treated the forest resource as a crop to be harvested as cheaply and intensively as possible and has adopted a sweeping mechanization program.

Clearcutting practices lay bare the land, stripping away whatever wood fibre is suitable for the mill, and leaving behind the environmental damage created by the machines. Clearcutting policies demand the use of large-capacity machinery and therefore the minimization of labour. A worker with a power saw can produce from 2-4 cords per day; a huge harvester machine, operated by one person, will fell, limb, buck, and accumulate eight-foot lengths of wood at a rate of 10-12 cords per hour.

Except for a small number of direct employees, Stora contracts out the bulk of its work on public lands to a small group of private operators who, with 20- to 30-person crews, carry out the actual harvesting. Control of the cutting operation is maintained through the corporation's ability to set prices to the contractor and through the mechanization policy. Contractors are encouraged to invest in the machinery (imported from Scandinavia) through a company policy of guaranteeing loans for such purchases. Keeping ahead of the heavy debt payments is adequate incentive to contractors to keep their machinery moving. The effect is to integrate the production of pulpwood into a highly-mechanized industrial process, from woodlot to mill.

A forest cannot regenerate under such an intensive clearing program. Industrialized cutting has necessitated the development of silviculture programs (of seeding, replanting, thinning, selective cutting, and so on) to encourage the forests to regenerate. In Nova Scotia, the silviculture program is paid for by the provincial government. Comparisons with the programs Stora has undertaken in Sweden raise serious questions concerning the effectiveness of the program here. Under the silviculture agreement, which began when the lease was renegotiated in 1971, the company paid the Department of Lands and Forests $2.75 per cord cut from crown land, and Lands and Forests returned $1.75 per cord to the company as a contract fee to carry out the silviculture program. In effect, Stora paid a stumpage fee of $1.00 per cord, one of the lowest in the country.

The arrangement allowed a yearly silviculture program budget of

$550,000. This money was supposed to provide adequate silviculture for the 18,000 acres of cut-over land each year. In practical terms, it amounted to only about $30 per acre. Stora claimed that this was sufficient to produce what the corporation calls the "New Forest."

In Sweden, however, where Stora operates on a similar scale, fully 15 percent of the total woodland cost went into silviculture. Of the 15,000 acres of cut-over land in Sweden, 85 percent were replaced, and natural regeneration occurred on less than 10 percent. Yet, according to the company, in Nova Scotia the majority of the "New Forest" could be reproduced by natural regeneration, and replanting took place on only 15 percent of the cut-over land.

Even more serious was the reduction of the cutting cycle in Nova Scotia. The cutting cycle there was reduced to 45 years even though in Sweden, after much more intensive silviculture, the cutting cycle was 75 years. A report commissioned by the Nova Scotia Department of Lands and Forests noted that Sweden and Nova Scotia have very similar climatic and soil conditions. These comparisons lead one to wonder whether the corporation's long-term plans are to develop the industry or, in the tradition of Canadian forest exploitation, merely to cut and run.

Industrialization of the forest has not brought security or prosperity to woodlot owners. Despite heavy and costly mechanization and growing corporate control, the price of pulpwood remains low. The price received by the woodlot owner for pulp does not reflect the real cost of production. Direct and indirect government subsidization to the companies for crown-land wood production, and the general rationalization of the traditional industry, are largely responsible for this distortion. Low stumpage rates charged by the government, the absence of provincial taxation, and government absorption of the costs of silviculture and some of the costs of road construction assist the company in holding down its production costs on the crown leasehold. With this amount of assistance, the company can afford to pay the private contractors relatively well for their cutting operations. This price, if fair for the contractor, is totally unrealistic for the woodlot owner.

Even though woodlot owners may receive a better price for a cord of pulpwood at the roadside, they cannot compete with the contractors, because the production costs of a private woodlot producer are more than those for actual harvesting. Added to the high costs of machinery are the costs of a 40-60 year cutting cycle and the maintenance of timber harvested only once in a lifetime. Without sufficient capital, no investment can be made in reforestation, and government assistance has not been forthcoming. From 1972-75, for example, the government spent merely $900,000 to aid small-woodlot owners. Even though independent woodlot owners receive more for their pulp than contractors do, their higher costs of production mean that the price they receive for pulp does not include the costs of labour.

Dealing with pulpwood solely on the basis of its market price means that the corporation does not have to bargain with the real costs of maintaining the resource and the people who produce it. The company keeps its input low by demanding and receiving government subsidies to cover many of its costs and by paying woodlot owners according to the demands of a market controlled by the company.

The decline in the market value of pulpwood in relation to the manufactured products demonstrates the squeeze on the small wood producer. In 1975, for example, pulpwood prices stood at $22 per cord at roadside, up 83 percent from the 1963 price of $12. Newsprint prices increased 94 percent (from $134 to $280 per ton) over the same period. Sulphite pulp prices leapt from $134 to $370 per ton, an increase of 175 percent.

The consequences for private-woodlot owners are clear. First, they are being forced out of the role of producer and into the role of resource caretaker, absorbing these costs for the benefit of the company. Between 80 and 90 percent of private producers no longer cut their own pulp. Instead, they make a contract with a private operator, who will clearcut, or else they abandon production altogether. Other than providing quick and cheap consumer items such as Christmas trees, a woodlot becomes of little economic value for the rest of an owner's lifetime. Second, having been forced out of production, the next logical step is to be forced off the land—and thousands of sale offers are received by the provincial government each year. The alternative employment opportunities are largely limited to pulp-cutting for the company or for a contractor. Such work is dependent on unemployment insurance compensation or on the employee's ability to support himself for at least a part of the year.

The independent producers thus face a false choice. With their revenue from pulp, they must choose to invest either in the maintenance of the resource or in their own individual survival. By choosing the latter, as they must, they sacrifice long-term interests to short-term needs and eventually lose control of their land. Faced with this pressure, woodlot owners have sought to organize but have faced tough opposition from government and pulp corporations to their demand for an effective marketing plan. Although the Nova Scotia Woodlot Owners Association was certified by the provincial Pulpwood Marketing Board as sole bargaining agent for wood producers in the province, weak legislation allowed NSFI to continue to resist the woodlot owners in the courts, and the woodlot owners have been repeatedly stymied in their efforts to bargain collectively.

Meanwhile, the corporations can afford to wait. One way or another, by direct acquisition or through the government's land purchase program, the industrial forest will fall to them.

Industrial forestry could be, if adapted to the needs of society and conducted in an environmentally responsible manner, a way of increasing the productivity of rural Nova Scotians and the economic viability of their communities. If work is organized more efficiently and the productivity of every hour of work is expanded by modern technology, then clearly the rural economy should benefit. However, precisely the opposite has happened. The expanded productivity of its workers has meant more gain for the company. The lower productivity of the independent producers has meant a lower return for their labour, thus reducing their contribution to the rural community.

Growing corporate control over Nova Scotia forest land is a far more important issue than the price of pulp. The development of the industrial forest has required that woodlot owners be kept in disarray and disorganization. It has required the consolidation of timberland holdings to make the forest accessible to modern technology. It has required the public to accept, without resistance, the corporate estimates of what the forest can produce and still survive. Most important, it has promoted the idea that local economies are barriers to the further development of the forest resource.

The experience of woodlot owners underlines the process of underdevelopment that passes officially for development. Government policy demands that development be equivalent to industrialization, and that industrialization take place by catering to private corporations. The older patterns of landholding, work, and resource use, and the communities based on these patterns, become obstacles to a development process which demands industrialization and consolidation—the industrial farm, the industrial fishing ground, the industrial forest.

The weakness of the woodlot owners' offensive reveals the eroded position of the independent producer and the rural community. Yet, their struggle and opposition have been the only significant obstacles to complete corporate takeover and the overexploitation of the forest resource. Nova Scotians have been slow to respond to this challenge, as they have been slow to see the real significance of the struggles of fishermen and other rural workers, but time is running out.

While the forest resource is being "strip mined," the rural population is becoming demoralized and displaced. The new industries being imposed by government policies do not adequately answer either the economic or social needs of the rural population, and do not represent a more-developed and rational use of the rural resource base over the long term.

The defeat of the woodlot owners is a crucial step towards a sell-out of the needs and interests of the majority of Nova Scotians. By ignoring the plight of the woodlot owners, Nova Scotians may forfeit their opportunity and their ability to create a development strategy rooted in the needs and capacities of the province's people and resources.

A Reader's Guide to the Spray

Christopher Majka

Every year it breaks out again like the annual budworm epidemic: the same controversy, the same disagreement over "facts," the same differences in values and visions of the forest; the head-to-head dispute which forester Michael Conway-Brown has called "The Longhair Emotional Obstructionists vs. the Nozzlehead Corporado Clones, with everyone sounding holier than Dow." What's going on beneath all of this? Is anyone right? Can there ever be a compromise solution which will please the forest industry, the government, the environmentalists, and the general public? Will it always be a polarized dispute with jobs and economic prosperity on one side of the coin, and healthy forests and healthy children on the other? What is this conflict really about?

There are, in effect, two separate areas of dispute in relation to the use of herbicides. The one which has received far and away the greater attention is the issue of potential health effects from the use of these substances. Don't, however, confuse this dispute with the one regarding the use of chemical *insecticides*, an issue which has also received a good deal of local press. Chemicals such as fenitrothion are used extensively in New Brunswick to combat the outbreak of spruce budworm. There are similar disagreements as to the effectiveness of such measures, and the potential health risks of these substances.

In relation to *herbicides* the health issue is this: The chemical substances used as herbicides are powerful and dangerous. The only reason they are used is that they are powerful and very toxic, at least to herbaceous plants. The chemical and forest industries, with the help of government, are always assuring us how safe these substances are for humans, but is this really so? We all know the story of DDT, documented so eloquently in Rachel Carson's *Silent Spring*. The lesson is that pesticides often have a myriad of side effects, many of which are not immediately obvious and may only make themselves known years or generations later.

In Nova Scotia, much of the concern about possible health effects has centred on the infamous dioxins. There are many different dioxins and there are many different sources of dioxin, one of which is phenoxy herbicides such as 2,4-D and 2,4,5-T. Dioxins are inevitable by-products of the manufacture of phenoxy herbicides. A number of dioxins are found in both of these substances, and some are very little studied in terms of their toxicologies. However, the one which has received the most attention is called

---

This chapter is based on an article first published in *New Maritimes* (February 1985).

2,3,7,8-tetrachlorodibenzodioxin, more conveniently referred to as TCDD. This little molecule is really nasty—it is often referred to as one of the most toxic synthetic substances known to humanity. Toxic effects have been found at the unimaginably minute levels of parts per trillion (most toxicities of substances are measured in parts per million or parts per thousand, not parts per trillion). Justifiably, many people have been concerned about what the broad-scale application of chemicals contaminated with TCDD would mean for the health of the forest, the plants and animals within it, and the neighbouring communities of people. It was this concern which took fifteen Cape Breton landowners to court to stop the application of Agent Orange (a 50-50 mixture of 2,4-D and 2,4,5-T) to the forests near their communities in what became known as "The Herbicide Trial."

This is where the issue gets complicated. The chemical companies contend that the current levels of TCDD in 2,4,5-T (this dioxin does not occur in 2,4-D) are acceptable. Current provincial standards in Nova Scotia require the level of TCDD to be less than 10 parts per billion. This is very much less than the levels of TCDD found in the Agent Orange which was sprayed during the Vietnam War, the effects of which have been the subject of a huge class action suit of Vietnam veterans in the United States. What levels of TCDD are "acceptable" is a matter for both conjecture and dispute, some authorities considering that the only acceptable level for such acutely carcinogenic (cancer-causing), mutagenic (causing mutations to the genetic material), teratogenic (causing abnormal growth), and embryotoxic (deadly to embryos) substances is a zero level.

TCDD is not the only culprit here. There are a number of other dioxins in phenoxy herbicides. The famous studies in Sweden which showed a six-fold increase of certain soft-tissue sarcomas and malignant lymphomas (different kinds of cancers) as a result of exposure to phenoxy acids and chlorophynols, were not able to distinguish whether these cancers resulted from the phenoxy herbicides themselves or from some of their contaminants such as dioxins or dibenzofurans.

Conducted by a leading Swedish cancer researcher, Dr. Lennert Hardell, these studies examined people who had been occupationally exposed to phenoxy herbicides while working in the forest industry. This research has been accepted by the International Agency for Research on Cancer (IARC) and the World Health Organization (WHO). Dr. Hardell said, in his written deposition to the court in the Nova Scotia herbicide trial, "It is possible that the phenoxy herbicides and their contaminants could increase the risk of soft tissue sarcomas and rare lymphomas in a population [i.e., Nova Scotia] exposed to lower levels [than the Swedish forestry workers] of these materials environmentally. I cannot say that they will, I can only state that there is no evidence to say that they will not."

This is, obviously, a complicated and difficult issue to resolve, fraught with questions of value such as "How safe is safe?" and "At what point do you barter health for economics?" There is obviously no one answer to these questions. It depends where you place your values in society, and as long as the case for and against herbicides is argued along these lines, we will continue to see a heated impasse. Before we have to face such a decision, however, we should carefully ask ourselves what these chemicals are being used for. Is this an intelligent use of such substances; if so, are they able to do the job for which they are intended, and if they are, are there any alternatives which can do this work as safely, efficiently, and effectively? In other words, only if there are really no options to using these chemicals in order to have a successful forest industry, should we have to face the difficult dilemma of what chemicals and in what dosages.

Herbicides are used for quite a number of different purposes, but the one that has been most hotly debated in the Maritimes is referred to, rather euphemistically, as "conifer release." The theory of this silvicultural technique runs something like this: In areas where young conifers have been planted or are regenerating, they compete for certain resources with other plants. If you can eliminate this competition, consisting of raspberries, hardwoods, and other herbaceous plants, then presumably more sunlight and soil nutrients will be available to the conifers. The thus "released" conifers will grow more quickly and get a head start in the crucial early years of their lives. The trees grow more quickly, therefore they mature sooner and can be harvested with a shorter rotation period. More growth leads to earlier maturity equals greater profits in a shorter time.

Thus far it all sounds great. The problem with this rosy picture, however, is that it is built on sheer conjecture. Dr. Jan Newton, senior economist with the San Francisco–based Environmental Service Associates, has carried out the most complete and comprehensive study ever done on the economics of herbicide use in forest management. She has, on numerous occasions, pointed out that there are simply no hard facts to support any of this theory. After a year of research she discovered that there are no statistics that show increased timber yields as a result of herbicide use.

Now, the absence of such information is not simply an accident or a gigantic oversight on the part of the forest industry. As a number of studies on herbicides are beinning to show, the simple scenario of herbicide use as outlined above just doesn't hold water. Ecosystems are much more complicated than this. Certain plants, such as raspberries, are very involved in the nitrogen metabolism of the soil. If you eliminate these plants you impoverish the soil, which in turn can affect the growth rates of young conifers. Many plants, including the raspberries and hardwoods, are very important in stabilizing the soil, something which is especially important in cut-over areas. By eliminating these plants you run the risk of greatly increasing soil leaching and erosion, again something which will negatively affect the young conifers.

In three separate studies undertaken by Groundwork Inc. in Oregon and Idaho it was shown that herbicides, aerially sprayed for conifer release programs, actually caused a reduction in the survival and growth of the conifers (pines, in these studies). Many young conifers with brush around them actually had better growth and survival rates than trees in the open, apparently because the brush protected the young trees from excessive frost and sunlight. Secondly, they noted that the application of herbicides actually damaged conifers and reduced their growth. One study area showed 70 percent of trees with herbicide-damaged needles.

There are many studies which show the negative effects of herbicides. One, by Gratowski, on the application of 2,4-D and 2,4,5-T on fir and pine, found that, "All spray treatments caused some reduction in height growth during the first two year period after spraying, even those where no visible effects were evident." Another study, done by Ahrens, found that "Glyphosphate (Roundup) severely injured conifers when sprayed overhead, but not when applied as directed sprays in established plantings." A study carried out by Sutton, comparing Roundup application to manual methods, found that, "Survival overall has been very significantly poorer in the herbicide plots than in the manual plots. . . . Glyphosphate therefore, almost certainly caused some mortality among spruce."

In a study carried out in the Siuslaw National Forest in Oregon, and published in the establishment *Journal of Forestry*, Walter Knapp and Thomas Turpin, both professional silviculturalists, and John Beuter, a professor of forest management, examined a number of different methods of managing forests, and were able to show that in the cases of both growth and net worth of conifers, eliminating phenoxy herbicides from programs of forest management would only decrease growth by a maximum of 1 percent and worth by 2 percent. Even eliminating all kinds of chemical release, phenoxies, glyphosphate, etc., would decrease the growth of the forest by only a maximum of 3 percent and worth by 6 percent. Clearly chemical release is simply not an important component of forest management even at its best, and at its worst, it can actually harm the species it is supposed to help.

Faced with this kind of information the pulp companies have countered with arguments that in today's competitive marketplace, it is necessary to intensively manage forests in order to maximize yield, and that manual methods are too costly and ineffective. All kinds of statistics have been conjured up in support of this argument. Costs for 2,4-D application have been cited at $25/acre as compared to $1,200/acre for manual control. Manual methods have been accused of everything from not working to causing worker injuries.

The costs of both herbicide application and manual release methods vary according to a number of factors, including the site, forest composition, the kind of equipment, the terrain, etc. Economist Jan Newton's study of these questions is perhaps the most comprehensive to date. In a typical case in the United States in 1978 her breakdown of information shows a per acre cost of aerial application of herbicides as $U.S. 82.86. This figure does not include a number of factors, however. Diesel oil is often used as a "carrier" for the herbicide and this use would add approximately $10.50 to the cost. It also does not include costs for "down time" as a result of weather conditions which do not permit the aerial application of herbicides (winds greater than 6 mph, rain, fog, etc.). Therefore a conservative estimate of the cost of aerial herbicide application is in the range of $U.S. 82.86-93.36 per acre.

How does this compare with the cost of manual methods? In a study published by Kowen and Miller in 1979 looking at the cost for all areas of the Pacific Northwest of the United States, they found that the average cost was $U.S. 115.57 per acre. In Siuslaw National Forest in Oregon, 1529 acres were manually treated for conifer release at an average cost of $U.S. 89.46 per acre. More recently, Michael Conway-Brown quotes an average bid price from contractors in the USA of $U.S. 106.86 per acre, probably the best current figure. Manual and chemical costs are very much in the same economic ballpark. All other considerations and complexities aside, manual methods may cost only as little as 14 percent more than chemical ones—certainly not 50 times more as has been suggested by the pulp companies.

In addition, manual methods are much more efficient. Chemical herbicides simply do not do the job of conifer release. Girdling tools (a manual method), for example, do an excellent and highly selective job. MacMillan Bloedel in British Columbia measured an 88-100 percent mortality on red alder with this tool. The British Columbia Forest Service found a 90-95 percent mortality.

Clearing saws are another manual method that is very efficient and selective. The U.S. Forest Service found a 100 percent mortality on four-year-old alder with this tool and a productivity rate of 2.4 acres per worker per day. They concluded their study this way: "The results were impressive and suggest, on an economic level at least, that this tool may be competitive with chemical release treatments." With manual methods you can cut exactly what brush you want, not damage the conifers, leave some brush to help shelter them, not threaten the soil with erosion, etc. Manual methods are cost-competitive and are more selective and efficient than chemical ones.

An important aspect of this whole issue is where forest management money is spent. A large proportion of funds spent on aerial herbicide application goes to purchase and transport chemicals, and to pay for aircraft, pilots, etc. The benefits to the local economy are marginal at best. In contrast, the largest proportion of funds spent for manual release methods goes into the wages of the people who do the work. The technology is inexpensive (girdling tools cost about $85 apiece), no chemicals are required, the methods are very safe, and there is far less "down time" as a result of weather, etc. "Consider this," said Michael Conway-Brown: "It costs $1,200/hour to put a large spray helicopter in the air. How many workers can be put in the field for that?" With a rural unemployment rate of approximately 20 percent in Nova Scotia, this is a question which many people should be asking themselves.

In the face of all this, why do the pulp companies persist with their chemical herbicide campaigns? Several propositions suggest themselves. Many of the executives of the pulp companies come out of a 1950s mindset which saw chemicals as a solution to all of society's woes. The use of herbicides in Nova Scotia and of insecticides in New Brunswick are both expressions of this overriding belief. They are both aspects of an approach to forests which has been called "armchair forest management." Herbicides permit "armchair forest management" rather than "people management." There seems to be reason to believe that forest industry management is willing even to risk loss of profits to sustain this method of management.

Consider the implications of initiating a large-scale manual release program in the Maritimes. This would involve hiring, on a continuing basis, a large number of workers, thus dispersing some of the power and control, inevitably, which the pulp companies have over their operations. What would happen for instance if these people, on whom the pulp companies would now be dependent, should demand higher wages and working conditions, and organize trade unions? This option makes chills run down the spines of pulp company executives. For them, it is to be avoided at all cost.

The overwhelming preponderance of information favours the use of selective manual conifer release methods over chemical herbicides, for reasons of cost, efficiency, efficacy, and employment benefits. All this can be concluded even before we have cause to examine the possible health and environmental problems associated with chemical herbicides.

The Political Economy of Pesticide and Herbicide Testing in New Brunswick

Bruce Livesey

Alfred Cain went to work for the New Brunswick Electric Power Commission in the 1960s, spraying the brush along power lines every summer with a 50-50 mixture of the herbicides 2,4,5-T and 2,4-D, better known as Agent Orange. Cain and the spray crew he worked with wore no protective gear. They were told by the commission's engineer that the defoliant was safe enough to drink. At the time, Cain broke out in a rash from the wrists to the elbow. Within ten years he experienced blistering, aching joints and nervous troubles.

Of the over 200 such sprayers who worked the lines with him between 1956 and 1964, 73 are now dead. Suicide as the cause of death among the group is ten times the provincial norm; half the survivors have been treated for nervous problems; and 90 percent of them have serious health problems.

These workers' struggle for compensation is the subject of a well-known court case by the Sprayers of Dioxin Association (SODA) against the power commission and the chemical companies.

What is less well-known is that the New Brunswick government in 1984 was spraying over 80,000 acres of forest with 2,4,5-T and 2,4-D; and that after all these years, the loopholes in the spray registration process that left Alfred Cain soaked in cancer-causing agents nearly every working day in 1960 are still a long way from being plugged.

Why spray herbicides? The answer is simple: chemicals such as 2,4,5-T are used by companies like J.D. Irving, Miramichi Lumber, and Fraser, in conjunction with the New Brunswick Department of Natural Resources, because softwood is in demand, hardwood growth competes with softwood, and herbicides kill hardwoods. As Ian Methven, chairman of the University of New Brunswick's Forest Resources Department, put it: "It's very possible we could be doing irreparable damage . . . but we've developed an industrial technology society and we can't depend on nature to take its course."

These are the benefits. The responsibility for assessing the risk lies with the governments' chemical registration processes. In order to register any herbicide or insecticide for use in Canada, chemical companies must submit data packages to the Pesticide Division of Agriculture Canada in Ottawa. These

This chapter is based on an article first published in *New Maritimes* (September 1984).

packages detail four areas of concern: health and safety, and environmental, aquatic, and agronomic impact. The data is based on tests carried out on the chemical by the company's own labs or by those of private testing firms contracted for this purpose.

The Pesticide Division cannot show the data it receives to provincial authorities without the permission of the chemical manufacturer but, because of the expense involved, Ottawa has no separate labs of its own with which to conduct long-term testing. Agriculture Canada officials are anxious to point out that they do not simply accept the companies' word that tests are valid; the manufacturers are required to produce scientific data. Yet Wayne Ormrod, Director of the Pesticide Division, explained candidly that, "it is not the basis of the system that we in Agriculture or our colleagues in Health Canada do the standard testing for chemical companies."

The case of Industrial Biotest (IBT) in Chicago shows the potential problems with this system. The U.S. Environmental Protection Agency audited the chemical testing laboratories of IBT in 1976 and found that over 800 of its tests on the health effects of 140 commonly used pesticides were invalid. IBT, now out of business, was at the time the largest private lab testing for chemical companies in the United States. As of 1983, over 40 of the invalid-test chemicals were still on the Canadian market, without being retested. The missing tests are for birth defects and cancer. Another audit done last year showed that the chemical companies themselves had repeated only 36 percent of the invalid IBT tests.

Wayne Ormrod said he doesn't know how many tests on these compounds have now been completed, but he is sure that fewer than 40 uncleared chemicals on the market have yet to be done. Asked what prevents laboratories from repeating IBT's actions, he said that federal health officials test the verification processes at the labs. When questioned further on whether or not regular audits are currently being done on the labs, Ormrod said he didn't know, and that, "Quite frankly I am not competent to speak out on that subject because toxicology is not our bag here in Agriculture."

This is evident. Ormrod was not aware that 2,4,5-T was being sprayed in New Brunswick in 1984; he called the controversy surrounding the chemical a "dead issue" because the province would not in future be able to get the product. Referring to the fact that Dow Chemical had withdrawn the compound from the market in 1983, Ormrod apparently did not know that it continued to be manufactured by Union Carbide, and that New Brunswick bought an almost new stock from this supplier.

Once a pesticide is registered by the federal government, regulations regarding its use are up to each province. In 1977, New Brunswick passed the Pesticides Control Act, creating the 10-person Pesticides Advisory Board (PAB). Although the Minister of the Environment gives final approval for pesticide applications, the board reviews requests, suggests standards, licences vendors and sprayers, and decides whether or not specific pesticides should be used in the province. PAB Chairman Ken Brown explained that a company applying for a spraying permit must list the product, the concentration, and how it is going to be applied, and the board reserves the right to deny companies the use of pesticides about which it is unhappy.

This registration process, too, is not very sound. During the board's first years of operation in the late 1970s, said PAB member Stephen Hoyt of the Department of Natural Resources, there was a lack of knowledge about pesticides on the board. PAB Secretary Gregory Shanks said that if it wasn't for the toxicologist the board hired in 1978, Dr. Donald Ecobichon, some potentially detrimental pesticides (on which Ottawa's expertise had been questionable) would have been approved without further scrutiny. The budworm spray Matacil, which has been accused of causing Reye's Syndrome, was one such pesticide.

Ecobichon, an enthusiastic supporter of pesticide spraying, has confidence in the current registration process, though he concedes concern with chemicals in use today that were registered when the system was less thorough. He claimed he had "caught" a couple of pesticides and refused to have them okayed until further assurances came from the companies. "The problem I have now is with the old products," he said. "Unless there is attention brought to them, without any constant watch, there is a possibility a product can slip through."

The registration of 2,4,5-T is "old," dating back to the 1950s. And improvements in the review process do not necessarily mean that it is now "thorough." The 2,4,5-T example is a case in point. The chemical is banned in the United States, many European countries, and some provinces in Canada. When Dow, formerly its largest manufacturer, reacted to its increasing unpopularity by removing the chemical from the market in 1983, forest companies were left without a herbicide they could apply from the air. The herbicide Roundup (which contains no dioxin) was widely favoured as an alternative to 2,4,5-T, but its 1976 federal registration was limited to ground application. Agriculture Canada quickly approved Roundup for aerial application in early 1984, and New Brunswick PAB member Hoyt admitted that he saw no information on the chemical when the provincial board approved its use. PAB Chairman Ken Brown conceded that the board didn't ask for any information from Monsanto Inc., the company which makes Roundup. Dr. Ecobichon's word that it was safe, and the federal registration, were simply accepted. Monsanto is one of the companies whose tests were falsified by Industrial Biotest in Chicago, and the company has refused to repeat five of the invalid tests.

It is what some of these pesticides contain that causes concern amongst environmentalists. Many people, such as Catherine Richards, president of the Concerned Parents Group, believe there is no such thing as a safe level of TCDD, the dioxin contained in 2,4,5-T. "There is no safe level for a carcinogen," she argues.

The Sprayers of Dioxin Association, too, is basing its lawsuit on the dangerous qualities of TCDD. Jerry White, one of the founders of SODA, says that documents revealed during recent hearings in the USA concerning Vietnam veterans and Agent Orange, show that Dow Chemical was well aware of the herbicides' hazardous properties in 1965.

Others point to the importance of the manufacturing process in determining the safety of 2,4,5-T. The lower the temperature during the burning process in which the herbicide is made, the lower the concentration of TCDD, although this makes the end product more expensive. David Walters, a member of the PAB and Fredericton's medical officer of health, argues that reduced levels of TCDD decrease the risk of danger to a low level. Still others talk about additional problems. Even when you bring the concentration of TCDD down, levels of another dioxin called "furin" rise, says Conservation Council of New Brunswick President Hajo Versteeg. "And that [furin] has not been adequately tested," he says. "It could be as dangerous or more dangerous than TCDD."

Versteeg sat on a New Brunswick task force which looked into cancer and the environment, one of many provincial attempts (there had been six or seven task forces by 1984) to study pesticides. The task force, working under McGill University epidemiologist Dr. Walter Spitzer, presented its final report in March 1984. It concluded that federal standards for evaluating the toxicity of chemicals were too lax and should include long-term animal tests. The report went on to say that the periodic review of chemicals, old and new, should be carried out, and that the chemical formulations of pesticides should be made public.

Information is the problem. The 1984 task force on chemicals in the environment and human reproductive problems, chaired by Dr. J. Donald Hatcher, Dean of Medicine at Dalhousie University, was unable to get essential information on Roundup from Monsanto. The task force went on to say that, for investigating the insecticide fenitrothion (the most widely sprayed budworm agent in New Brunswick), "the available information was very limited," and that what was available was unacceptable by present-day standards.

Catherine Richards of Concerned Parents says it has always been difficult to find out what pesticides contain, especially the chemicals' emulsifiers (used to dissolve them in water). The chemical companies refuse to release information publicly because they would be giving away "trade secrets" to competitors. For while the ingredients of a chemical may themselves be well known, what toxicologist Ecobichon calls the "black art of formulation" remains strictly company property.

The issue, once again, is economics. The forests must be sprayed with herbicides because of the demands of the market for softwood, the make-up of many highly suspect chemicals cannot be released because of the demands of the competitive market for chemicals, and on it goes. Two recent federal studies have shown that Canadians may be exposed to unacceptable levels of dioxin, and that this and other toxic chemicals are far more widespread than is generally thought. Over 65 studies, costing more than $100 million, are presently in progress trying to learn more about TCDD. The chemical is being sprayed on the say-so of regulatory authorities, practically all of whom agree that much more needs to be learned about it. "Learn first, spray later" should not seem so radical a proposition.

Underdeveloping Nova Scotia's Forests, and the Role of Corporate Counter-Intelligence

Aaron Schneider

The Nova Scotia Royal Commission on Forestry (NSRCF), formed in response to worries about a future pulp shortage in the province, held its hearings between August 1982 and December 1983. At the same time, a small group of Cape Breton landowners challenged the way a Swedish multinational corporation (Stora Kopparbergs Bergslags AB) managed Cape Breton's forest resources, in a case which became famous as the "Herbicides Trial."

A major issue raised both in the trial and at the hearings of the NSRCF was the danger of pesticides to human health and their dubious advantages in forest management. Although the commissioners were invited (by this writer) to hear the evidence at the trial, they declined, even though it was made clear to them that the witnesses would be world authorities on pesticide use.

As preparations for the trial proceeded, it became increasingly obvious that herbicides were not a means to an end (that is, an effective and efficient method of conifer release) but an end in itself—the firm entrenchment of a parallel chemical industry under the foresty umbrella. The continued use of the herbicide mixture of 2,4-D and 2,4,5-T (Agent Orange) put Nova Scotia in its accustomed position of being just another Third World market for toxic chemicals. The trial's outcome was a disappointment to most Cape Bretoners, but it did not diminish the overwhelming public rejection of 2,4-D and 2,4,5-T as forest herbicides, and these were replaced by Roundup in later spray programs, although with continued opposition. (Roundup's registration was based on tests by the Industrial Biotest Laboratories, later convicted of fraud.)

The report of the NSRCF in November 1984 was a second disappointment. The commission's report was assailed from all quarters. Perhaps the report's most significant quality is its implicit blueprint for underdeveloping Nova Scotia's forests through the control of private woodlands management. Uniform management, as dictated by the province along the guidelines set out by the Royal Commission, would secure a viable market for "input" industries supplying pesticides, fertilizers, and seedlings. This would impose a capital-intensive technology on wood production, which had previously been labour-

This chapter is based on two articles published in *New Maritimes* (August 1985 and March 1987).

intensive and heavily dependent on natural regeneration and sustained fertility.

The danger with this scenario lies in creating a highly competitive market where, in order to compete, a private producer would feel compelled to use expensive inputs, which he could not afford without government assistance. Such assistance could only then be obtained by accepting a provincial management plan, complete with all the constraints suggested by the Royal Commission. This would ensure the continued production of cheap fibre (at low stumpage rates) for the pulp mills, but it would also establish wood production as an adjunct to input industries, with forest practices secondary to chemical sales. Such a situation would be of great advantage to the respective industries, but of dubious benefit to the private producer, the taxpayer, and the unemployed.

The wood producer would lose his independence and his choice of management options while being condemned to produce at appallingly low stumpage rates. The taxpayer would watch helplessly as revenues were drained away from the province and the country to buy foreign-manufactured inputs or were paid out as subsidies to foreign-owned pulp companies. In short, most of the capital would fly abroad rather than remain to be invested in local development. For the unemployed, the preference for herbicides over manual clearing in conifer release (the elimination of non-softwoods so as to promote the growth of wood destined for pulp) has cruel social and economic implications. It amounts to a preference for foreign corporations' and helicopter contractors' profits over the development of skilled forest workers in a province with unusually high unemployment.

One of the Royal Commission's recommendations was particularly high on the agenda of the Minister of Lands and Forests, Ken Streatch. The rescinding of the Forest Improvement Act, along with its provisions for public input, stands to isolate the public from all major decisions regarding the development of forest resources, thus rendering a service of great convenience to the forest industry. This would allow the continued underdevelopment of resources and labour for the benefit of industries which are largely foreign-owned, a situation well known both in the Maritimes and throughout the Third World. It will also allow the establishment of agribusiness-type input industries in relation to forestry and will bring the same consequences of capital drain and financial crisis that this process has brought to farming.

What, one wonders, is a nice government like ours doing in a shady deal like this?

Agriculture Canada's announcement of its intention to review the registration of the herbicide 2,4-D in late September 1986 made the front page of the *Globe and Mail*, as well it should have, considering the level of public interest on both sides of the herbicide issue.

In Sydney, where the infamous Herbicides Trial is still well remembered, there was nothing but a small mention buried in the back pages of the *Cape Breton Post*. Yet, it was the very question of the safety of phenoxy herbicides (2,4-D and 2,4,5-T) that was the centrepiece of evidence presented by the plaintiffs in the trial that attempted to stop the spraying of the Cape Breton Highlands. The 1979-81 Swedish epidemiological study[1] of forestry workers by Hardell, Eriksson, Lenner et al. that connected certain cancers, including non-Hodgkin's lymphoma, with exposure to phenoxy herbicides such as 2,4-D was presented as evidence at the trial, with Michael Eriksson himself as a witness.

If the work of Hardell, Eriksson, Lenner et al. failed to impress Justice Merlin Nunn, who decided against the herbicides plaintiffs, it did lay the basis for further studies that have since eliminated the objections raised against the Swedish study. A new study from the U.S. National Cancer Institute was done on Kansas farmworkers in 1986. As reported in the September 5th edition of the *Journal of the American Medical Association*, the Kansas research, conducted by Sheila K. Hoar and others, upholds the Swedish study's association between phenoxy herbicide use and non-Hodgkin's lymphoma. The Kansas study has also been judged by American Medical Association (AMA) peer review to be stronger than the Swedish study in several respects.

While no one is suggesting a review of Justice Nunn's decision in the Herbicides Trial, some mention of this new evidence would be of more than secondary interest to the people of Cape Breton, a majority of whom, according to the Gallup poll conducted at the time, supported the goals of the plaintiffs. Of more immediate relevance, 2,4-D was still being used on 4,000-6,000 acres of power lines and roadsides in Nova Scotia that summer against the strong opposition of environmental groups.

Following the September 1986 registration review announcement by Agriculture Canada, New Brunswick banned the use of 2,4-D; then Nova Scotia Minister of the Environment Guy LeBlanc said that his department would no longer issue permits for 2,4-D pending the federal review; and the Canadian Environmental Law Association called for a federal ban on 2,4-D.

While local media found the issue a sleeper, the pesticide industry displayed an immediate and keen interest. Representatives of a thirteen-company task force met with researchers to discuss the Kansas study. One of the spokesmen for the task force, Dave Dietz, who made his Canadian debut as an herbicide advocate at a 1984 "educational seminar" discussed later, did not think the news was all bad. He was quoted in the October 1986 edition of *Science News* to the effect that the overall incidence of lymphoma among farmers who wore protective equipment was not as greatly elevated. "That for us is interesting and probably good," he said. Given Mr. Dietz's history one could predict that the company task force will see that 2,4-D dies hard. Will we get a ban on 2,4-D, more protective clothing, more label directions, more indecision, or more Roundup?

To see what forces are acting here, it is useful to look at the way the

---

[1] L. Hardell, M. Eriksson, P. Lenner et al., "Malignant Lymphoma and Exposure to Chemicals, Especially Organic Solvents, Chlorophenols and Phenoxy Acids: A Case-Control Study," *Br. J. Cancer* 43 (1981): 169-76.

agricultural chemical industry customarily responds to opposition towards its products. In April 1986 a private meeting and workshop between forest-industry officials and a "counter intelligence consulting firm," as the Edmonton *Journal* referred to it, was organized by Champion Forest Products of Hinton, Alberta, at an Edmonton hotel. The agenda for the meeting billed Ian Fraser of CML Consultants, Halifax, as the seminar leader. "Ian Fraser and his Associates," the agenda read, "have considerable experience and success dealing with 'environmental activists.' Their military backgrounds . . . include extensive training and experience in counter-intelligence and conflict situations. This has proven to be very effective when dealing with the 'anti's' who, as we have all come to realize, do not always play by the rules."

The workshop cost $60 per delegate, with lunch hosted by Dow Chemical. Alberta's Environment Department boycotted the meeting, much to its credit. Champion was trying to get approval to use Roundup and Velparin in an herbicide-spraying program on 450 acres of forest land it leases from the Crown. The "anti's" are the local townspeople of Hinton, who had delivered 1,500 names on a petition asking for a moratorium on aerial spraying. Bob Udell, Champion's Forest Manager, described the seminar as aimed at "those of us who are either in the trenches or soon will be" over the spraying issue. Alberta moved to reject the spraying proposal sooner than might have been expected, possibly in reaction to the bizarre nature of the tactics proposed by Champion, CML, and Dow.

This whole approach is best understood as a reaction to the declining credibility of forestry and agriculture herbicide advocates. Reports of high mortality to crop-tree seedlings, the growing debate about whether conifer release (the removal of competing vegetation) actually helps or hinders crop-tree growth, the many studies indicating the carcinogenic nature of herbicides, indications that herbicides increase the incidence of insect pests and soil pathogens, and the notorious Industrial Biotest Laboratories fraud, are causing the chemical manufacturers and their lobbying organizations to attack their critics rather than stress the ever more dubious merits of their wares.

This "counter-intelligence" approach is not new. On October 25, 1984, an interoffice memo was distributed with the New Brunswick Ministry of Natural Resources' Forestry Service. The government memo describes an "educational seminar" sponsored by the Atlantic Vegetation Management Association, a central premise of which was that "the philosophy of environmental movements is provided by Marxist-Leninists who are using environmental concerns as a way of furthering the Marxist struggle."

The purpose of the seminar was to discuss the promotion of grass-roots movements to fight the environmental movement. One such group highlighted at the meeting was Oregonians for Food and Shelter (OFS), which was organized by the law firm of Dave Dietz to reverse some of the "antipesticide momentum" in Oregon. Said Dietz to the Halifax seminar, "OFS as a citizens' group can attack environmentalists in ways that industry never could, forcing them to divert time and money to defending themselves."

This outlook can also be traced back through the annals of the Canadian

Agricultural Chemical Association (CACA). In its paper to the 1982 Industrial Vegetation Management Association seminar in Calgary, CACA described itself as a small organization consisting of 50 active and associate company members plus a "large number of organizations and personnel who belong to and work solely within the Provincial Councils . . . putting out local 'brush fires.' " Their primary concern, the organization said, was with improving the relations of agricultural chemical producers with the government and the public in the harassing atmosphere of environmentalists, and the "stranglehold with product specific registration." This industry has been assailed, said CACA, "by a well-organized, well-financed and well-orchestrated anti-pesticide movement. . . . We should first of all stop complimenting our adversaries with the label 'environmentalists.' I prefer to apply the term 'activist' or even 'obstructionist.' "

The CACA paper continued, describing "cells of activists in urban areas." In its outline of CACA's public relations plans, item 9 is "monitoring activists' groups—who they are, how they operate, who their officers are, how they are financed, etc. In other words, military intelligence." Item 10 is also revealing: "Monitoring the Ottawa and Provincial Capital scenes and cooling adverse political reaction." The paper ends with a call to support organizations like the Atlantic Vegetation Management Association.

In an earlier, 1978 CACA newsletter announcing the election of D.E. Webber, General Manager of Dow Chemical's Agricultural and Specialty Chemicals Department, as President of CACA, Mr. Webber's strategy to create a better climate for production and sales of pesticides was discussed: "This will involve the launching of a campaign against 'political' environmentalists." Mr. Webber, we are told, will "call on those in government responsible to join him in this important effort." "Webber feels that if the 'political environmentalists' are not stopped now, they could do irretrievable harm to the industry. . . . The campaign however will be low key. The emphasis will be on involving government pesticide control authorities in refuting charges resulting from 'political' environmentalism." It is interesting to note that CACA made a submission to the NSRCF in April 1983. CACA was further consulted by the NSRCF as an authority (however biased) on the consequences of pesticides with regard to human health.

In the same newsletter the outgoing president of CACA, G.H.S. Malcolmson of DuPont Canada Limited, is quoted as saying, "Those who charged that pesticides are dangerous hazards are really saying that the government regulations and the people who enforce them are not doing their jobs. It seems to me that this entirely undeserved allegation should be vigorously refuted by the people concerned." Malcolmson is further quoted, urging the growers and their associations to speak up: "Who can more effectively refute insinuations about mysterious pesticide-caused diseases than the people who have used these products as directed year after year without ill effect?" Perhaps the Kansas farmers who are dying from 2,4-D-induced lymphoma would have something to say.

CACA's militaristic counter-intelligence tactics, as the examples from

Halifax and Hinton make clear, have moved increasingly into the mainstream of chemical-corporation public relations. It is one of the ironies of underdevelopment that the Maritimes can export counter-intelligence to help a western lumber company expose people to herbicides, while the west sends us kiln-dried lumber because our own forests have been reduced to pulpstands.

Perhaps it is time, if we are to deal with forestry management as activists, that we pursue a far more creative program. Although we are promoting manual clearing as a better way to release conifers, we do not in fact support monoculture forestry at all. We also question whether or not "release" of any kind actually promotes optimum conifer growth. We could press the Department of Lands and Forests to explore integrated pest-management techniques as a real alternative to pesticides. Rather than forcing on the province, at great expense and future risk (economic as well as ecological), the type of forest that is compatible with the present forest industry, we could lobby the provincial department to investigate alternative forest-industry technologies that are compatible with, and complementary to, a diversified forest, and less prone to pest and disease infestations.

There is no guarantee that the pulp mills will still be here in 40 years when the new forest is ready. We cannot predict the changes in markets and technology that could put us in a predicament opposite to that of the pulp scarcity outlook put forward by the Royal Commission. One indicator of change is represented by a new cardboard and paper mill in Cuba, which uses *bagasse* (the fibre left from the pressing of sugar cane) in place of pulpwood—an efficient use of the abundant waste product of that country's primary industry. It is entirely possible that we could end up with an oversupply of trees good only for pulp, and with nowhere to sell them. Diversity is common sense.

Both the Royal Commission and the Herbicides Trial are examples—of a kind increasingly familiar as the real political economy of regional underdevelopment—of dependency disguised as growth. The wolf of underdevelopment has been wrapped in the sheepskin of jobs and prosperity. We need to be aware of the consequences. Who will prosper and who will not? We also need to be aware of who the real actors are who shape these policies and portray mock realities in their own interests.

Further Reading: Forestry

History

Hiller, James. "The Origins of the Pulp and Paper Industry in Newfoundland." *Acadiensis* 11, No. 2 (Spring 1982): 42-68.

Hunt, Russell, and Campbell, Robert. *K.C. Irving: The Art of the Industrialist* (Toronto, 1973).

Johnson, Ralph S. *Forests of Nova Scotia* (Halifax, 1986).

Lower, Arthur R.M. *Great Britain's Woodyard: British America and the Timber Trade, 1763-1867* (Montreal, 1973).

Robertson, Barbara R. "Trees, Treaties and the Timing of Settlement: A Comparison of the Lumber Industry in Nova Scotia and New Brunswick, 1784-1867." *Nova Scotia Historical Review* 4, No. 1 (1984): 37-55.

Wynn, Graeme. *Timber Colony: A Historical Geography of Early Nineteenth Century New Brunswick* (Toronto, 1981).

Theory

Bahro, Rudolf. *Socialism and Survival* (London, 1982).

Clow, Michael. "Marxism and the 'Environmental Question': an Assessment of Bahro." *Studies in Political Economy,* No. 20 (Summer 1986): 171-86.

Present Perspectives

Baker, Howard. "New Brunswick Sprays Again." *New Maritimes* (December 1982): 10-11.

Lansky, Mitch. "Lessons in Forest Degradation." *New Maritimes* (April 1985): 11-12.

May, Elizabeth. *Budworm Battles: The fight to stop the aerial insecticide spraying of the forests of Eastern Canada* (Tantallon, 1982).

Nova Scotia, Royal Commission on Forestry. *Forestry: Report of the Nova Scotia Royal Commission on Foresty, 1984* (Halifax, 1984).

Orton, David. *Pulpwood forestry in Nova Scotia.* Gorsebrook Research Institute for Atlantic Canada Studies, Occasional Paper, 1983.

Peabody, George. *Forestry* (Halifax: Ecology Action Centre, n.d.).

Royce, Rachel, and Tom Ptacek. "On Trial: A Look at the Plaintiffs of the Herbicide Trial in the Supreme Court of Nova Scotia." *New Maritimes* (July-August 1983): 5-8.

Senopi Consultants Limited. *A Report on Noranda Mines Limited for Conseil Régional d'Aménagement du Nord* (Petit Rocher, 1979).

Swift, Jamie. *Cut and Run: The Assault on Canada's Forests* (Toronto, 1983).

Wanamaker, Glenn. "Herbicides Plaintiffs Hang Tough." *New Maritimes* (November 1983): 5-6.

Part IV

Mining and Energy

Introduction: The Hidden Injuries of Dependence

The Premier had a vision. The future of the province, he explained to the House of Assembly, lay in its rich energy resources. Corporations from around the world would flock to them, providing jobs and economic development to thousands of local people and finally putting the province and the region on the map. Geological discoveries, the latest scientific methods, a host of industrial spinoffs—all these lay within reach, provided that the honourable members would vote to give money and concessions to the interested foreign companies. Without such concessions foreign capital might not come, and local people would be denied access to the rich New England markets. Of course, any great project would attract the attention of carping critics, worried about "monopolies" and "political control" and so on, but these were just the sort of people to hold up any sort of economic development. . . .

Which Premier is this? Which province? The secret to the history of mining and energy development in the region is that it could be almost any Premier in any of the three provinces that have important mining or offshore sectors. It could be W.S. Fielding in the 1890s, explaining the permanent industrial benefits Nova Scotia was to receive from the coming of American capital to the Cape Breton coalfields, or it could just as well be Richard Hatfield in the 1970s, informing New Brunswickers of the great advantages to be had from exporting nuclear power from the expensive new plant at Point Lepreau. It could be John Buchanan, expounding the wonderful benefits Nova Scotia was soon to receive from the boom in offshore natural gas, or from exporting Fundy tidal power to New England, or from starting a tin mine in Yarmouth County; or perhaps Brian Peckford of Newfoundland, enthusing over Newfoundland's prospects with the oil of Hibernia.

In the mining and energy sector, what passes for development policy has been a broken record that continually repeats what W.S. Fielding said in 1893: "I believe the people will support any government or party that brings in capital and skill for the development of our mines, and I believe too that the people will not be particular whether that capital and skill comes from Great Britain or from any part of the world, provided it comes." Repeated development policies have had recurring effects. Mining throughout the region has followed the pattern of the area Fielding so confidently predicted would prosper following an infusion of "capital and skill"—industrial Cape Breton, whose economy today is the epitome of everything that has gone wrong with regional development.

Since the mid-nineteenth century, whenever provincial governments have looked at their fossil fuels or other energy resources, they have concentrated on just one policy: building up their government revenues by exporting energy, fossil fuels, and minerals in relatively unprocessed form out of the region—either to the rest of Canada or, very frequently, to the northern United States. This has been the fixed star in mainstream thinking about the region's non-renewable mineral resources and fossil fuels for over a century. No provincial government has ever seriously tampered with the basic formula, which is one of complete dependence upon foreign capital, foreign expertise, and foreign markets.

It is helpful to keep this unifying theme in mind when approaching the extraordinary variety of enterprises and conditions that are lumped together under the heading of mining and energy. From the iron mines of Labrador to the gypsum quarries of Nova Scotia, from the base-metal mines of northern New Brunswick to hydro-electricity at Churchill Falls, from the tin mine started up with great fanfare in the 1980s in Yarmouth County to the Cape Breton coal deposits exploited since the seventeenth century, the pattern has been, and remains, remarkably consistent: The resource is first discovered, perhaps by local residents. Foreign capital is interested in it. The state provides assistance of various kinds, often on a massive scale.

Brian O'Neill shows, in his two chapters on today's offshore exploration, that nothing has changed since the nineteenth century—the region's politicians still milk the last drop of short-term political advantage out of energy megaprojects. They still look longingly at New England markets. They still put the interests of workers and communities to one side in their pursuit of what they think is "development."

The problem is that while the capitalist state pursues policies that pay off in the short term, mining and offshore energy developments are long-term propositions for the workers and communities dependent upon them. A resource (a coal seam, for example) is discovered; a mine is sunk; a town grows up around the mine. For generations, everyone depends upon the non-renewable resources which lie far beneath the homes of the community. Then the mining stops, sometimes very quickly and disastrously (as Ian McKay notes in his chapter on Springhill) or sometimes more gradually but no less painfully (as Alan Story describes in his chapter on St. Lawrence). It is no longer profitable for the company to exploit the resources: markets have changed, better investment opportunities have opened up in Latin America, difficulties have intensified as the mines grow deeper and less competitive. The (usually foreign-controlled) company leaves. Suddenly the government is expected to pick up the burden of the hidden injuries of short-term, dependent development. It has to deal with miners dying of occupational diseases; communities suffering from crippling rates of unemployment; polluted landscapes pockmarked with deep, water-filled holes; and dependent local economies whose reinvestable surpluses have long since been drawn off to London, New York, or Toronto.

"The pattern is familiar enough," writes J.D. House. "The metropolitan companies exploit the raw materials of the hinterland region; they are shipped out in a raw or semi-processed form, economic surplus is appropriated, control remains firmly in Head Office (or, where this is mainly a front for foreign parent companies, as for the Iron Ore Company of Canada, in the head offices of the company's parent firms), and the whole operation can be phased out on short notice at the whim of the multinational corporation" (House 1986, 178).

One can readily understand why foreign capital has participated in these profitable exercises in resource depletion, but why would the state and local workers support it?

Politics in dependent regions is a short-term business. In the short term, a program of rapid resource depletion, even when the resource is non-renewable, is a political winner. Resource megaprojects have a ready-made constituency in poor regions. W.S. Fielding's scheme to bring in American capital and methods to revolutionize Cape Breton's coal industry (see Macgillivray 1979) did not, from a historical perspective, guarantee the island the vigorous industrial capitalism he promised, but it did entail generous profits for promoters, handsome royalties for the provincial government, and huge political advantages for the Liberal Party, which, largely on the basis of its development policies, set the Canadian record for the number of consecutive years a provincial political party has ever held office. Cape Breton coal, from its point of view, was a glittering success story. It was only in the 1920s that the devastating price was paid for this strategy of development—primarily by the workers whose lives were inextricably tied to the coal industry (see Frank 1977). In other words, what may appear at first sight to be "gross mismanagement" of the region's resources is, on closer inspection, often revealed to be "politically adept management" from the points of view of both capital and the capitalist state; what may appear as "mismanagement" to workers with black lung and stranded coal communities may appear as just the opposite to capital and its local boosters.

New Brunswick's mining history, documented in an excellent report by Senopi Consultants (1979), graphically illustrates the pattern. Although coal mining had been conducted in a marginal way in New Brunswick for years (see Seager 1980), far larger developments began with the discovery of rich lead-zinc-silver ores in northern New Brunswick in the 1950s. One large multinational mining company monopolized the resource, which it neglected for fear of undermining its position in unstable lead markets. The reform-minded Liberal government of Louis Robichaud, elected in 1960, was eager to break this pattern of arrested development, and pulled off a major coup in 1967 when it announced the coming of the giant mining multinational, Noranda Mines Limited, and plans for a large zinc smelter. There followed the predictable giving of tax concessions and outright grants. The Department of Regional Economic Expansion (DREE) provided incentive grants of $3,839,290 along with a $750,000 no-interest repayable loan, and DREE's predecessors gave $3.5 million to the chemical-fertilizer plant at Belledune and

$2,988,549 to the particle-board plant at Chatham shortly before Noranda acquired these companies.

As with Nova Scotia's coal development, a short-term political coup for the provincial government represented an immense long-term gain for the controlling corporation, whose appetite for other New Brunswick companies was whetted by many government favours. Over the next decade, Noranda became the owner of the rich lead-silver-copper deposits in the Bathurst area, a refinery and sulphuric-acid plant and a chemical-fertilizer plant at Belledune, pulp mills at Edmundston and Atholville, a planer mill at Plaster Rock, a sawmill at Kedgwick, a particle-board manufacturing plant at Chatham, a wire and cable plant at Saint John, and a car-recycling plant at Moncton. By 1978 it employed a work force in the province of 3,847 and owned or held government leases on 1,944,856 acres of land (Senopi 1979, 13). Noranda became the principal employer in New Brunswick towns and cities such as Edmundston, Bathurst, Kedgwick, and Plaster Rock. However, there was still no sign of the crucial smelter the Liberals had announced with much publicity ten years earlier.

The implications of this style of dependent development have been predictable. The multiplier effects of mining are low because of the low level of transformation carried out within the region and the few interindustry purchases made by the mining industry. Noranda, operating on a world scale, cut back its heavily subsidized operations in Bathurst in 1977 while investing millions in a rich copper deposit in Chile. Although Noranda's operations had a high level of unionization, the effectiveness of unions was undermined by high unemployment rates. As in Cape Breton, what the state had advertised as a way out of chronic poverty and underdevelopment merely led to further and deeper dependence on a multinational corporation and unstable world markets.

An even starker illustration of mining dependency is provided by gypsum in Nova Scotia, as documented in a study by Kuusisto and Williams (1974). Nova Scotia is an important source of gypsum for North America. In 1973, Williams and Kuusisto note, approximately 21.5 million tons of raw gypsum were consumed in the United States and, of these, about 7.7 million tons (36 percent) were imported—75 percent from Nova Scotia and the rest from Jamaica and Mexico. Nova Scotia also accounted for 75 percent of Canadian production. By 1965, three big multinationals (Canadian Gypsum, a subsidiary of American Gypsum; National Gypsum Co.; and Georgia-Pacific Corporation) controlled the resource. Never a crown mineral, gypsum was taken out of Nova Scotia without any payment of royalty or tax until 1953, when the Nova Scotia government imposed a tax of 33.33 percent on the profits of the mining operations to secure at least some of the substantial capital surpluses derived from gypsum, which were almost entirely exported.

As Kuusisto and Williams demonstrate, Nova Scotia's attempt to control the outflow of economic rent was systematically thwarted by the multinationals. Substantial gains in productivity from 1950-73 allowed them to cut the work force from 638 to 350, reducing employment for Nova Scotians. The multinationals evaded local taxes by setting an artificially low price for gypsum. Through vertical integration, they consolidated the mining, shipping, manufacturing, and marketing operations and facilities for the mineral. They then branched out to gain control over other aspects of the construction materials industry. As a result, and in collusion with other giants, they were able to manipulate prices "vertically" within the gypsum-production process, and "horizontally" for other products.

The impact of these market manipulations on Nova Scotia was drastic. The local mining operations could be run at a loss or for break-even returns because the company wanted to make its profits in another place or at another level within its operations. If no profit was made in producing the raw material, the manufacturing or marketing operation would be able to increase its earnings. By means of such "price transfers," the company could avoid a local tax on profits and relocate its earning power in places where taxes were more lenient. By minimizing their production costs here (in wages, capital investment, and taxes) and selling raw gypsum to their U.S. manufacturing operations at a break-even price, the gypsum corporations transferred the profitability of the mining operation to their parent corporations. In effect, Nova Scotians were indirectly giving the American multinationals a multimillion-dollar subsidy (Kuusisto and Williams 1974, 4-5).

Will offshore oil and gas break with this pattern of dependent development? Conceivably it will, argue those who write from a perspective sympathetic to Newfoundland nationalism—the lessons of past resource disasters might have been at least partially learned, and a far different perspective might prevail than was the case in the short-sighted past (House 1981, 1986). No, it will not, answer critics writing from the political-economy perspective. The politics of the Nova Scotia's non-existent offshore, like those of New Brunswick's imaginary smelter, are classically those which will perpetuate dependency. Even Newfoundland's unusual effort to master the details of the multinational oil-and-gas game (rather than merely giving the multinationals everything they wanted) hinged on its having a position of power in a healthy international market. Its initial hard-bargaining position has collapsed along with international oil prices. It is bargaining with corporations with annual budgets far greater than its own. Moreover, as the case of the Ocean Ranger suggests, the health and safety of the workers who explored the resource were ignored, as is customary in the exploitation of resources in situations of dependency. The likelihood is for some refinement but not the abandonment of the crude export model that has dominated the region for over a century.

Mining and energy development raise, to the most acute level, the central moral contradiction of dependent development: those with the most to lose have the least control over their future. Even if the mines and rigs clearly seem to pose an immediate danger to life and limb, it is hard for workers to say so, or, if they do, to have their words be taken as seriously as those of politicians and experts. It is inconceivable that workers and primary producers could, within the present system, reshape capitalist development strategies, whose disastrous results can be documented in sector after sector. As Kuusisto and Williams have observed, the case of mining suggests broader lessons to be learned:

> Historically, in the agriculture, forestry, fishing and mining industries in general, we have been producers of cheap primary products under conditions of external control. We have traditionally allowed the value of our economic activity to be 'marginalized', and the underdevelopment we now suffer is a direct consequence. We must face the painful truth that it is not coal or fish or gypsum that we have exported, but the wealth and human energy with which to build a healthy, diversified and self-reliant economy. . . . Our lands and our productivity will be of marginal importance as long as we depend on others to decide and exploit their value (1974, 8).

Genuine development, in mining and in the other resource industries, will be possible only if workers and primary producers in the region face the painful truth of underdevelopment and break free of the bankrupt strategies that continue to perpetuate it.

The Political Economy of an Illusion: The Strange Case of Nova Scotia's Vanishing Offshore

Brian O'Neill

In a rousing speech to the Tory faithful at the Party's annual convention in January 1982, Premier John Buchanan claimed that offshore oil and gas developments would end "going down the road" for Nova Scotians in search of jobs. Predicting "a great future in oil and gas," Buchanan said he believed that "all our young people will be able to stay here and be gainfully employed." Such expressions of optimism by the Premier and his ministers have been quite routine since the discovery of the Venture gas field in 1979. Although this hype has not and will not help to produce the promised offshore bounty of jobs and revenues, it certainly has succeeded in enhancing the political fortunes of the Tory establishment in Nova Scotia.

In fact, that is what the offshore is really about: politics. Oil, gas, jobs, development—these are terms used by Buchanan and company to sell the offshore to a Nova Scotia electorate that has long been waiting for a solution to the problems of economic underdevelopment and dependence on federal transfer payments. Energy Minister Joel Matheson described the future deliverance in a January 1983 *Globe and Mail* report on the Nova Scotia economy: "When we look back at the decade, I think 1984 will be recognized as the year, in a developmental sense, that the economy of Nova Scotia moved from that of a 'have-not' to a 'have' province."

The fact that Nova Scotia's 1984 "official" unemployment rate is 13.3 percent presents us with a blessing in disguise: the Buchanan government will not have to go to the trouble of importing South Korean labour for the oil and gas boom as the Saudi Arabian government was obliged to do. As for equalization payments from Ottawa—perhaps the major indicator of the province's "have-not" status—help in reducing this dependence is surely on the

---

This chapter is based on three articles published in *New Maritimes* (October 1984–January 1985). The reader should note that the vantage point of this chapter has not been altered but remains that of 1984, as it was written then. Although some minor facts had changed by 1987, the continued relevance of this piece demonstrates that even in the "optimistic" days of 1984 it was possible to discern that the tremendous political and economic energies being spent on the offshore were based primarily on myth and opportunism. The author has provided comments from the vantage point of 1987, which appear in a note towards the end of this chapter.

way. Thanks to the lucrative provisions of the Canada–Nova Scotia Offshore Agreement, the province could now collect taxes on cigarettes and other items used in the offshore.

Contrary to what the Tories would have us believe, offshore exploration, as well as potential development and production, will have little positive impact on the province's underdeveloped economy. The petroleum industry is highly capital-intensive in any situation but, in the Nova Scotia offshore, the number of jobs created, both directly from drilling operations and indirectly from onshore "spinoff" activities, is minimal compared to the hundreds of millions of dollars spent drilling for oil and gas on the Scotian Shelf. Moreover, the whole offshore business is controlled by the federal government and the oil companies. It is difficult to conceive how Nova Scotia is to become "developed" according to the wishes and potential of Nova Scotians when the agenda is set by external forces. Another major feature of the industry's operations is that there are invariably very few onshore sites of industrial and commercial activity. The May quarterly report of the Atlantic Provinces Economic Council (APEC) noted that virtually all of the economic growth in Nova Scotia related to the offshore is occurring in the Halifax-Dartmouth area.

John Buchanan and his coterie of offshore optimists are well aware of these economic limitations, but it is the changing political climate in the offshore that really generates the election juices in provincial Tories. The primary and probably the only reason why in 1984 there were seven holes being drilled on the Scotian Shelf at a minimum daily cost of $350,000 each is the generous allowances provided to the oil companies under the terms of the former federal Liberal government's National Energy Program (NEP). Politics, not economics, has dictated the course of drilling off Nova Scotia. As such, it is the federal government, not the oil companies, which has been covering most of the costs of these expensive drilling operations.

While in opposition, federal Tories never relented in their criticisms of the NEP. Pat Carney, now federal Energy Minister, charged in March 1984 that the NEP's drilling grants regime, the Petroleum Incentives Program (PIP), was being used "to drill dry holes." Indeed, all of the political parties and the petroleum industry know that, as Calgary oil analyst Wilfred Gobert puts it, "The private sector is bleeding this program [PIP] for all it is worth."

There are obvious problems in curtailing or eliminating the PIP, not the least of which is the fact that some of the major players in the Nova Scotia offshore are U.S. multinational oil companies, whom the federal Tory government of Brian Mulroney does not wish to offend. In the midst of concern about the size of the deficit, however, the general thrust of the new government will undoubtedly favour energy developments in the proven "oil patch" of western Canada. Ironically, John Buchanan, stalwart supporter of "free enterprise," knows that he had a much better offshore ally in the federal Liberals than in the more market-oriented Mulroney administration.

From 1981-84, approximately $1 billion of taxpayers' money has been spent in the form of PIP payments for drilling on the Scotian Shelf. Yet there is still no commercially viable discovery of oil or gas out there. Speaking at a U.S. energy conference in early 1984, Ian Doig, editor of the East Coast energy newsletter *Doig's Digest*, predicted that most of the Canadian companies, having "had their fill of the high-profile frontier romance," will soon "head back to the Western Canadian Basin," leaving the east coast—once again—to the multinationals. Oil finds and the announcements of heavy oil "mini-projects" in the west confirm its attractiveness, in stark contrast to the Nova Scotia offshore, for those companies interested in actually producing oil and gas. In August 1984, Petro-Canada and its partners pulled out of a projected $500 million Scotian Shelf drilling program which had been announced with great fanfare by John Buchanan and former federal Energy Minister Marc Lalonde in July 1982. Two wells were drilled at a total cost of $90 million, less than one fifth of the optimistic spending projection made by Buchanan and Lalonde two years earlier.

1986 is the year when the first—perhaps only—phase of the National Energy Program, including the PIP, comes to an end. The presence of nine Nova Scotia Tories in the federal government caucus of 211 members is bound to provide little influence for the continuation of expensive, unproductive drilling off Nova Scotia at the rate which has prevailed over the past two years. Moreover, there is a decidedly Western tilt to the composition of the Mulroney Cabinet.

Western politicians and their constituents, including virtually all of the oil companies that are not committed to long-term frontier drilling off the East Coast or in Northern Canada, felt burned by the National Energy Program. Looking at the Nova Scotia offshore, they are inclined to ask some pointed questions, such as: Why hasn't there been a commercial discovery of oil and gas on the Scotian Shelf, given the fact that 100 wells have been drilled there since 1967? If this area is supposed to be a good prospect for hydrocarbon development, why should hundreds of millions of taxpayers' dollars be spent there on drilling programs? If there is only natural gas on the Scotian Shelf, who needs it? John Buchanan and his ministers know the answers to these questions. From them, it can produce only one response: a last political kick at the offshore cat.

What is probably most remarkable about the Buchanan government's political success in the offshore is the startling fact that the actual physical resource which has generated so much political hype is, not only in global but also in national terms, quite insignificant. The size and nature of the resource on the Scotian Shelf hardly furnishes the basis for any springboard to a full-employment, broadly developed economy, the fantasy so often evoked by government leaders.

Estimating the reserves of hydrocarbons on the Scotian Shelf is anything but an exact science. When we take a comparative look at Alberta and the

North Sea, it appears that there is some consistency to the estimates for the Nova Scotia offshore: the deposits there are reckoned consistently to be small.

There is an important distinction to be made between proven/recoverable reserves of oil and gas, and potential deposits. As well, there is an important equation for standardizing the relative value—in the ground—of oil and natural gas: one barrel of oil equals 6,000 cubic feet of natural gas. In other words, 1 billion barrels of oil (1B bbl oil) equals 6 trillion cubic feet (6 tcf) of natural gas.

Husky Oil's "best guess" is that the area off Nova Scotia contains "potential" reserves of 20-25 tcf of natural gas. The federal Department of Energy concludes that "proven" gas resources on the Scotian Shelf total 1.514 tcf, and "potential" reserves could reach 18 tcf.

Government leaders in Nova Scotia often describe the petroleum-based economic potential of the province as comparable with Alberta and the North Sea. The magnitudes of the hydrocarbon resources in these areas, however, beg the comparisons. About 5 B bbl of oil have already been produced in Alberta, and normal production methods are expected to yield at least an additional 4.8 B bbl. Alberta's "marketable" natural gas reserves are 65.3 tcf. These figures do not include the approximately 300 B bbl of oil contained in oil sands and heavy oil deposits. In the British sector of the North Sea, recovered and recoverable oil deposits total at least 14.8 B bbl. The same classification of natural gas indicates a minimum of 40 tcf. According to this data, the Alberta and North Sea oil and gas resources are vastly larger than even the most optimistic estimates for the Nova Scotia offshore.

More qualifications must yet be added about the make-up of the Nova Scotia offshore. First of all, although there may be the generalized presence of natural gas on the Scotian Shelf, it has been known for almost a decade that the resource is dispersed into numerous small accumulations because of the high degree of geological faulting in the area. This appears to be one of the problems confronting the proposed Venture gas development. Despite enormous amounts of political and corporate enthusiasm for the economic activity which will supposedly be generated by the construction and production phases of the Venture development, the field has still not proven large enough to be commercially viable. With the threshold of viability—at least 2.5 tcf of natural gas—not having been reached, Mobil Oil, the operator for a consortium of companies, has been obliged to consider other possible options for development. One suggestion involves the inclusion of surrounding fields in the development plan, although none of these fields has been subjected to delineation drilling. Consequently, their sizes and features are unknown. Moreover, the development costs of hooking neighbouring gas fields into the Venture operation might possibly be prohibitive.

All in all, the treatment of this viability problem is scandalous. Ten years ago, then Premier Gerald Regan reported that Mobil and others had estimated known natural gas reserves in the Sable Island area at 1.7 tcf. Despite billions of dollars worth of deep holes and considerable volumes of hot air in the intervening period, government and the companies have not been able to come up with that extra .8 tcf in the right place.

Secondly, as far as both Nova Scotia and Canada as a whole are concerned, natural gas is a significantly less valuable energy resource than oil. Provincial, regional, and national demand for Sable gas is insufficient to warrant its production, so markets must be found in the United States. In order to reach this market, a trunk line will have to be constructed along with thousands of distribution lines to residential and industrial consumers. Gas pipelines have considerably higher costs per unit of energy delivered than oil pipelines, since the energy content per unit of transported gas is much lower than that of oil: approximately 20 percent lower. A study by the Economic Council of Canada concluded that Alberta gas transported by pipeline to the Maritimes would cost less than Venture gas at the gate of the proposed refinery in Canso. Even if we exclude for now the profound limitations involved in accumulating Nova Scotia government revenues from a "buyers' market" in the United States, the small and fractured nature of the province's offshore gas resources, combined with the costs of transportation, certainly weakens the prospects for significant public revenues from the proposed Venture development.

Thirdly, the presence of either land-based or marine-based hydrocarbon resources provides no guarantee that the surrounding economy will be developed, diversified, and fully employ the local labour force. For example, Alberta has had over 30 years of opportunity to broaden its economy based on a proven resource infinitely larger than what is known to exist off Nova Scotia. When the recession hit Alberta in the early 1980s, the economy slipped further and faster than that of any other province. Alberta's official unemployment rate was over 10 percent for 1982-84, and its growth is expected to lag behind the rest of the country until at least 1985 because of low demand for petroleum products, a clear indication of the failure to establish a diversified economy. The presence of a $13 billion Heritage Fund had little, if any, beneficial impact on the tens of thousands of Albertans who lost their jobs when the "boom" of the late 1970s went bust. "From how you define development," says industrial economist Joyha Sen, "the Alberta economy wouldn't even qualify as developed because manufacturing is so low. If we keep on appeasing companies, instead of making them invest in workers and in the country, we'll become like a Third World country."

In the North Sea, where the oil and gas resources dwarf even the most optimistic potential scenario for the Scotian Shelf, total Scottish employment (most of the oil and gas fields in the British sector of the North Sea are off Scotland) related to offshore developments peaked at 60,000 in the late 1970s and has been diminishing ever since. This figure included the labour involved in the construction of 90 offshore production platforms. According to Brit-Oil planner Michael Fenwick, "a very jaundiced view of what was to be a boom has arisen in many parts of Scotland" as offshore-related activities wind down.

Could we expect the government of John Buchanan to handle oil and gas developments any better than that of Alberta or Britain? Hardly. Indeed, outside of the arena of political opportunism, Tory leaders in Nova Scotia do not know how to deal and negotiate with the petroleum industry. Although some of this is the result of sheer ignorance of oil and gas affairs, much of the weakness is due to nineteenth-century notions that the oil companies will do the right things for Nova Scotia as long as they are left alone.

Nevertheless, it must be said that John Buchanan knows how to deal with Nova Scotians.

Well into October 1984, the Tory election campaign in Nova Scotia was being buffetted by a series of setbacks related to drilling programs and plans in the offshore. The much-touted application to Canada's National Energy Board for the export of Venture gas to the United States was already 18 months overdue and would now be delayed until at least the New Year. Meanwhile, Mobil Oil was still having trouble finding enough of that elusive gas to make export possible: the drill casing in its all-important N-91 delineation well cracked, bad news which was compounded by preliminary indications that the well did not contain sufficient volumes of natural gas to make the proposed development of the Venture gas field viable. The international price of oil began to drop, producing a negative market-price scenario for natural gas. Husky–Bow Valley started moving two drilling rigs and all of its supply vessels from the Scotian Shelf to the Grand Banks off Newfoundland. Hardly a word was mentioned by John Buchanan about the offshore boomerang.

Relief for the sputtering Nova Scotia offshore, however, was announced on October 17 in this headline from Halifax's *Chronicle-Herald* and *Mail-Star*: "Shell Discovery Stirs East Coast Optimism." Yes, indeed, some more gas had been found on the Scotian Shelf. Although it is doubtful—at best—that this gas will ever provide thermal energy onshore, it generated the predictable volume of political energy on the campaign trail. Quickly rehooking his deflated respiratory system to the offshore, John Buchanan gushed forth with the old story to the Tory faithful of Bible Hill. "It is a foregone conclusion," he said, "that several more significant gas and condensate discoveries will result from this [drilling] activity." In a word, the Premier was "excited" about the future of the offshore.

It's remarkable to see Buchanan still striking the same upbeat chord as offshore drilling activity enters its inevitable downturn phase. The man's psychic resources cannot be underestimated, particularly where political mileage is to be gained. The story of the Buchanan government's offshore "development" probably tells more about politics than economics or geology. From the beginning, with a poorly endowed offshore, John Buchanan wittingly set Nova Scotia up for political prostitution to Ottawa. In exchange for a big economic quickie, the provincial government handed Ottawa control over offshore operations, dovetailing thereby with the federal political agenda.

Why would a deficit-ridden federal government commit $1 billion in direct grants (or roughly a total of $2 billion if you include corporate tax deductions) to induce oil companies to explore for natural gas which both the region and the country will not need? To get an understanding of this federal bankrolling of the Nova Scotia offshore, we need to look at the details surrounding the implementation of the National Energy Program.

In the fall of 1980, the federal government introduced the NEP with a number of objectives in mind, all of which were to ensure Canadian oil self-sufficiency by 1990 along with at least 50 percent Canadian public and private ownership of the petroleum industry. In order to exercise control over the direction of energy developments, Ottawa required a greater share of oil and gas revenues.

During the 1970s the petroleum industry was by far the fastest-growing and most profitable of Canada's non-financial industries. As the price of oil skyrocketed, most of the profits went to the oil companies, mainly the multinationals, and to the provinces, mainly Alberta. By 1980, 82 percent of the revenues generated by the oil companies were foreign controlled. Translated into terms of capital flowing out of the country, $3.7 billion in oil and gas revenues left Canada from 1975-79.

Through the NEP the federal government enlarged its portion of the revenue pie by imposing new taxes and increasing domestic oil prices. This enabled Ottawa to shift a substantial amount of exploration activity away from the so-called provincial lands in Western Canada to the Canada lands—the east-coast offshore and the North—where, despite opposition, it has exercised political jurisdiction. Although influenced by the recession and stagnant world oil prices, this shift was primarily a result of the generous benefits package provided to the oil companies by the federal government under the NEP.

Chief among these federal allowances is the Petroleum Incentives Program, characterized by former Liberal Energy Minister Marc Lalonde as a series of the "richest fiscal incentives in the world." The PIP grants specifically favour the exploration and development of oil and gas resources on Canada lands versus provincial lands. They are also tailored to benefit primarily individual, or consortia of, Canadian companies. For instance, a 75 percent Canadian-owned company or consortium drilling on the Scotian Shelf is eligible to receive 80 percent of its drilling costs outright in the form of a PIP grant. When you include tax deductions, the federal government actually picks up 93 percent of the tab for a drill hole. In other words, a $50 million exploration hole sunk off Nova Scotia can cost the companies as little as $3.5 million. Canadian taxpayers cover the rest of that cost. Even the multinationals like Mobil, which receive smaller PIP grants, can write off up to 60 percent of their after-PIP costs in the form of tax deductions.

Although the idea of Canadianizing the petroleum industry is quite supportable in theory, many practical problems have afflicted the NEP. Despite the federally sponsored drilling programs on Canada lands (about $8 billion will have been spent on PIP grants by 1984), no commercially viable discovery of oil or gas has occurred since the introduction of the NEP in 1980. In some cases, drilling has been carried out at inflated prices (this is called "gold-plating" in the petroleum industry) solely to collect PIP funds. Some observers have even suggested that PIP grants are so generous that money can be made drilling dry holes under the program. "The pure geology of a drilling site," notes E.W. Kulsky of Westmin Resources in Calgary, "is well down the list of priorities."

This was certainly the case in August 1982, when federal Energy Minister Marc Lalonde, aware that the Petro-Canada drilling rig Bow Drill One was idle in Halifax Harbour, induced Petro-Canada to spud a hole at West Esperanto on the Scotian Shelf. This is the sort of underwater turf that Senator Earl Hastings, chairman of the Senate Energy Committee, has referred to as "moose pasture" as distinct from "oil and gas patch". After sinking the second of eight planned holes in this vicinity, Petro-Canada and its partners, including the provincial government's Nova Scotia Resources Ltd., quit this drilling program in August 1984. The cost to Nova Scotia and Canadian taxpayers: $90 million.

The abuses of PIP grants are too numerous to mention here. In summary, despite the noble intentions of the NEP, it seems that foreign exploitation of Canada's energy resources has been replaced by mismanagement of the country's financial resources. This situation arose because the federal Liberal government, eagerly assisted by the Tory government in Nova Scotia, subordinated economics to politics on its offshore agenda. Hundreds of millions of dollars have been wasted in the Nova Scotia offshore because of faulty and opportunistic decision-making. At the same time, minimal benefit has accrued to working people and the public as a whole in Nova Scotia from gas exploration. What short-lived activity has occurred off Nova Scotia is solely the result of John Buchanan's playing puppy dog on the lap of Pierre Trudeau. While Ottawa wielded a stick against intransigent Newfoundland with one hand, it dangled the carrot of Nova Scotia from the other.

One of the factors involved in the content and timing of the NEP was the discovery of the Hibernia oil field on the Grand Banks off Newfoundland in 1979. Estimated to contain between 1.5 and 2 B bbl of recoverable high-quality crude oil, this remains the only commercially viable discovery of petroleum on Canada lands. Until the Supreme Court of Canada ruled in Ottawa's favour in March 1984, the federal government had been locked in a heated dispute with the Newfoundland government over ownership and control of the Newfoundland and Labrador offshore. Along with physical and environmental problems, the lack of a management agreement between the two governments postponed the development of the Hibernia field, much to the chagrin of the federal Liberals. While the Newfoundland and federal governments were at loggerheads over negotiating a satisfactory resolution to this contentious issue, a couple of other significant agreements concerning energy policy were established between Ottawa and each of two provincial governments, Alberta and Nova Scotia. In both cases, there was an implicit focus on Hibernia.

In September 1981, the federal and Alberta governments reached a five-year agreement on oil and gas prices (including offshore oil) and revenue-sharing amongst themselves and the petroleum industry. Shortly afterwards, federal energy officials began two sets of negotiations with their counterparts from Newfoundland and Nova Scotia in order to devise management and revenue-sharing formulas for oil and gas developments in the respective offshores of both provinces. The governments of Newfoundland and Nova Scotia, however, began these deliberations from substantially different backgrounds on offshore affairs.

Dating back to the early 1970s, the Newfoundland and federal governments had been involved in a protracted dispute regarding jurisdiction and management of the hydrocarbon resources lying off Newfoundland and Labrador. The same was not the case with Nova Scotia. Indeed, in February 1977, the Nova Scotia government and those of New Brunswick and Prince Edward Island signed a memorandum of agreement with Ottawa over management and revenue-sharing of the Maritimes' potential offshore oil and gas resources. In exchange for a larger share of royalties (which, under closer analysis, reveals only modest economic prospects for the Maritimes), the Premiers surrendered administrative control over offshore developments to Ottawa. The then Liberal Premier of Nova Scotia, Gerald Regan, commented: "The only real problem I have is wiping the smile off my face." Meanwhile, the Newfoundland government refused to join this accord and proceeded to complete its drafting of oil and gas regulations.

In fact, along with claiming ownership and control over its offshore, the Newfoundland government was developing a high degree of expertise in legal, technical, and financial aspects of oil and gas affairs. Such was not the case with the Nova Scotia government. (This point was frankly conceded by a spokesperson for the Nova Scotia Department of Development at an offshore conference in December 1980: "I think I shall be quite candid in saying that the Nova Scotia government was behind other jurisdictions in its planning efforts, notably Newfoundland," he said.)

Following the 1978 election of the Tories under John Buchanan, Nova Scotia revoked its participation in the 1977 agreement with Ottawa. The Buchanan government then decided to take its offshore cue from Newfoundland, publicizing its legal case for ownership of the offshore in a booklet modelled on the 1977 Newfoundland government publication "Heritage of the Sea," and passing offshore legislation virtually identical to the Newfoundland government's Petroleum and Natural Gas Act. Buchanan opted for shortcuts through the morass of petroleum details while he developed a careful political strategy for offshore negotiations and discussions with both the federal government and the oil companies.

In approaching the fall 1981 meetings with Ottawa, Buchanan and his colleagues were clear on two very important factors: (1) The hydrocarbon resource in the Nova Scotia offshore is "gas prone" and contained in fractured deposits which tend to diminish the feasibility of development. (2) The federal government was more interested in striking a deal with Newfoundland so as to bring Hibernia, and potential neighbouring oil fields, on stream as quickly as possible. Not only is oil a significantly more useful energy resource for Canada, which has been experiencing a gas glut for some time, but, in strict terms of energy equivalence, Hibernia oil has at least four times the energy value of Venture gas.

Moreover, Buchanan apparently realized that, if Newfoundland and Ottawa struck a deal, the bulk of regional offshore-related business would probably end up in Newfoundland (as indeed was the pre-agreement situation when both provincial governments began their negotiations with Ottawa in the fall of 1981). Thus, in contrast with the Peckford government, John Buchanan and his ministers heightened their traditional pro-corporate appeal in tandem with their political deliberations on the offshore.

The oil and gas legislation, which contained preferential regulations for the use of local labour and business, was intentionally not enacted. While government officials compared the anticipated "boom" with that of the North Sea and described Halifax as the "Calgary of the future," Premier Buchanan took his pitch to business groups at home and away. The Foreign Investment Review Agency (FIRA) had to be dismantled, he said, in order "to get outside companies interested in locating in the area and participating in offshore development." In formulating a "ravage us" invitation to New York businessmen, he solemnly declared that, "frankly, . . . there is no such thing as acid rain." A *Globe and Mail* report at the time concluded: "Short of presenting the oil companies with a key to the province, a brighter corporate lure couldn't be imagined."

With the offshore stage thus set, the Buchanan government—like its predecessor in 1977—surrendered control over offshore developments to Ottawa in March 1982. This was a step which the Newfoundland government of Brian Peckford was determined—predictably—not to duplicate. The Buchanan strategy of endeavouring to reap political and economic gain from both Newfoundland's economic nationalist stance on the offshore and Ottawa's politically motivated largesse paid off (at least in form, if not in substance). As a final stab in the back to the Peckford administration, the Nova Scotia Offshore Agreement contains a provision whereby, if the Newfoundland government negotiates a better deal with Ottawa, Nova Scotia can automatically opt for this new agreement in its entirety.

For their part, the federal Liberals wished to demonstrate to Brian Peckford and his ministers, but more especially to the business community and the labour force in Newfoundland, that much could be gained by meeting Ottawa's terms on offshore control and management. To make this point abundantly clear, within eight months of the signing of the Nova Scotia Offshore Agreement, the federal government announced drilling programs on the Scotian Shelf totalling $1.6 billion, with more than $1 billion of this amount to be paid directly to the oil companies in the form of PIP grants. Each of the four announcements was stage-managed to attract the maximum degree of media attention. While presiding over the fourth such event in Halifax on November 17, 1982, Energy Minister Jean Chretien said that he hoped the Newfoundland government would look to the Nova Scotia experience and realize that resource development off its coast would be spurred by a settlement with the federal government. Needless to say, in the 24 months following this binge of spending commitments, only half as many programs have been announced.

The consummately political and uneconomic nature of the commitment of over $1 billion in taxpayers' funds for Scotian Shelf drilling cannot be exaggerated. A fraction of that spending in numerous other directions in Nova Scotia would have benefitted the people significantly more. Pouring it down useless, three-mile holes in the Atlantic is almost a criminal act when you consider the desperate need of many people in the Atlantic Provinces, let alone the rest of the world. The questionable geological characteristics of the Scotian Shelf were well-known beforehand. Neither the Maritime Provinces nor any other part of Canada can use natural gas from offshore Nova Scotia in sufficient quantities to make development viable. Ten thousand wells containing inexpensive natural gas in western Canada have been "shut in" because market demand and prices were low, resulting in little gas exploration activity in that region. The only potential market always has been the United States and when the buyer is in a monopoly situation, watch out! Finally, the surge in exploration activity off Nova Scotia began when the international price of oil—which is ultimately the bench mark for all energy prices—started to fall, dropping US$5 to $29 per barrel one year after the signing of the Nova Scotia Offshore Agreement.

John Buchanan would probably defend this sleazy romp with the federal Liberals by commenting that it's a dog-eat-dog world when you're underdeveloped. You have to take advantage of whatever opportunities present themselves. The bottom line on this behaviour, however, is that it is morally sordid. Economically, it presents us with nothing more than a shallow, fly-by-night operation. But politically, it helps to win elections.

"**W**e are Number One!" This was the repeated claim of John Buchanan during the 1984 Nova Scotia election campaign. He was referring to the province's current and projected rates of economic growth as compiled by the Royal Bank of Canada. Election day had barely passed, however, when the Conference Board of Canada, the country's pre-eminent private think tank on economic matters, presented a substantially different set of figures on Nova Scotia's economic performance. At 4.7 percent, the province's growth rate in 1984 would be fourth among the provinces, and a projected 1 percent rise in 1985 would put Nova Scotia in a tie for sixth place. So much for Nova Scotia's brief moment at the economic pinnacle!

Economic growth statistics alone provide little understanding of what is really happening to the vast majority of the population. Almost all feel no impact on employment, disposable income, quality of life, etc., if the province's economy grows or declines by 4 or 5 percent annually. There are, however, elite groups, as well as political leaders, to whom these figures represent a numerical god. Much of this deity's spell in Nova Scotia of late has been cast by the offshore.

According to provincial government economists, two or three rigs drilling for a full year off Nova Scotia produce 1 percent growth in the economy. With an average of seven rigs operating on the Scotian Shelf during 1983 and 1984, offshore expenditures can be seen as the key to Nova Scotia's statistical growth.

The hundreds of millions of taxpayers' dollars that have been committed to offshore drilling, and the Buchanan government's red-carpet treatment for outside business and capital, have combined to produce "business confidence." There are two practical features to this phenomenon as it affects Nova Scotia. First of all, the smell of oil and gas, or even a hint of their odour, tends to trigger a stampede response among business promoters and their financial backers. Secondly, although they can cut their losses through creative accounting and tax loopholes, we should not underestimate the capacity for some business people and bankers to be stupid. The pixie-dust character of the "business confidence" in Nova Scotia's economy is glaringly manifested in the Halifax skyline.

Nine major commercial developments either have been completed in 1984 or are scheduled for completion in 1985. According to Lyndon Watkins in *Atlantic Business*, the office building boom is "mostly in anticipation of off-shore oil-fuelled demand." The result of this construction activity is a high vacancy rate in office space. To illustrate this situation, the North American Life Centre on Brunswick St., which was completed in mid-1983, by December 1984 was only 50 percent leased. By the time all of the office building construction is finished, the amount of empty office space in Halifax will be equal to the area of the Halifax Commons.

Nevertheless, there are those who might argue that these office buildings will be fully occupied as Halifax emerges as eastern Canada's "oil capital." This indeed was the thrust of a task force set up by Halifax City Council in 1981 to inquire into offshore opportunities. In fact, the report contained a recommendation that Halifax "Houstonize" itself. Although the task force cannot be faulted for lack of ambition, the participants failed to take account of petroleum industry reality. "All the task forces in the world," notes off-shore analyst Mark Shrimpton, "will not move Hibernia any closer to Halifax." Simply put, the east-coast operations of the oil companies and their major contractors involve—both now and in the future—the employment of technical personnel, with some office backup, in the cities closest to offshore activities: Halifax for the Scotian Shelf and St. John's for the Grand Banks. Calgary is and will continue to be Canada's oil capital with Toronto performing an administrative and financial role. The departure to Newfoundland of Husky-Bow Valley's main personnel along with their rigs and supply ships emphasizes the portability of their offshore operations. There is, and will be, no regional headquarters; rather, there are and will continue to be local "legquarters."

All of this points to the fact that, as far as the "offshore boom" is concerned, what you see is what you've got. With the possible exception of a political frenzy inspiring some more construction during the Sable gas development phase, the speculation-induced contribution to Nova Scotia's economic growth is pretty well over. What's left is the actuality of how much local business and employment have been generated specifically through offshore exploration. The evidence indicates that there is a considerable gulf between the promise of the offshore and its reality.

In the fall of 1982, Nova Scotia's Minister of Development, Roland Thornhill, toured the province with the message that every community could benefit from offshore oil and gas business. Whether naively optimistic or simply a means of encouraging entrepreneurial spirit, such comments conflict glaringly with the site-specific operations of the offshore oil and gas industry, particularly when it functions in a free-enterprise political climate such as has been furnished by the Buchanan government. Indeed, the only jurisdictions where the offshore industry has decentralized its operations to any extent are Norway and the Shetland Islands, and this has been solely as a result of the enforcement of strict government regulations.

In Nova Scotia, almost all of the business inputs into the offshore come from the Strait of Canso and Halifax/Dartmouth areas, with the latter attracting the great majority of business activity. This is the direct result of the government's decision not to regulate the operations of the petroleum industry, a policy enunciated by Thornhill himself early in 1982. Stating that the province will rely on "subtle persuasion" in its dealings with the industry, Thornhill continued, "We know the oil companies. All we have to do is tell them what we want and they will co-operate." Since that time, however, the Nova Scotia government has discovered that the petroleum industry has a will of its own.

According to provincial government figures in 1984, some 250 Nova Scotia firms are directly and indirectly involved in offshore business. Even a brief look at their operations indicates a low level of overall activity. About 50 of these companies are located in Dartmouth's Burnside Industrial Park, but most have opened only small offices on the speculation that, as one businessman put it, "Nova Scotia's offshore could develop into a booming gas field." Regardless of whether the gas field booms or sputters, the odds are against any significant benefit accruing to Nova Scotia businesses.

Mobil Oil and the other offshore operators contract much of their work out to international consultants. They tend to rely on traditional, experienced suppliers, especially where there are no local regulations to constrain their contracting practices. Barry Lohnes, president of Dominion Diving of Halifax, comments: "When the first couple of rigs arrived we were pretty busy. Now, with eight rigs out there, we haven't any work on them, nothing." As more international offshore companies have moved to Nova Scotia, his company's profile has become increasingly smaller. "It's like David and Goliath," says Lohnes, "our $1 million company against the $10 million operations." The problem with free enterprise, concludes Lohnes, is that the big get bigger and the smaller companies, who don't stand a chance, become demoralized. Another local offshore supplier has suggested that the only businesses in Halifax making any substantial gain with the oil companies are the hotel and restaurant people.

According to federal and provincial government figures, about 24 percent of the $630 million exploration program off Nova Scotia in 1983 was spent in the province. Both governments obviously have a vested interest in magnifying local business content; an independent consulting firm has put this figure at approximately 15 percent. In any case, most of the materials purchased in Nova Scotia are manufactured outside the province. In addition to the offshore operators' traditional reliance on external suppliers, the major costs of offshore drilling are accounted for by the leasing of drilling rigs and supply boats, most of which are not constructed in Canada, let alone Nova Scotia. Indeed, the business people who are probably reaping the greatest benefits from Nova Scotia's offshore "boom" are the owners of these vessels, whose capital costs are being secured primarily by federal government grants.

Given this situation, an exasperated Roland Thornhill has changed his tune somewhat in 1984. He has been heard to complain that the oil companies "have not been totally co-operative with the provincial government's efforts to ensure that the province gains maximum benefits from offshore development."

The disappointing results on the business side of the offshore enterprise have been duplicated with regard to employment. Once again, a gap has emerged between the political projections of offshore job creation for Nova Scotians and the reality, especially when you consider the total expenditures for the offshore drilling programs.

Trying to determine the number of offshore-related jobs held by Nova Scotians is a difficult task. One thing which is very clear, however, is that the future does not approach the provincial government's 1982 projection of 8,000 jobs to be created by offshore exploration activity. Nor does it represent much significance in the context of Nova Scotia's labour supply.

Turning again to the dubious estimates provided by government, in 1984 1,400 Nova Scotians were working on the drilling rigs and in support industries. When this number of jobs is compared to those who were in agriculture (9,000) or the fishing industry (20,000), we get a perspective on the offshore which clashes with the glitter and excitement of political pronouncements on offshore employment. Even if you include all of the jobs which were induced through the spending of offshore wages in Nova Scotia retail stores, hotels, etc., the total figure is still substantially less than 1 percent of the province's labour force of 390,000.

Official unemployment statistics tend to bear out the fact that the offshore has done little to alleviate Nova Scotia's most pressing problem. The only positive comment which might be made is that the leap in unemployment has not been as critical in the Halifax/Dartmouth area. Much of this is due, no doubt, to the office-building construction binge.

All of this points to the fact the offshore is an incredibly capital-intensive industry and a very poor job creator in relation to the money spent. If you exclude potential revenue calculations, each direct and support job for Nova Scotians costs about $450,000 per year. (This is not to deny that much of the estimated $600 million annual expenditure on the Scotian Shelf drilling programs creates jobs elsewhere. Indeed, this is one of the critical features of this type of "development.") By contrast, a report on the economic impact of Dalhousie University's operations for 1982-83 revealed that the $96.6 million spent by this institution created 3,174 jobs. In other words, each job cost just over $30,000 annually. This clearly demonstrates that government money spent on education and, similarly, on other social services creates employment for Nova Scotians at more than ten times the rate for offshore exploration.

To summarize the provincial business and job impacts from offshore exploration, the benefits are quite unspectacular. Of course, there are those who will argue that Nova Scotia's transformation to prosperity will arise with the later phases of offshore activity: the construction of facilities for the development and the transportation of offshore natural gas, and the production and marketing of the resource. But once again, the chasm between myth and reality widens.

Some of the geological and economic problems facing the proposed Venture gas development were outlined earlier. Perhaps the most crucial element in determining the feasibility of extracting natural gas from the Sable Island area, however, is the market price for the product. In this regard, U.S. demand for Venture gas is vital to the project. Of the expected maximum daily production rate of 400 million cubic feet, approximately 100 million cubic feet will satisfy requirements for the Maritimes' market: the remaining 300 million cubic feet will have to be exported. Three consortia of American corporations and utilities have already indicated interest in purchasing Venture gas, and the Nova Scotia government "is determined to make the U.S./Canada energy partnership a strong and mutually advantageous commitment to the future," but a close look at this commitment reveals that the advantage will be clearly one-sided, because the Buchanan government has overlooked the key ingredient in the marketing matrix—price.

Traditionally, because of the high capital costs associated with constructing extensive networks of trunk and distribution pipelines, gas producers have required long-term, fixed-priced contracts when negotiating sales of their land-based products. In the case of Venture gas (or any other field which might be developed on the Scotian Shelf), the capital outlay is increased considerably because of the difficulties involved in recovering the resource from, and transporting it by pipeline under, a hostile marine environment. Therefore, this gas will warrant a premium price, especially if the government of Nova Scotia is to realize any significant revenues from its sale. By no means is this assured when you consider the various factors affecting the only outlet for Sable gas, the northeastern U.S. market.

From 1981-83, U.S. gas buyers purchased only half of the Canadian imports for which they had contracted because the price of Canadian natural gas was too high. Consequently, the U.S. Department of Energy established a new regulation early in 1984 governing the contract prices of new gas imports. They will have to be flexibly priced so as to be competitive both with each other and with other energy sources, notably oil. It is in this context that we can see the squeeze applied to Nova Scotia offshore-gas revenues.

The benchmark for all energy prices is the price of oil, because it is highly transportable and is the source of more than half the energy needs of the industrialized countries. Although there were two large increases in the price of oil in the 1970s, the likelihood of a similar occurrence extending beyond a brief period within the next 20 years is minimal. First of all, the Organization of Petroleum Exporting Countries (OPEC) produces at only a fraction of its capacity in order to maintain its offical price of US$29 per barrel. Any crisis which might cause a shortfall in oil exports and tend to raise prices (such as a blockade of the Persian Gulf) would dissipate within 90 days. A host of unaffected producers, such as Nigeria, Venezuela, and Mexico, would eagerly fill the void so as to relieve the strains on their debt-ridden economies. Moreover, the recent downward pressure in oil prices will be intensified significantly when the Iran-Iraq war ends and both countries try to reconstruct their economics by pumping more oil out of the ground. Second, in the wake of oil price hikes in the 1970s, the industrialized countries developed a myriad of conservation and oil-substitution practices which could be vigorously accentuated in the event of a threatening oil crisis. Third, the industrialized countries' economies need to maintain a collective growth rate of at least 2 percent—the experience of the international recession in the early 1980s reminds us that there is no guarantee of this—so that the demand for oil will keep the price from falling. Putting all of these factors together, if Sable gas hits the New England market at the end of the decade, it will be competing with cheap and abundant oil.

There is also the problem with other gas suppliers. Again, a study conducted by the Economic Council of Canada concluded that Alberta gas transported by pipeline to the Maritimes would cost less than Venture gas at the gate of the proposed processing plant in Canso. Small quantities of western Canadian gas have now started to flow into the northeastern U.S. market through existing pipelines, and an American pipeline consortium is planning to construct a new natural gas pipeline from the Saskatchewan border through the United States to Pennsylvania. Estimated to cost $800 million, this pipeline will be roughly 50 percent longer than the one proposed to bring Venture gas to New England, although the latter will be comparable in cost. So, even if we assume that the northeastern U.S. market will be able to absorb both western and eastern Canadian natural gas, establishing the market price on a contract-by-contract basis will not be in Nova Scotia's favour. Although political and corporate figures currently express confidence and satisfaction over the apparent eagerness of New England utilities to purchase Venture gas, offshore analyst Ian Doig observes that the potential buyers "know that Nova Scotia only has one place to sell the gas—to them. It's a buyer's market and there's a signficant surplus."

With pricing as a critical weak link in the Venture development scenario, what are the economic implications for Nova Scotia? After all, as we heard in the 1983 Speech from the Throne in Nova Scotia and have been told on countless other occasions, offshore development revenues "will help lay a solid base for economic growth into the next century." In its Environmental Impact Statement for the Venture development, Mobil Oil forecast total "government take" for Nova Scotia of $13.5 billion over the eighteen-year life of the project. Not a bad prospect, but subsequent evaluations have determined that Mobil's estimate is unduly optimistic for a number of reasons: they relied on increasing oil prices, low interest rates, and few problems in developing Venture gas. Because of these factors, the Buchanan government, ordinarily noted for its penchant to slightly enlarge any statistic related to the offshore, has even diminished its revenue expectations to $5 billion. By comparison, this is the annual government take in recession-plagued Alberta. Divided over eighteen years, it also equals less than half of what Nova Scotia received in 1984 in equalization payments, one of the true indicators of the province's "have-not" status.

Comments by Mobil President Bill Mason in 1984 that "Venture field economics look pretty damn lousy," and by federal Energy Minister Pat Carney promising changes in the "fiscal regime" governing offshore gas development, point to lower government revenues. It should be noted that the first call on these revenues is by the companies. Federal grants and tax allowances notwithstanding, Mobil Oil and its partners have spent millions of dollars drilling on the Scotian Shelf. The Canadian subsidiary of the third largest oil company in the world (its annual revenues are roughly equal to those which the Canadian government receives from all of its sources) does not invest such sums of money unless there is a firm assurance that it will receive a substantial return on its investment. Government sabre-rattling against Mobil tends to obscure the real power of Mobil and the rest of the "Seven Sister" multinational oil companies. Because of the latter's ongoing influence with the U.S. government—and hence its Canadian clone—both the National Energy Program and the Canada–Nova Scotia Offshore Agreement will be changed so that the oil companies will receive their specified profits from offshore gas development. What will be left over for government will be negligible. Indeed, the word circulating around Ottawa is that Venture will be an "economic development project"—in other words, a make-work project in the time-honoured tradition of the "develop-or-perish" mentality of desperation that has always characterized resource extraction in this region: we get some work for a brief period of time while others benefit from both the product and the profits of our labour.

The underdeveloped character of the Nova Scotia economy stands out clearly when the commercial features of the Venture project are examined. During the construction and development phase, Mobil estimates that 75 percent of the $2.4 billion in expenditures will originate in Canada. Twenty-three percent of this will be placed in Nova Scotia, 21 percent in Ontario, and 13 percent in Quebec, while the remainder will be distributed among the other Atlantic Provinces and western Canada. When you look more closely at these figures, it turns out that the central Canadian content is much higher than first indicated: approximately 60 percent. This is because manufactured goods purchased in Nova Scotia for Venture will tend to originate in Ontario and Quebec, the provinces which stand to gain most from this project. Even during the production phase, when direct employment and income payments occur only in Nova Scotia, Ontario and Quebec will still account for almost one-half of the total incomes earned as a result of purchases of goods and services attributable to Venture. In fact, this model provides an excellent example of one of the strongly implicit elements in the National Energy Program: the enhancement of the manufacturing industry in central Canada. This is one of many points on which the federal Liberals and Tories see eye to eye.

Understandably, the limited provincial business opportunities contained in Mobil's development proposal provoked much criticism during the Socio-Economic Review hearings in the fall of 1983. With the Nova Scotia content concentrated almost totally in both the Halifax/Dartmouth and Strait of Canso areas, one Sydney speaker at the hearings complained: "Maybe we are paranoid, but we really feel that we have been left out." This sentiment was echoed by Merritt Crawford, president of the Pictou County Research and Development Commission (PICORD), who criticized Mobil's plan to have most of the metal-fabrication work performed outside the province, even though the industrial infrastructure for this kind of construction activity exists in Pictou County.

The limited participation factors and consequent criticisms also apply to the level of Nova Scotia employment arising from Mobil's projections of the development and production phases of the Venture project. In the year of maximum construction activity associated with the development of the Venture field, the total peak direct employment for Nova Scotians is estimated to be 1,875 person-years. Potentially, almost 5,500 additional indirect and induced person-years of work may be connected with the Venture spending impacts in that year. Putting this in a practical perspective, PICORD's Merritt Crawford notes that the peak provincial employment for metal fabrication, 673 person-years of work (one-third of the total peak employment), is less than the average employment at Hawker-Siddeley's Trenton Works Division for 1981. When development ends and the production phase begins—two years after the peak construction activity—an estimated 560 direct jobs will be provided for Nova Scotians through the eighteen-year life of the project. Again, to express this in comparative terms, economist Michael Gardner, who assisted in the preparation of Mobil's Environmental Impact Statement, says that employment from the production stage of the Venture development will constitute about one-third the number of jobs at a Michelin plant. In short, Venture—or any other possible gas field development—will hardly put a dent in Nova Scotia's unacceptably high unemployment rate.

Despite the gloomy market prospects for Sable gas and the fact that the resource has been unco-operative in not locating itself in large quantities in one area, the Venture gas field, by itself or in costly combination with nearby fields, will almost certainly be developed. There are too many political and financial forces pushing in its favour. Although least influential, the Buchanan government desperately wants this development at any cost to salvage whatever credibility it still has.

For its part, the federal government wants Venture to go ahead for two reasons. Like their predecessors, Mulroney's Tories are keen on mega-projects as a means of attempted reinvigoration for central Canada's crumbling manufacturing industry. As well, this would represent the first step in the fulfilment of Brian Mulroney's cherished dream of encouraging U.S. corporations to "invest" in Canada. With the doors held wide open and the blank cheques already signed, the oil companies are quite willing to "develop" uneconomic gas fields because they are assured a profit for their work.[1]

There are many negative aspects of the offshore phenomenon with which this chapter has not been able to deal. Among others, there is the tremendous pressure which has been put on social services in Halifax/Dartmouth because of the unceasing hype the Buchanan government has irresponsibly projected about offshore opportunities. There is a desperate housing shortage in Halifax and there is neither work nor income for the increased number of transients who, according to Father Peter McKenna of the Roman Catholic–sponsored food relief program at Hope Cottage, have come here "for the offshore boom that isn't."

Politically, the Buchanan government has triumphed. Socially and economically, however, it has blown it. The whole faulty approach to the offshore is summed up in Development Minister Roland Thornhill's comment that, "The offshore is the only game in town, and we are out to milk it for everything it is worth." The vaunted role of an industry over which there is so little local control and from which are derived so few benefits, is truly indicative of the continuing underdeveloped status of the Nova Scotia economy.

---

[1]**Author's Note (March 1987):** When this chapter was published in three parts in *New Maritimes* over the winter of 1984-85, there existed the possibility of a plunge in oil prices—and hence a decrease in prices for all energy sources, including natural gas—but such an occurrence was generally regarded as improbable. The fact that this happened one year later warrants a revision to the assumption that the offshore resource is going to be developed anyway, even though the development of the Venture and neighbouring

natural gas deposits was not even feasible at higher prices (US$29 per barrel of oil until November 1985 versus US$15-18 from the summer of 1986).

The influence of both the Canadian governments and the multinational oil industry had tilted the balance in favour of Scotian Shelf gas development, even if this meant that American consumers of the resource would have to be subsidized by Canadian tax-payers. Although the federal Progressive Conservative government was willing to pay a small price both to bolster the declining manufacturing industry of central Canada with the initiation of a megaproject and to gain political points in the Maritimes from the temporary effects of this kind of regional development project, the perceived pricing scenarios simply provide too prohibitive a cost for a government with a heavy deficit to reduce, and the subsidy required to do so would arouse an unprecedented storm of op-position from politicians and from the petroleum industry in Alberta.

By the end of 1985, the federal Tories had announced the end of the National Energy Program and any new PIP grants.

Venture will not be developed in the foreseeable future, despite the considerable in-fluence of Mobil Corporation of New York and the federal government's favourable at-titude towards its American counterpart, which in turn has always actively represented the interests of the major oil corporations. The political and economic cost for the Canadian government is simply too high.

This does not mean that Mobil will not find—or has not found—some way to get a return on the capital that it sunk into the Nova Scotia offshore (from 1981-86, this amounted to at least $100 million). The 1986 sale of Canadian Superior Oil Co. by Mobil Corporation to its wholly owned subsidiary, Mobil Oil Canada Ltd., at a hyperinflated price has provided one means of recovering its offshore costs. The fact that, after a year of negotiations up to March 1987, Mobil was still holding up final agreement on the fiscal regime for the development of the Hibernia oil field off New-foundland (while another partner in the project, Petro-Canada, was willing to com-promise for less revenue) suggests that Mobil's proposed return on investment for the Hibernia development incorporates its investment in the Nova Scotia offshore. One way or the other, and keeping the broad picture in view, Mobil will not lose on its Nova Scotia venture.

The Sinking of the Ocean Ranger, 1982: The Politics of a Resource Tragedy

Brian O'Neill

The sinking of the Ocean Ranger during a violent storm on the night of February 14-15, 1982, was a terrible and shocking landmark in the modern social history of the Atlantic region. It was so, for most people, because 84 crew members died, but the Ocean Ranger tragedy had a deeper, and perhaps even more disturbing, significance. It revealed how little the needs of workers count when governments pursue get-rich-quick development schemes. It demonstrated that those primarily responsible for a preventable disaster could escape without blame. It was shocking because federal and provincial governments put their own "jurisdiction" over the offshore resource far ahead of the health and safety of the workers on the rigs. The Ocean Reanger tragedy was really the tragedy of a whole style of development which has, repeatedly, placed the needs of corporations for profits and the needs of governments for tax revenues far ahead of the needs of the people of the Atlantic region.

The Ocean Ranger was the largest semi-submersible oil rig in the world: 396 feet long, 262 feet wide, and as tall as a 35-storey building. Valued at $120 million, it was referred to by spokespersons for the offshore oil industry as the "Cadillac" of the drilling fleet. Initial reports of its loss naturally prompted the obvious question: how could the Ocean Ranger—built to withstand storms more severe than the fateful mid-February blizzard during which it sank—succumb, while two smaller neighbouring rigs survived?

Shortly after the sinking of the Ocean Ranger, three inquiries were established to investigate the causes of the accident: the first two by the U.S. Coast Guard and the U.S. National Transportation Safety Board (the Ocean Ranger had U.S. marine certification), and a third by the joint federal-provincial Royal Commission on the Ocean Ranger Disaster (hereafter referred to as the Ocean Ranger Inquiry). Evidence presented at the three hearings led to general agreement as to the specific cause of the Ocean Ranger's sinking. The rig had a unique and complicated ballast system, described as "fail-safe" by a senior ODECO (Ocean Drilling and Exploration Company) engineer. Yet, evidently, it failed. Shortly after 7:00 p.m. on February 14, water broke through one or two portlight windows in the rig's ballast control room, short-

---

This chapter is based on an article first published in *New Maritimes* (February 1984).

circuiting a panel controlling valves in two gigantic underwater pontoons. While it appeared that the problem had been fixed by 9:00 p.m. (a 10:00 p.m. radio message to shore indicated that everything had been restored to normal in the ballast control room), a Mayday (distress) call was suddenly sent from the Ocean Ranger around 1:00 a.m., February 15. The rig was listing badly, and it ultimately capsized around 3:30 a.m. due to the uncontrollable intake of 5,000 tons of sea water into one of its ballast-containing pontoons.

The two U.S. inquiries have both concluded that the tragedy could have been prevented if better safety and training procedures had been followed. In reviewing what occurred on the night of February 14-15, the U.S. Coast Guard report states: "This chain of events was not an inevitable progression and could have been broken by competent human intervention." Both U.S. investigating bodies have blamed ODECO for the tragedy. The safety record of the Ocean Ranger was abysmal. The Coast Guard had determined in 1980 that the rig's two lifeboats were substandard; it was only around the time of the sinking that new ones were installed. A couple of months earlier, a Coast Guard official had reported 200 deficiencies on the rig, including insufficient maintenance on the remote control valves for the ballast tanks. Former captain Karl Nehring described the required abandon-ship drills as "a mess." Often, the emergency radio channel did not work. The Ocean Ranger was operating in one of the most hazardous offshore environments in the world without any certificate of inspection of its seaworthiness—its last certification had expired 50 days before the sinking.

Injuries were more common on the Ocean Ranger than on the nearby rigs, Zapata Ugland and Sedco 706, and there was a comparatively high turnover of workers there. Allan Rowe worked for seven months on the rig before quitting in August 1981. "I didn't want to lose any fingers. My friends on the Sedco 706 would look at me like I had three heads or something for working on the Ranger." The angry widow of another worker said that her husband had told her that if anything ever happened to him on the rig to "sue ODECO for all it was worth." She claimed that her husband frequently mentioned the company's poor attitude towards safety. On radio calls to and from the rig, it was often referred to—lightheartedly but reflectively—as the "Ocean Danger".

If the Ocean Ranger had been operating in an area over which no government or agency claimed any jurisdiction or regulatory responsibility, it would be quite appropriate for its demise to be blamed solely on ODECO, or perhaps for the blame to be shared with Mobil, the oil company which had contracted ODECO to drill in the Hibernia oil field. However, such was not the case.

Since the early 1970s, the Newfoundland government pursued a vigorous and incessant campaign of asserting provincial ownership and control over Newfoundland's and Labrador's offshore mineral resources. Newfoundland's ownership claim had been just as resolutely—but less noisily—countered by the federal government. What underlay the federal and provincial claims is very straightforward: both levels of government, as well as the oil companies, stand to earn tens of billions of dollars from the exploitation of offshore oil and gas. (In October 1982, the federal government estimated combined provincial and federal revenues from Hibernia alone to be $87 billion.) In this very significant respect, political and corporate goals—and priorities—converge, and this convergence of interests dominated the relationship between these two entities at least until the sinking of the Ocean Ranger.

With ownership comes the responsibility to manage the development of public resources in a safe and secure manner, whether on land or on the continental shelf. The Ocean Ranger disaster reveals a surprising degree of government negligence in this respect.

Most people who are even vaguely aware of offshore developments in Newfoundland have probably heard references to the Peckford government's "tough" regulations. Enacted in 1978 the Newfoundland and Labrador Petroleum Regulations are quite comprehensive and reveal a surprising level of petroleum-related expertise for such a small, and only potential, petroleum producer. However, these comprehensive regulations deal with only one aspect of offshore development: the maximization of economic benefit to the Province of Newfoundland. They cover matters such as the granting of drilling permits and licences; preferential purchase of Newfoundland goods and the hiring of Newfoundland workers for the offshore; and a generous tax and royalty scheme for the Newfoundland Government. For all the province's studious efforts at the time to understand the nuances of petroleum development on a global scale—fluctuations in the price of "marker crude" at Ras Tanura, Saudi Arabia; the federal/state offshore jurisdictional dispute in Australia; Norwegian petroleum taxation and royalty schemes—no effort was expended simultaneously to examine safety problems, practices, and regulations elsewhere, particularly in the North Sea. Consequently, by the time the Ocean Ranger sank, there were no provincial regulations concerning any aspect of safety in the offshore. (The province came forward with its first drilling regulations in June 1982, four months after the Ocean Ranger sank.)

For its part, the federal government has looked after its economic and jurisdictional interests through the National Energy Program (1980) and the Canada Oil and Gas Act (1982). It did, however, enact the Canada Oil and Gas Drilling Regulations in 1979, thirteen years after the first exploration hole was sunk off the east coast. When asked why it took so long to officially establish these regulations, Tom Dexter, the former East Coast Manager of the Canada Oil and Gas Lands Administration (COGLA), replied: "We had those drilling regulations in draft form some five or six years before that, and we intimated to industry that, although these were not promulgated as regulations, we would expect them to adhere to them." Intimations notwithstanding, it seems that the oil companies and their drilling contractors were officially left to police themselves over drilling operations and safety matters at least until 1979. In the case of the Ocean Ranger, the evidence indicates that ODECO was effectively granted an almost free hand until the rig disappeared.

The question of offshore safety covers a broad range of activities. Basically, there are three elements in a complete safety system: ensuring the seaworthiness of drilling rigs; minimizing the risks posed by down-hole drilling operations at sea (blowouts, etc.); and assuring safe working conditions for offshore employees. The fact that both levels of government adamantly claimed jurisdiction over the area where the Ocean Ranger was drilling should have provided duplicated coverage of safety requirements. Tragically, this was not the case.

As far as the seaworthiness was concerned, the marine safety of the Ocean Ranger had never been checked by federal authorities, as the Minister of Energy at the time, Marc Lalonde, was obliged to confirm. The province had never conducted a marine inspection either. When questioned about this inspection gap at the Ocean Ranger Inquiry, Gordon Gosse of the Newfoundland Department of Energy conceded that the Petroleum Directorate was "weak" in marine matters. Both levels of government were unaware that the Ocean Ranger's U.S. marine certification had expired at the end of 1981. (In the time-honoured east-coast tradition of locking the barn door after the horse has fled, the Newfoundland government has required its own marine inspections for rigs drilling off its coast since January 1983.)

The Newfoundland government's record on the safety of down-hole drilling operations was not much better than that for marine safety. Up to the time the Ocean Ranger sank, the province's Petroleum Directorate had no official drilling regulations, and there was only one provincial inspector to look after every aspect of safety for all the rigs in the Newfoundland and Labrador offshore. The day after the Ocean Ranger sank a former crew member complained bitterly: "If Peckford cares so much about oil for Newfoundlanders, then where were the provincial safety inspectors? The only ones we ever saw were from EMR" (the federal Department of Energy, Mines and Resources—COGLA now has this responsibility). The reason why most offshore workers never saw a provincial inspector is that, as Gordon Gosse told the Ocean Ranger Inquiry, the Petroleum Directorate's sole inspector usually visited a rig only when someone complained of a safety problem. (The Petroleum Directorate now has five inspectors.)

Federal drilling regulations had been in effect since 1979, and inspectors had been checking each rig for about a day and a half every two or three weeks. What was the quality of these inspections? How rigorously were the drilling regulations enforced? Both questions are best answered by the story of the events surrounding a serious listing incident which occurred on the Ocean Ranger on February 6, 1982, nine days before the rig and its 84 crew members were lost.

The captain of the Ocean Ranger when it sank was Clarence Hauss. It was his first shift aboard the rig. His only instructions regarding the operations of the Ocean Ranger, including its unique ballast system (for which the captain of any sea-going vessel has ultimate responsibility) were contained in a ten-minute conversation with the departing captain, Geoffrey Dilks, on January

25. On February 6, while the Ocean Ranger was taking on drill water, Captain Hauss incorrectly opened two sea-inward valves and upset the stability of the rig. It immediately began to list to one side. Twenty minutes later, the list was worse and there were repeated warnings on the public address system to prepare to abandon the rig. Although the seas were calm and the list never exceeded seven degrees, panic prevailed. Many crew members did not either know or remember their emergency stations, which constitutes a violation of Canadian drilling regulations. Virtually the whole crew gathered around one of the four lifeboats on the rig.

Steve McIntyre was one of them. "The boat couldn't have held everyone. There was a feeling of anxiety, of helplessness. We were confused and we didn't know what to do." One crew member tried to start the engine of the lifeboat. But it would not start, reflecting either ignorance or poor maintenance of the lifeboats. Perhaps most disturbing, said McIntyre, was the fact that some members of the crew were not awakened during the emergency call.

The list was corrected within a half hour. Crew members such as Steve McIntyre, who went through the February 6 experience but were on leave from the Ocean Ranger when it sank, said it was fortunate there were perfect sea conditions at the time. There was a safety meeting afterwards, at which crew members later reported the rig superintendent as having said the rig could never sink.

The incident also pointed out poor training in vital operations of the rig. Testimonies at all three inquiries have indicated a very informal process for training ballast control operators on the Ocean Ranger, and most of the operators did not know how to use the manual backup system. Frank Jennings, who spent five years on the Ocean Ranger as a ballast control operator, said that his approach towards problem solving if a crisis arose regarding the ballast system was to try and find someone else to fix it. Federal and provincial authorities had no standards or training requirements for any offshore workers.

According to federal regulations, the February 6 listing incident, because of its severity, had to be reported to COGLA "immediately, by the most rapid and practical means." This was not done. The Petroleum Directorate found out about it a few days later when a reporter called to confirm rumours. The Petroleum Directorate then contacted Mobil, which confirmed the incident, having only heard about it on Feburary 8 from a Mobil official who had been on the rig at the time. COGLA, whose regulations were violated, only learned of the list on Feburary 12, when someone from the federal agency called Mobil to check the unofficial reports which had been circulating. No reprimand, fine, or corrective action was taken against Mobil or ODECO over the listing incident and the surrounding violations of regulations.

When Premier Peckford and his Energy Minister William Marshall were questioned about this matter the day after the sinking, they said it had been checked out and was found to be the result of "human error." Peckford added that the provincial government had the power to shut down any rig that Newfoundland inspectors felt was unsafe. "We have not found anything so far of a nature serious enough as to cause a shutdown," he said—an interesting assertion, considering the limitations on inspecting all the offshore rigs when there is only one person to do the job.

Apparently, neither the sole provincial inspector nor a federal counterpart was on the Ocean Ranger at the end of September 1981, when it developed a five to ten degree list, another unreported incident. In fact, according to testimony given at the Ocean Ranger Inquiry, the rig had developed three severe lists between August 1981 and February 1982. Former captain Karl Nehring said that the rig had a tendency to take on an unexpected, severe forward list of seven to ten degrees while it was being ballasted or deballasted.

Following the February 6 episode, it appears that officials within the Peckford administration knew that something was awry with the operations of the Ocean Ranger. Ray Hawco, the Community Relations officer with the Petroleum Directorate, had been scheduled to take a helicopter flight out to the Ocean Ranger on Saturday, February 13, to hold discussions with the workers. His trip—unusual for an onshore community impact official—was necessary, said Hawco in an interview, because "their morale was so low." "Without a union," he added, "there is no avenue for the workers to voice their concerns." Fortunately for Hawco, the helicopter had mechanical problems that weekend and was grounded.

As a matter of fact, an "avenue" did exist for workers to voice their concerns: the province's Occupational Health and Safety Act. However, the provincial government seems to have kept that avenue closed, at least until the summer of 1982, half a year after the disaster. Newfoundland Federation of Labour President Bill Parsons has described this legislation, enacted in 1978, as "on par with any other legislation in North America on the issue of occupational health and safety." Through the application of this Act, workers have the right to form committees in their workplaces to express their grievances collectively over matters such as safety problems. The legislation specifically prohibits discrimination against workers who lodge complaints or who take part in health and safety committees.

This Act was not enforced in the offshore despite numerous appeals by the labour movement, including a formal brief to the Peckford government in 1980 requesting "that the government not grant any further licences or permits to explore and develop the oil fields until agreement is reached on safety regulations and a decent standard of working conditions." Provincial government inaction on this issue prevailed, leaving individual workers to fend for themselves.

Rig worker Byron Prior explains the difficulties for offshore employees to express, on an individual basis, their concerns over safety on some rigs: "I found that on a number of the rigs individuals have been ignored to the point where they have had to quit and go ashore. Or else, if they're not ignored and the problem is fixed, they're given a hard time for bringing it up because they're disturbing a process.''

Shortly after the Ocean Ranger sank, provincial Labour and Manpower Minister Jerry Dinn was asked about the enforcement of the Occupational Health and Safety Act in the offshore. He replied that every complaint regarding safety was throughly investigated (presumably by the sole Petroleum Directorate inspector, who was not one of the province's 50 trained occupational health and safety inspectors). Federation of Labour President Bill Parsons commented on Dinn's assertion: ''I don't doubt that. But, my question is: why on earth would he have to wait until a complaint came to him? You have to realize that a person who gave him that complaint put his job in jeopardy!''

While reports from offshore workers and the labour movement had indicated that there was no protection for rig employees under the province's occupational health and safety legislation, official confirmation of the fact was difficult to obtain. In a May 20, 1982, CBC Radio interview with the then Executive Director of the Petroleum Directorate, Steven Millan, he said: ''Occupational health and safety inspectors have been on the rigs and continue to be out on the rigs. We have our own inspectors as well, and usually the inspections that we do are done jointly with the occupational health and safety people. Quite often the two inspectors go out together.''

Millan's remarks were contradicted a month later by Robert Langdon, Assistant Deputy Minister of Labour and Manpower in charge of Occupational Health and Safety. He was asked if, up to that time, occupational health and safety inspectors had been on any of the rigs. He replied: ''No. We were just in the process of commencing, initiating, in co-operation with the Petroleum Directorate, and, as it will be in the future, a joint inspection program.'' When asked, ''Given that the drill rigs were out there for a long time and the Occupational Health and Safety Act has been around for a few years, why has it taken so long to get involved in the offshore?'' Langdon answered: ''Well, I suppose it's an evolving thing and I guess it ties in with the direction in which the province intended to pursue this matter.''

On the federal side, Labour Canada officials never set foot on the Ocean Ranger; Lionel Brandon, Director-General of Engineering for COGLA, said that this responsibility ''belongs with the provinces.''

The storm that hit the Grand Banks on the night of February 14-15, 1982, packed winds of 90 knots and churned up waves of 60 feet. Yet, all 84 crew members who abandoned the Ocean Ranger need not have perished. As the lifeboats were lowered into the stormy seas, they were apparently smashed against the rig's support columns, producing holes in their sides. Few of the victims were clad in survival suits, which turned out to be both deficient in number and quality. At least two of the three nearby supply vessels were in violation of federal regulations because they were not equipped with all of specified rescue gear. Moreover, while the regulations called for the stationing of "stand-by craft" near the rigs at all times, Captain Baxter Allingham of the supply boat *Nordertor* testified at one of the U.S. inquiry hearings that the supply vessels were "not stand-by vessels. We're not equipped for taking bodies over the side." The manager of one of the companies leasing supply vessels to oil companies on the east coast did not even know that these vessels were to be used in a safety stand-by capacity until after the disaster. One of his company's boats, the *Seaforth Highlander*, was nominally the "stand-by craft" for the Ocean Ranger the night it sank.

According to offshore safety specialist Hamish McDonald of the Robert Gordon Institute of Technology in Aberdeen, Scotland, if the same sort of rapid intervention safety vessels present in the North Sea since the mid-1970s had been stationed on the Grand Banks the night of the disaster, some crew members might have been saved. One damaged lifeboat capsized within six feet of the *Seaforth Highlander*, but everyone in the lifeboat perished.

This grisly episode also demonstrates the meagre financial resources allocated to safety equipment and technology. Former Ocean Ranger control-room operator Bruce Porter commented poignantly on this issue at one of the hearings conducted by the U.S. Coast Guard: "It strikes me as very sad that this wonder of modern technology and ingenuity didn't have a way of transferring people to a safety ship. . . . Hundreds of millions of dollars of modern ingenuity can drill miles into the ocean, but we haven't yet devised a contraption that can move men 100 yards to save their lives." Indeed, as much as $4 billion (in 1982 dollars) had been spent on east-coast offshore exploration by the time of the Ocean Ranger disaster. Roughly 80 percent of this amount—over $3 billion—was provided by Canadian taxpayers in the forms of tax allowances and outright grants to the oil industry. The proportion of this money which was spent on safety inspections, equipment, research, and technology was, and still is, pitifully small.

The sinking of the Ocean Ranger occurred at a politically inopportune time for the Peckford government. Private polls had indicated that this was the right time to call a provincial election on the theme of Peckford's leadership in "standing up for Newfoundland" against Ottawa over the offshore jurisdictional dispute, but Premier Peckford and some of his ministers must have felt somewhat apprehensive about the political liabilities which could potentially arise for them out of this incident. Shaken but undaunted by the disaster, Premier Peckford and Energy Minister Marshall maintained a measured offensive in dealing with occasionally awkward questions from the media regarding safety inspections, the February 6 listing incident, etc. Friday, February 19, was declared an official day of mourning, and requiem services and events were organized in churches and schools throughout Newfoundland and Labrador. It was not a conducive atmosphere in which to pursue a thorough line of questioning and apportion blame.

On the federal scene, there were a few days of heated questions and charges in the House of Commons, but challenges to the Department of Energy's regulatory operations had faded by the end of the week. After some initial haggling between Newfoundland and Ottawa as to who had been the first to appoint a board of inquiry, the joint federal-provincial Royal Commission was announced. It was mandated to investigate the cause(s) of the disaster and to look at the full safety and regulatory regime in the east coast offshore. Initially, the Ocean Ranger Inquiry commissioners were expected to submit their final report within two years. This deadline was then stretched to three and one-half years, perhaps a suffcient period of time to dissipate whatever immediate demands had existed both to determine all the causes of the disaster and to see justice carried out with respect to those found culpable.

The Peckford government emerged from the Ocean Ranger disaster and its immediate aftermath virtually unscathed. So remarkable was the government's triumph over the threatening political, and possible legal, liabilities surrounding the deaths of 84 people, including 54 Newfoundlanders, that Premier Peckford could confidently, and quite successfully as it turned out, go to the electorate one month and a day afterward on the issue of the province's right—meaning the Peckford government's right—to significant control over the offshore.

The loss of the Ocean Ranger and its 84-man crew shocked and saddened everyone, including those in government and the oil industry associated with the rig's exploration on the Grand Banks. However, the consequences of the tragedy for either of these two groups have not really been all that severe. ODECO, a subsidiary of Murphy Oil, has a somewhat tarnished reputation, and it may have to pay out as much as $50 million or more in legal suits and fees, a figure approximating one-half the cost of a new drilling rig (the Ocean Ranger, by the way, was insured). Mobil's legal expenses will likely be much smaller. (The families of the 54 Newfoundlanders who died reached a $23 million settlement with ODECO and Mobil. Settlements for the families of deceased American crew members have not all been reached and are expected to be substantially higher.)

Politically, the Trudeau government seemed virtually unaffected by the Ocean Ranger disaster. As far as the Peckford government is concerned, its shrewd political use of the safety issue since the offshore deaths has—perversely—almost enhanced the stature of the administration. During the 1982 provincial election campaign, Premier Peckford reminded his audience in St. Alban's that: "I have always said, Newfoundland owns the oil and gas on the continental shelf in the same way as Alberta owns the oil and gas on land." Up to that time, his government had indeed acted as if these resources were on land—but their diligent regulating of offshore operations was confined to just the economic sphere. Both levels of government had set a course for offshore development which differed little from industry's. Former Ocean Ranger Captain Karl Nehring, who had been frustrated in his attempts to conduct safety-training exercises aboard the rig, aptly expressed the impact of these similar political and corporate priorities: "The most important thing . . . is to keep that bit turning. Keep that drill turning. Never mind the safety of the people. Never mind if they get injured. Keep it turning."

Springhill 1958

Ian McKay

It happened at 8:06 p.m. on Thursday, October 23, 1958. The people of Springhill were doing a variety of things when they felt the ground shake and heard a booming noise. The Wolf Cubs were just concluding their meeting, and Mayor Ralph Gilroy was just bringing the Town Council to order. Many people were at home watching Lucille Ball in "I Love Lucy."

Some people thought the noise was the sound of a car crash, or their children falling out of bed, or "just the TV aerial falling down again." One miner who was walking down the street remembered,

> I thought some kids put a bomb under Jim Brown's house. I said, "What in the hell's that?" and he said, "I don't know!" And then a neighbour came out and she hollered, "What was that?" and I said, "I don't know." So I ran home, and I said, "Mary, did you feel that bump?" And she said, "It knocked me off the couch." And I said, "Lord God! It's the whole three walls must have went!" and I ran to the pit.

Many miners' wives said afterward they knew at once what had happened. "It is hard to explain, but it just felt like the whole world hit the house; it was terrific. I knew it was a bump and I thought of my husband in the mine. I said right out loud, 'My God above, it happened!' "

The telephone system was jammed with calls, and rumours started to spread along the streets. Some people said that the tremor had affected only the waste portion of the mine—nothing to worry about, they said nobody had been hurt. However, the crowd which gathered at the pithead soon learned that a bump—a sudden shifting of underground strata—had closed down most of No. 2, the town's only functioning mine.

George S. Calder, the Manager of No. 2 mine, tried to phone the mine as soon as he felt the bump at home. He couldn't get through to the underground, so he rushed to the mine himself. When he finally did get through on the phone, he found out that there was no communication from the mine's lower levels, where most of the men had been working on three walls. At 8:45 p.m., the manager led the first contingent of rescue workers into the mine. They braved the mine gases without wearing masks.

This chapter is based on an article first published in *New Maritimes* (December 1983–January 1984).

At the pithead the crowd grew larger and more anxious. The Red Cross unit arrived, and the Salvation Army pitched three huge tents, two of which had been used during a disaster two years before. Inside the tents many residents waited around potbellied stoves. Then the draegermen—specially trained rescue workers who carried equipment for breathing in a mine choked with hazardous gases—arrived from Stellarton and New Glasgow. There could be no doubt that a major calamity had taken place.

At 5:40 p.m. on Friday, October 24, 1958, the first body was brought to the surface, and then taken to the Canadian Legion Hall, which served as a temporary morgue. That same Friday, Harold C.M. Gordon, Vice-President and General Manager of the Dominion Coal Company, and the General Manager of the coal operations of the Dominion Steel & Coal Corporation (Dosco), operators of the mine, announced that there were no men left alive on the 13,000- and 13,800-foot levels. "The way things look, those still listed as missing must be presumed dead," he remarked. "There is virtually no hope left."

From Friday to Wednesday morning, the community waited anxiously for news. On Tuesday Gordon held his fifth conference. He reported that the rescue crews were making very slow progress in reaching the "13,000 wall." They could fight their way through only 10-12 feet per eight-hour shift. When a reporter asked him what that meant, he replied, "It means that there is no further hope. There just can't be. We cannot hold any reason to believe that men will be found alive when we finally do reach them."

On the morning of Wednesday, October 29th, the total stood at 81 men rescued, 26 known dead, and 67 still missing. Some wives had made funeral arrangements for their missing husbands, and it was feared that all of the men left in the mine were dead.

But they weren't.

When the bump hit No. 2, it affected 174 men on the afternoon shift. Shortly after 3 p.m. on October 23rd, these men had gone down in the rake (a mine train) to the "7,800 level," and there changed into a second rake which took them to levels over a mile beneath the surface. Most of the men worked on three adjacent walls at the 13,000-, 13,400-, and 13,800-foot levels. About 80 worked at the coal face digging coal; the rest did other jobs, such as keeping the machines in good order and moving the coal to the surface.

Before the bump came, Fred Hahnen was working on the 13,800 wall, about ten or eleven feet away from miners on either side of him. It seemed to him that the coal face was easy to work that night. He told the men beside him that the coal was so easy to work that it seemed to be trying to get ahead of him. When the overman (boss) of the wall came along, Hahnen remembered him saying, "You are right in to the berries, your coal must be working good," and Hahnen replied, "You should have seen how hard I had to dig to get this out."

Shortly after 8:06 p.m., James McManaman, the overman, was talking with two other men, when they suddenly heard a tremendous roar and felt a blast of air racing up the wall. Then the dust rose in great clouds, and they could hear the sounds of men moaning.

Another miner remembered that at the moment of the bump, he was talking to his friend. He was bringing up the issue of a small tremor that had been felt in the mine earlier that shift, and he started to ask, "Oh, by the way, did you feel that bump a while ago?" Just at the time he said the word "bump," the mine suddenly let go. His friend went flying, and so did he, right up to the mine roof.

Other men felt that the coal face had just come towards them. They were thrown back, tossed into the air, bounced off the roof of the mine. The walls seemed to have closed in, the floor had risen about seven feet, pans and rails were smashed and driven into the timber packs (roof supports) and the roof of the mine. Timber was shredded, and where men had been at work, there was a solid wall of coal.

Here and there, though, the bump had left enough space between the pavement and the roof for men to survive. Two groups of survivors were trapped: twelve men at the bottom of the 13,000 wall, and eight men about 400 feet away from them. These groups were unaware of each other. The first group included two injured miners; the second a miner whose arm was trapped in the wreckage of a mine pack, and a semiconscious miner who was separated from the others in a hole the size of a coffin.

It was hard to breathe at first in the dusty atmosphere after the bump. After the men recovered from their shock, they set about digging out their fellow miners. The first days were spent looking for ways of escape. The men explored all the passages which might have led them out of the mine. They explored the waste, where normally miners would not go because of the dangers of the roof coming down on them. They explored pockets that were full of gas, and only by waking each other up from the sleep induced by the gas did they escape alive. They found it hard to believe how much damage the bump had done.

Herbert Pepperdine, who was in the group of eight men, remembered that the first two or three days of entrapment went by quickly. There was a lot to do. But after the third day, any hope of escape was gone. The men were fatigued and almost out of water. They now knew that there was no way they could get themselves out of No. 2.

Why did these things happen? The historian Marc Bloch once described the situation of a man walking along a mountain path, who tripped and fell off. For this accident to happen, Bloch observed, a number of things were necessary: the existence of gravity, a mountainous terrain, the pathway connecting the alpine village with its summer pastures, but anyone asked why the man fell off the mountain would simply say, "He tripped."

Anyone who was asked why these 20 men were entrapped in No. 2 mine would say, "They were caught in a bump." Many people would not see the need to say anything more. If they did, they might mention the fact that coal mines are notoriously dangerous places to work, and that death and entrapment are inevitable consequences of this kind of workplace. "Presumably there will be such terrible disasters as this as long as there is mining, as there are drownings while men go to sea in ships, but we must have coal and we must have fish." These words were written after Springhill's first great disaster in 1891, but they might just as well have been put down in 1958.

Bloch goes on to say that it is dangerous to look only at the immediate and obvious causes of historical events: the causes in history cannot be assumed, they must be looked for. The causes of the Springhill disaster of 1958 are to be looked for in the history of the region's coal industry and in the way decisions were made in the workplace. The Springhill disaster was man-made.

The town of Springhill was threatened with economic disaster in the years leading up to 1958. The citizens of the town had gathered in large meetings to try to stave off the closing of the mines, and the newspapers had already started talking about emergency measures. The bump made the crisis much worse, but it didn't by itself cause Springhill's long economic disaster.

In the nineteenth century, Springhill was Nova Scotia's boom town. Springhill was then one of the province's largest coal producers. Without Confederation and the railway to central Canada, this would never have been. Confederation built this town, as it built no other community in Nova Scotia. The railway opened up the interior of Cumberland County to prospectors, speculators, and investors—among them Charles Tupper, the province's leading Confederate and a future prime minister—and provided a guaranteed market for the coal. Local businessmen sold the mines and the railway connecting Springhill with Parrsboro to Montreal interests in 1882 and 1883, and since those years the mines had been under external control. After 1893, the year the provincial government helped form the Dominion Coal Company in a giant merger in Cape Breton, the Cumberland Railway and Coal Company felt more and more pressure from its Cape Breton rival, and it was swallowed up by the merger in 1910. (Technically the Cumberland Railway and Coal Company still ran the mines, but the Dominion Steel Corporation owned the capital stock of the old company and leased the property to the Dominion Coal Company.) By the 1950s the mines were in the grip of Dosco, the region's largest employer.

The town which grew up around the mines sprawled across the top of a high Cumberland County hill. In the 1870s and 1880s, "Springhill" was synonymous with "progress." The town was even compared with the Klondike. Immigrants came from far and near, from England and continental Europe and from Pictou County and northern New Brunswick. The town's major economic worry was a shortage of houses for the immigrants. There was not much company housing, and the miners were anxious to establish homes of their own. It was said that trees growing on nearby Maccan Mountain in the morning were the same evening standing in Springhill, as part of a new house.

After the 1880s, Springhill was not a backwoods, primitive village dominated by substandard company housing, with company-owned streets and company-owned people. Instead it was a community of home-owners, of coal miners who were proud of their skills, of merchants who sold everything a workingman would need. In the early twentieth century, Springhill prided itself on being a modern town. The water system was of the most advanced type, the town's clergymen were interested in social issues, and the place was crammed with temperance societies, sports clubs, fraternal orders, and well-supported churches.

There were few radical ideas which did not find support in Springhill, and from the 1880s on, labour candidates did surprisingly well in the town. During the big labour battles in the early twentieth century, socialists attracted support, and after the First World War the Springhill vote went heavily in favour of the Farmer-Labour Party. The coal miners here made a very large contribution to the labour movement. Both of the two great trade unions that have represented the Nova Scotia miners were born in Springhill—the Provincial Workmen's Association in 1879, and District 26 of the United Mine Workers of America (UMW) in 1908.

Springhillers were proud of their town. Mayor Ralph Gilroy, who struggled so hard to attract new industries in the wake of the disasters, came from a long tradition of civic pride. When the government sent in the troops to help break the great strike of 1909-11—which collapsed only after 22 months—the mayor declined to sign the request form, and the government had to find someone else. There was a solid sense of community in Springhill, a sense of belonging.

By the 1920s the dreams of prosperity which had been prompted by Confederation were over, as were the province's dreams of building great industries on the basis of foreign control and rapid resource depletion. After the financiers and promoters had done their work, the coal economy was in shambles.

In the nineteenth century the provincial government had looked to the coal industry for its revenue and its economic direction; now the coal industry looked to both levels of the government for subventions and concessions. Although Springhill was cushioned by the steady demand for its coal from the C.N.R., that would rapidly change when the railway converted to diesels in the 1950s.

From the 1930s to the 1950s, the community lost its bargaining power with the coal company and the government. Whenever local people raised questions about what the company was doing, it could threaten to pull up stakes. Although the coal was a public resource, and technically all the private companies did was lease the right to mine it from the government, in practice the government was not about to step in and tell the coal companies what to do. It would set safety limits and give financial assistance, but direct control over long-term corporate strategy was, for ideological reasons, out of the question.

In 1932, three mines were active in Springhill: Nos. 2, 6, and 7. No. 2 had been going since 1873; the other two were relatively new. That year, at a hearing called by a Royal Commission on coal, many voices from the community expressed profound concern about making the town completely dependent on the No. 2 mine. People were worried that the mine was going very deep, and they urged the company to look at other ways of doing things. Why not reopen pits which had been closed because of various mining accidents, but which could be reopened with a little effort and money? Was there not something the company could do about making everyone depend on a mine known to have bumps? The company kept on driving No. 2 deeper and deeper.

The community's worries were allayed for a time by the opening of a new mine, No. 4, which helped solve the town's unemployment problems, and by the company's commitment to putting new equipment in No. 2 mine. (The installation of a new 1,000-horsepower electrical hoist in No. 2 in 1956 was hailed by the *Chronicle-Herald* as "a great achievement.") Then an explosion, caused by faulty mining practices, killed 39 men in No. 4 mine and damaged the main slope.

Although the coal miners, local merchants, and the town council all agitated for the reopening of No. 4 mine, they did not succeed. Nor could they reverse the C.N.R.'s plans to switch to new fuels, which cut out as much as one-third of the market for local coal. By 1957 the town faced a terrible economic crisis.

The community united behind a citizens' committee: its meetings packed the miners' hall, and people lined the streets outside as well. Unemployed miners, merchants, clergymen—they all appealed to the government for help. What they got was a federal assistance grant of $100,000 (announced with great flourish at a public meeting) to tide the town over for a while. Nobody thought the seven-month program announced by the Diefenbaker government was a solution.

Through 1957 and 1958 the coal company and the citizens' committee discussed the future of Springhill. By October 1958, there were bitter suspicions that the community had been taken in. Joe Tabor, Springhill delegate to the UMW convention that year, complained that the company still refused to look seriously at reopening No. 4, even though it contained more than a million dollars' worth of equipment, and there were additional criticisms of the citizens' committee for agreeing to the scrapping of the Springhill-Parrsboro line and its acceptance of a company scheme to relocate Springhill men in Cape Breton. A spokesman for the committee denied that they had given the company any mandate to scrap the railway, and urged the UMW to put more pressure on the company to live up to its promises.

There was little the community could do to change company policy. If short-term economics dictated that No. 2 mine be driven deeper and deeper, there was little local men and women could do. From the 1930s to the 1950s the community's alternative plans for less exclusive concentration on a very deep No. 2 mine had fallen on deaf ears. The size of the controlling company kept growing, and by the 1950s Springhill was just one small star in a vast economic firmament. In August 1957, control of Dosco passed to A.V. Roe Canada Ltd. There were grave local fears that the takeover might harm the region, but A.R. Williams, assistant to President Crawford Gordon, told Maritimers that the corporation was honest and sincere in its intentions. Why would the holding company put up $100 million in shares and cash, he said, just to "close down or slow down Dosco or the Maritimes?"

In October 1958, the month of the disaster, A.V. Roe Canada Limited issued its annual report. It noted a 57.8 percent increase in consolidated net sales, a 15.2 percent increase in consolidated net profits, and a 113 percent increase in consolidated assets during the past fiscal year. The company's 77 percent interest in Dosco had boosted its consolidated assets from $145,754,527 to $310,400,714. Altogether it employed 43,000 people. Dosco, meanwhile, had a combined net profit of $2,707,717 in 1958, 92 cents per share of ordinary stock. That was down from the previous year's total of $7,112,996 and $2.42 a share.

By the time of the disasters in the 1950s the community was under siege. The number of men on the company payroll, 1,425, was 50 fewer than the total in 1901. With a population of 7,348, the town had expanded only slightly since 1941, and the number of people per company employee had risen from 3.09 in 1901 to 5.15 in 1956.

Nobody knew what the company's plans really were, although it was no secret that the mines were not considered that important to the corporation. To the people of Springhill, of course, they were essential. These people knew that under the town there were still vast reserves of coal to be won—52,748,000 net tons, according to one conservative estimate—and they knew that their town in the past had provided a tidy profit for external interests. They still wanted the company to pursue a more balanced policy and to reopen the mines it had abandoned instead of depending exclusively on one very deep mine. They knew they held little power in this situation. They didn't know whether or not their town would be allowed to live. In the end, the whole town was trapped as surely and terribly as were the coal miners in the creaking ruins of No. 2.

Six men faced a dilemma as they lay trapped in No. 2 mine. They had to decide what they could do for the seventh member of their group, whose arm was caught in a shattered pack. His arm was crushed, and the pain was unendurable. Some aspirins had been used, but after awhile they did not ease the pain. The trapped miner wanted them to amputate his arm. There was a saw available. One of the miners wanted to try it, but the other five thought not. It seemed that an operation of that sort would almost certainly kill the man, and who could tell if rescuers might not save him?

It was hard for the miners to listen to the pinned miner, who continued to plead with them. They did not know what they could do for him. By Sunday the pinned miner had escaped the mine, in his own way. He was on a farm, in his delirium, hauling water up from the brook. He had his horses hooked up, and he was going to haul up a barrel or two of water. Everyone would have lots, because he had lots to share from his spring.

He died late Tuesday afternoon.

No. 2 mine was a vast complex of passages, roadways, machines, telephones, ropes, walls, and levels. It was only six years younger than the Dominion of Canada, and much of its coal had powered the railway which held the Dominion together.

Many people in Springhill did not think No. 2 should have been the sole support of the town, given its reputation. The poet Danny Boutilier, who penned many of his best lines during breaks in the mine, had this to say:

When a man works in a place that "kicks"
He is up against no joke;
For he doesn't know when she might let go
(And she hits a nasty poke).
He holds his breath, he is scared to death;
Every noise he hears, he jumps;
For a man's in dread, fear he'll lose his head
When he's in a place that bumps.

It had been doing just that for over 40 years by 1958, although never had any bump been as heavy as the one which had trapped the miners.

We know why the community was unable to stop the company from cutting back its production until Springhill depended completely on an uncertain and ever-deepening mine, but what caused the bumps here, in particular the great bump of 1958?

This bump was man-made. It was foreseen by a number of rank-and-file miners who did everything they could to avert it. Their protests were not listened to because the opinion of the men who worked in the mine mattered less than the opinion of the officials of the company and the people who had money invested in it.

Coal mines are rather unusual workplaces. The workplace and the work itself are intertwined, because the place of work is also its result. You make the mine by working in it. Nothing could be less useful than thinking of a mine as a hole in the ground from which coal is drawn like water from a well. In fact, a mine is a very complex structure, much like a huge building, and subject to all the dynamic forces of the underground. Every mine is unique. No. 2 mine, for example, was based primarily on a seam of coal which varied between 6 and 10 feet in thickness, and which was considered one of the best in the province for steam and domestic uses. The Springhill coalfield had a major fault cutting the seams about 3,000 feet from the surface, and as you moved away from the main slope of the mine the coal seams deteriorated in quality to the east and west. These factors limited the horizontal extent of the mine, while giving every impetus to increasing its depth. It was more economical to push the mine deeper.

By 1958, No. 2 mine was a huge, solid, historial document. Its upper levels had never been left with enough support in the 1870s, a fact which still plagued mining engineers in the 1920s. These upper levels had been worked on the "room-and-pillar" system, which was one of two basic ways of producing coal. The room-and-pillar method involved driving a series of parallel passages (or "roads") through the coal and connecting them at right angles with other roads. This makes a checkerboard pattern of passages and blocks of coal called "pillars." The pillars did the job of holding up the roof of the mine while the coal obtained by driving the roads was removed; then the pillars themselves would be taken out or "drawn" and the roof allowed to subside.

On the lower levels of the mine, an entirely different system was in effect: longwall. As the name suggests, longwall involved working the whole of the face of the coal simultaneously, without leaving supporting pillars, along long walls of coal. Longwall came in two varieties, longwall advancing and longwall retreating, the difference between the two being that in the first, you "advanced" or worked outwards from the main slope to the boundary of the mine, while in the second, you "retreated" or worked towards the main slope from the boundary of the mine, having first put in the levels and headings (passageways used for travelling or as airways).

Both these methods could work well, but it was necessary to adapt to local geological and mining conditions. Both methods had to deal with a fundamental fact: when you extract minerals from the ground, you place stress on the strata above and below. The strata above the mined-out area, unless supported, will come down eventually to meet the strata below the mined-out area, and it is impractical to hold the space between them open indefinitely. If the subsidence of the strata is to be effectively controlled, you must consider such things as the depth, inclination, and thickness of the coal seam, the nature of the adjacent strata, the faults in the coal seam, the rate at which mining is being conducted, the nature and arrangement of roof supports, and the thickness and distribution of top coal not taken out during mining.

In the room-and-pillar system the space was kept open by the coal pillars left standing after the first mining operations; once these were drawn the roof subsided. (Drawing pillar, as can be imagined, could be hazardous.) Beyond a certain depth, most mining experts agreed, this kind of mining was not really appropriate, because the strength of the pillars would not be enough to bear up under the pressure of overlaying strata, unless the pillars left were uneconomically large. In Springhill this critical depth at which room-and-pillar was no longer thought suitable was about 2,000 feet from the surface.

In the longwall system, roof subsidence is supposed to take place gradually, while the immediate coal face is protected by timber. In Springhill "midwalls" were also used for support in mined-out areas. Longwall involves a steady push of the wall through an enormous pillar of coal, with the roof gradually collapsing in the "gob" or waste, and as such many think it better suited to deep coal mining.

By the 1950s, No. 2 mine had walls which were approximately 400 feet long. Twenty-two men would work on the upper walls, with 30 men on those on the bottom. The coal was worked with handpicks and, in contrast with most mines, it was not "undercut" first but taken out straight from the face. No. 2 had a good system of ventilation and a two-stage transportation system, very large pumps to handle the unending challenge of water, and an up-to-date communications network. It was an advanced mine, even though the mode of getting coal was not mechanized.

The mine had made the transition from room-and-pillar to longwall in the 1920s, and the story behind this transition takes us into the history of bumps in No. 2.

Bumps have been noted in the United States, South Africa, Poland, Germany, France, Britain, and the USSR. A bump is conventionally defined as "a sudden bursting of the coal or of the strata immediately in contact with it." Bumps are often accompanied by a loud report and by tremors, sometimes felt a good distance from their place of origin. Although bumps may be accompanied by outbursts of gas, mine gases are not their causes. Bumps entail the sudden failure of the coal seam and/or the strata associated with it and are caused by excessive stress. The coal face may be expelled into the open areas of the mine, and sometimes the floor heaves and the roof collapses. This is roughly what happened in 1958.

Most authorities agree that one of the biggest factors in bumps is the kind of roof in the mine. Contrary to what one might expect, a strong roof which would bear up under the strain imposed by overlying strata could be a problem. The very strong sandstone strata which made up the roof of No. 2 helped to make the mine dangerous, because the roof would not subside in a gradual and predictable way. When both the roof and pavement of the coal seam consist of strong sandstone or shale, bumps or sudden rupturings of the coal seam will take place during mining operations at depth.

Perhaps the hardest aspect of bumps to visualize, and one of the most crucial, is that the coal seam being mined is being subjected to stresses. What happens when a coal seam fails is that the coal behaves more like a fluid than a solid. The coal face might be projected by a yard or more, bending conveyors and other mine equipment. When mining engineers bored holes into seams known to be prone to this sort of thing, they found the volume of coal in one hole would be 70 times the expected volume. The coal was virtually flowing into the borehole, because it was under high confining pressure.

There is no way of entirely eliminating bumps in a deep mine, but one can adapt the layout of the mine and the plan of mining operations so as to reduce the hazard. They are rather hard to deal with, because they involve the entire system of mining and not just one isolated problem (such as poor ventilation or defective pumping).

According to the official records of the Cumberland Railway and Coal Company, there were 653 bumps from 1917-58, of which 525 occurred in No. 2 mine. This is undoubtedly a low estimate, because the company missed minor bumps which did not damage the mine or injure individuals. Also, the miners pointed out in 1959 that they had heard of bumps going back to as early as 1904—and there is newspaper evidence to back them up. The official company record lists fewer than 50 bumps in the last two years of No. 2, but other evidence lists at least 91 bumps in the same period. Since much effort was put into trying to portray the 1958 bump as an unforseeable calamity, preceded by only minor bumps of little significance, this evidence is important.

Over the years the men in charge of No. 2 had worried about bumps and tried to come up with plans for getting rid of them. The first major attempt to understand the bumps of No. 2 mine was made by J.C. Nicholson, who was in charge of No. 2 in the 1920s. In a paper called "Past and Present Methods of Working No. 2 Mine," Nicholson explained that the bumps had become a serious problem right after the First World War. Nicholson came up with a novel suggestion to correct the problem: reduce the size of the pillars, and change the mining cycle so the pillars don't have to bear up for a long time. Nicholson thought, on the basis of his own experience, that bumps tended to be more severe when bords were driven with a large pillar rather than with a small one, and so he reasoned that leaving a small pillar might reduce the number of bumps.

His plans worked for a while, but all he had really managed to do was buy some time. As the mine went deeper, the bumps started again. In 1923 70 bumps were recorded, followed by 80 in 1924, a record.

Bumps in the room-and-pillar mine were hard on the men who went through them. Memories of these days in Springhill are sombre ones, as are the pages of the union's minutes, which record funeral after funeral and a mounting level of alarm. "I remember the last bumps they had in room-and-pillar," says one mining veteran:

> Remember a young fellow who was driving a horse, Bobbie—he was driving a horse in one of the levels, and they were working room and pillar and she bumped. She closed in ahead of him and closed in behind him. And he was in the front box, and the horse was kicking the box. And they were two days getting him out. And of course by that time the horse had kicked itself so it was half dead, they had to destroy it. They got the young fellow out, he never was the same, though. . . .

Some men never did get out. On July 18, 1923, a bump on the 5,400-ft. level killed one man and blew out fifteen boxes of coal. Two miners were killed on September 25, 1923, when a bump in the same location wrecked the bord for 70 feet and caused the roof to fall in large slabs. On August 4, 1924, a bump collapsed five sets of timber in a head on the east 5,400-ft. level; two miners were killed.

The plan didn't seem to be working, and the government called in an outside authority, George S. Rice, Chief Mining Engineer of the United States Bureau of Mines, to look at the problem. His report was quietly critical of the way coal was mined in Springhill. He noted the sharp rise in the number of bumps, and among the causes of the bumps, Rice listed, "The method of mining both past and present in connection with heavy cover." He recommended adoption of a longwall system and put his case bluntly in one sentence: "I never heard of bumps being experienced in longwall mining."

The bumps did not stop after the mine was switched to longwall. There were still mine fatalities from bumps: two men died from 1925-30, and 47 more were injured. Walter Herd, who analyzed the situation in 1929, was not convinced that the problem had been solved, but he did note that the men had evolved their own early-warning device. Whenever the mine became very quiet and you could no longer hear the coal "working," it was time to leave. It signalled that the normal weighting in the coal was no longer being taken care of, and a bump was imminent.

After the 1920s the bumps in No. 2 receded, and it looked as if the advancing longwall system brought in by Rice had really helped solve the difficulty. From 1930-50, only one man died in a bump. There had been 80 bumps in 1924 alone; there were only 87 in the years 1930-50. But the bumps started in No. 4 mine, especially on the 5,400-ft. longwall. As this problem worsened, the union pressed for some answer from the company. In response, the company came up with an important idea. In Rice's report, and in the mine itself, the general practice was to develop the walls in a step-wise fashion. If you had three walls moving into the same pillar of coal, you would try to develop them unevenly, so that on a map the walls looked like a stairway.

Company officials, operating largely on the basis of personal experience, had come to the conclusion that this step pattern had to be avoided. For General Manager Harold Gordon the better way of developing the mine was to avoid any step between the faces. As he explained to a reporter in 1958:

> The whole question of working in an area with strata such as exist here is in getting pressures relieved. If they're not relieved there will be a sudden release and a bump is produced. And if there is a long line of face then the tendency is for the pressures to be relieved more frequently and more gently. . . . If . . . you have a long face, the tendency is for the stone—the overlying stone—to break at much more frquent intervals before those pressures are built up.

The policy of straightening the walls became the major component of the company's strategy in the fight against bumps.

In 1944, in response to the union's request for action, the company proposed to straighten the walls of No. 4 mine. The consensus which approved this decision would later be cited by the company as evidence that this change had been universally commmended. However, such later use of the meeting took the decision out of the context of a relatively shallow mine and implied that consent had been freely given to line up the walls in all mines. It is hard to understand why a decision in 1944 should have been thought binding upon men 14 years later.

Although the bumps in the 1940s were largely a problem in No. 4 mine, the problem made an unwelcome reappearance in No. 2 in the 1950s. Here the coal miners and the mine management had two entirely different assessments.

In the nineteenth century, and well into the twentieth, the coal miner was commonly considered a man with very important skills. In bord-and-pillar mining, the coal miner, his butty, and a helper ran their "place" with a good deal of independence. When a man was responsible for the safe timbering of his part of the mine, and for laying track and keeping the work straight, he felt able to deal with his employer on terms of rough equality. The employer wasn't thought to know a great deal more about mining than his workers, and some workers were not afraid to say that he probably knew a lot less.

This was no longer the case by the 1950s. Now coal miners no longer controlled their own places or set their own pace of production; they were more closely supervised. They no longer made the same range of decisions the old craft miners had made. Their union had accepted a subordinate place in the workplace and advocated harmonious relations with the employer. Its main priority was maintaining wage levels. In every UMW contract in Nova Scotia was a provision which left the mode of operating the mines solely in the hands of the employer—as the UMW representatives were quick to point out in the aftermath of 1958. The workers' ability to go on strike was hemmed in by restrictive labour laws and by the union itself, which had long stood for the "sanctity of the contract."

These developments in the labour movement help us understand why the protest against the company's policies in No. 2 mine was unsuccessful. To push such a protest very far would have meant going beyond what the union, and society, regarded as the proper business of labour.

The miners' faith in the company was shaken with a severe bump on December 18, 1954. The 11,800 longwall face and the 12,200 face below were out of alignment by about 120 feet, and the company decided to bring these walls into line. After the two walls were aligned, a heavy bump occurred, resulting in five deaths and the pushing out of the coal on the 12,200 longwall face for a distance of 84 feet. This bump is now largely forgotten, but it was both tragic and important. It shocked many coal miners and made them look hard at the company's mining policies. Some coal miners thought the bump had been precipitated by the lining up of the walls.

The miners' faith in the company was further undermined by a terrible explosion in 1956 in No. 4 colliery. This explosion was caused by a dangerously located power cable, and by working the mine when the methane content in the atmosphere was greater than the permissible legal level, among other difficulties. Although infractions against the law were listed by the Royal Commission which investigated the explosion, charges were never laid. The miners of Springhill asked that the methods used in No. 2 mine be added to the mandate of the Royal Commission, but this request was not granted.

The consensus on mining policy evident in 1944 had now completely broken down. The miners no longer believed that lining up the walls would control bumps; they thought, rather, that leaving a step between the walls would protect them. This clearly was the traditional, accepted way of mining in No. 2. There was little hard scientific evidence for either side in this debate. The study of such problems was in its infancy. Both sides were guided by practical experience, not by theory. Some studies were in progress. A team of researchers linked with the Mines Branch of the Department of Mines and Technical Surveys began a survey of ground stress in collieries. They tried seismographic tests to see if there was a connection between mining and bump activity, and took various convergence measures which helped measure movements of strata. The terrible irony, as one scholarly account of the disaster has noted, is that had this research been done with more perseverance (and more funds), the warnings being sent out by the mine might have been understood. The removal of seismographic equipment from Springhill in June 1957 was justified by the completion of the specific research the team had in mind, but it meant the best means of predicting the bump had been taken away. Even more ironically, the measures taken of the convergence in the mine carry a clear warning that seismic events in the mine were increasing from the August holiday on, but nobody was able to draw the correct inference from the data.

The last act of No. 2 mine was about to begin. Early in 1956, three new walls were started, and as usual they began in a stepped formation. By March 1957 there were approximately 210 feet between the 13,400 and the 13,800 walls; this had increased to 290 feet in September 1957. Then a bump occurred on October 9, 1957, which the company thought was caused by the step between the walls. They resolved to bring the walls into line, but without undue haste. On March 18, 1958, there was a bump on the 13,400 level, which killed Alfred White, a timberman. It was the beginning of the end.

In March 1958, union men debated the question heatedly in their local, and word of their arguments reached the ears of management. It came up at a meeting with the company on March 5, 1958. As the minutes make clear, the union was willing to go along with a reduction in the size of the step between the walls, but did not want the distance eliminated.

Mr. Calder [manager] said the Union wants the 13000 longwall kept ahead of the 13400, and they also want the 13800 stepped up to bring it more in line with others. He has no objection to these measures but takes exception to statements allegedly made at the last Union meeting. It is rumoured that one statement advised the men that a distance of 40 feet must be kept between longwalls, otherwise a dangerous condition would exist. Rumour also states that it was reported at the same meeting that the

13400 was 7 feet ahead of the 13000 longwall. Mr. Terris [Union representative] said he is informed that Underground Manager McKay stated that the 13400 was 7 feet in advance of the 13000. In so far as the instance between longwalls is concerned, the Union feels it should be maintained at 40 to 50 feet.

Discontent was growing, partly over disruptions in the sharing out of work caused by stopping the two forward walls so that the lagging wall could catch up, and partly over safety.

It is clear that the issue was very much alive in early April. At a meeting on April 8, 1958, Harold Gordon told union representatives that "Danger of bumps is minimized when all faces are kept in line, or very nearly so. While a straight line is ideal the most feasible practice is to maintain 10 to 15 foot steps between the faces." He claimed that enough had been proven by the researchers to show that this was the safest method of mining. Just that morning men had walked off the 13,800 wall, and Gordon warned the union that the company would not put up with any more.

Who was right? After the bump, three kinds of explanations emerged. Some men, like William F. Campbell, retired resident superintendent of the Cumberland Railway and Coal Company, believed that the bump was caused by an external force—most probably an earthquake. There was not much evidence for this view, and nothing has emerged since 1958 which lends it greater credibility. More people, including the company officials and the Royal Commission which reported on the disaster, believed that while the bump was clearly related to ground stress, there was no way of determining the probable causes. George S. Calder, manager of No. 2, put it well when he said, "In our ignorance of ground stress we did upset something of the law of nature, and what it was I am not in a position to state." Some speculated that a large roof fall in the waste precipitated the catastrophe. In any event, no blame could be placed at the door of management.

Finally, coal miners believed that certain mining practices had greatly contributed to the bump. Elroy Tabor told the Royal Commission in 1959, "I think that bump was man made, caused by the people that control this company." Donald Beaton, a mines inspector, testified that in his experience as former underground manager of No. 2 mine, he had always found the step system suitable.

In the quarter-century after the disaster, much work was done in the field of rock mechanics and on the particular problems of stress in mining. New insights were gained from many countries, since there are now more longwall coal mines working at depth, and new techniques involving more complex reasoning have come into play. This more sophisticated analysis of rock mechanics has borne fruit in a 1980 Ph.D. thesis by Keith Roger Notley, *Analysis of the Springhill mine disaster (October 23, 1958)*.

Notley is a student of rock mechanics, and he is not interested in the social aspects of the decisions made in 1958. He is strictly concerned with the technical and theoretical implications of the disaster for the field of rock mechanics (and he believes it unfair to speculate on what would have happened had given company policies not been followed). Notley summarizes six contributing factors which caused the bump in Springhill. Four of these are aspects of the physical conditions of deep mining: (1) the overburden loading was higher than the uniaxial strength of the coal at a depth of 4,000 feet; (2) with a mining thickness of about 8 feet, a large amount of caved roof material was required to fill the void left by mining and establish load transfer through the gob, and the greater the distance back in the gob to the point where load transfer was reestablished, the greater would be the pressure on the coal ahead of the face; (3) the presence in the roof of massive sandstone beds with poor caving properties; and (4) the absence of a clay floor, which led to a steeper stress gradient in the yield zone ahead of the face. These points of Notley's make more specific and precise the well-known difficulties of mining at depth, and while they do not bear directly on the debate between the miners and management in 1958, they do tell us of the dangers implicit in the strategy of deep mining in Springhill.

The next two factors listed by Notley bear directly on the issue. Notley first argues that mining towards a rise heading on a parallel face created a uniform and accelerating stress buildup in the pillar. On this point, Notley notes the experience of European collieries, and cites this passage from an article by O. Jacobi in the *International Journal of Rock Mechanics* about conditions in the Ruhr:

> The risk [of bumps] is particularly great in the case of a rise heading which is approached by a longwall face parallel to it whenever roof and floor consist of thick sandstone bands. A rock burst occurs when the face has advanced to about 25m from the rise heading. The coal rib is smashed by the rock burst over a considerable distance and is pushed into the rise heading. . . . Such narrow coal pillars should be avoided at all costs in seams which are prone to rock bursts.

As Notley notes, this is almost exactly what was happening in Springhill in 1958, and the greater distance of the Springhill faces and the rise heading is in proportion to the greater depth of Springhill's mine.

Notley therefore suggests that such adverse geometrical configurations in the mine probably had a significant role in causing the bump. At the time of the bump, he notes, the three walls were almost exactly in line and were straight on the full dip. The lower two walls were approaching the rise heading on the full dip. By straightening the walls, the company created a configuration of faces especially conducive to bursting. There appears to be an abundance of international literature on this point. The miners' worry that the company was making things worse by aligning the walls was apparently justified.

On the second point, Notley finds that through a long process of empirical trial and error in mining No. 2, the operators became skilful in avoiding situations which would lead to localized face bumping, but they thereby created conditions suitable for much larger bumps, because without the energy release allowed by small-scale bumping, more energy would be stored for eventual catastrophic release. Notley's argument is substantiated by a computer simulation of the stress and deformation patterns during the mining of the last three longwalls in Springhill. He discovers that the energy release with a stepped configuration was well below the peak found when the faces were in line. The way mining was conducted in Springhill allowed the stress on the remaining pillars to build up to a very high level; there was no "weak link" to act as a safety valve. When walls were staggered and approached headings obliquely, failure could take place gradually from the weakest point, but when the faces were aligned and parallel to the head, this gradual failure could not occur. This argument is almost the exact opposite to the argument advanced by Gordon in 1958.

Notley does not claim that the problem of bumps would have gone away had these mining policies not been followed, but he does suggest, as the miners did, that the severity of this bump had a lot to do with the way the ground was worked to a "highly tuned level of unstable equilibrium." The most detailed and sophisticated research on the problem of the bump had borne out the miners' position almost completely. The miners' practical knowledge of the pit turned out to be something which, if anyone had acted on it in 1958, might have averted this particular disaster.,

However, the company acted as any efficient corporate enterprise could have been expected to, preferring the advice of its own engineers to the opinion of its workers. It should be pointed out, too, that there is no reason to think the men running the company were not sincere in their advocacy of this position. Instead of giving us an example of an unreasonable employer neglecting the safety of the men, the disaster offers us a much more modern case of the way expert knowledge can mislead, and how the decline of workers' control in production can harm an entire community. The blame rests not on this individual company, but on the entire system which made it impossible to place a moratorium on mining in No. 2, without destroying the local economy, until the phenomenon of bumping was better understood.

On September 27, 1958, the distance between the top two walls was 22 feet and the bottom two 18 feet. That month Harold Gordon came to Springhill to deal with miners. This is what he told them:

> The Company had suffered terrific losses due to the setbacks suffered by the operation and the loss of markets for Springhill coal owing, largely, to the loss of C.N.R. orders due to diesel locomotives replacing coal burning locomotives. . . . The Federal Government had granted a special subvention to assist the movement of Springhill coal to Quebec. That had been done to help out the Town of Springhill and its people, but as soon as that had been done the men went on strike. Such action not only caused the

loss of the sympathy of the general public but would lead directly to the closing of the one mine left. It had been said that the tie-up was caused by one or two men but that was not quite good enough. . . . He did not want to be understood as making any threats—he was merely saying what would happen if that course of action be persisted in.

On September 25th, the *Chronicle-Herald* reported a strike at No. 2 mine, and described the issue involved as a "minor technicality." No other information was released.

On October 4th the distance between the top two walls was 18 feet and the bottom two walls 25 feet. Arthur Noiles remembered what it was like to work in No. 2 mine as the walls were being aligned:

Since they started taking the walls close together there's been many gray hairs come in my head. Why? Well, self-preservation. I was a working man. I worked for my living and in my job did what I was told. Every shift of the pans that we got closer to that 13,400 wall the sands were running out fast I figured. The overman at the 13,400 wall is gone now. Many a night we sat together and prophesized a big one. That's just my own feelings.

On October 11th the distance between the top two walls was 12 feet; between the bottom two, 19 feet. Men were sick to their stomachs before they went to work in No. 2. It was a very quiet mine. Stanley Whitewood would afterwards reflect, "If she stayed quiet I was scared, I was nervous, and when they lined up those walls, that done it."

On October 18th the distance between the top two walls was 7 feet and the bottom two walls 13 feet. Elroy Tabor: "Half of our miners were scared to go down because they knew when they lined those walls up there would be a major bump and a lot of men would get killed." On October 23rd the faces were almost exactly in line.

Six days later, men and women were living with the consequences of the bump. During the first two or three days, when it seemed that escape might be possible, the miners consumed a good deal of their supplies of food and water. Only later did they resort to rationing. Now they were forced to adopt desperate measures, such as chewing coal and bark from mine timber.

The six surviving miners at the top of the 13,000 wall were gathered in the engine space. The five and one-half days were an ordeal for them. They listened to the coal working in the waste. They feared that the waste was about to close in on them, and they tried to make their underground quarters safer. By a stroke of good luck, one of the miners found a ten-cent chocolate bar in the dark. It served the men for two meals. On Monday the miners had a birthday party for Garnet Clarke, who had just turned 29. One sandwich was divided equally among them. Each man had a bottle capful of water.

Sometimes the sound of the rescue crews could be heard, but there was no telling if they were getting closer or not. Men turned to hymns and prayer. Maurice Ruddick led them in singing, and he would later explain that the Lord had had them live through the bump for a purpose.

Barney Martin, the isolated and semiconscious miner, was clawing the coal to give himself an air hole.

The group of twelve trapped miners also sang hymns and prayed. They heard the thumping noises and vibrations from the rescue crews, but it was hard to keep hoping. By Wednesday they had prepared themselves to die, and asked God to be merciful.

On the surface, news of the disaster brought reporters from radio stations, newspapers, and that new medium, television. The disaster was covered by *Time, Newsweek, Maclean's* and *Life*; by the Toronto *Globe and Mail,* the Montreal *Gazette*, the Boston *Tribune* and *Globe,* and by the *New York Times*; by the wire services; by the radio stations CJCH and CHNS; and by the television networks NBC and CBC. (These are only some of the organizations that sent reporters to Springhill.) Probably the greatest impact was made by television, even though the new medium had not yet reached every household. Television kept people all over Canada in constant "on-the-spot" touch with the small mining town.

Suddenly the whole country was watching Springhill. As one story from Ottawa put it, "In the nation's capital people mourned in their own simple way. People who have never been to the mining town in the Cumberland hills wore shocked expressions as they visited their churches to pray for men they had never known."

More than 40,000 telegrams and letters came to Springhill, with contributions to the disaster fund totalling nearly $2 million. Contributors ranged from ordinary children to Pope John XXIII. Money was raised in colleges and churches, at race tracks and in taverns. John Diefenbaker spoke for many when he said, "The people of Canada are shocked and saddened by the news of the terrible tragedy which has struck again in Springhill. . . . All Canada pays tribute to those who go down in the mines." Earlier, Diefenbaker had said that the whole "family of Canadians" had been drawn together in sorrow and sympathy for families of the men killed and missing in the accident.

It was in fact one of the biggest news stories of the year. Springhill became a famous place. It would become the subject of an article on psychology, at least one novel, a decent factual account (*Miracle at Springhill* by Leonard Lerner, who covered the disaster for the Boston *Globe*), and many poems, including an epic poem in French (*Tragédie à Springhill* by Michel Aubier). Sociologists were particularly interested in the Springhill disaster because they believed it could teach them a lot about small-group interactions. The existence of two separate groups of trapped men made it possible for them to carry out tests reminiscent of those by scientists studying rats escaping from a maze.

The people of Springhill in 1958 were courageous, loyal, and determined. The memory of their heroism has not been dimmed after 25 years, and the reporters who came there were genuinely and deeply moved by this town and its spirit. However, the way they covered the story did not do justice to this real heroism. They turned Springhill, a real community in crisis, into an unreal symbol, and they turned their eyes away from complex truths to concentrate on the stark human drama unfolding before their eyes.

In the process, the media promoted a myth about the disaster—that it was the result of natural causes. The idea that the disaster was a natural event was conveyed in many ways. The *Reader's Digest* carefully selected the evidence it cited to make the point that nobody could have foreseen the tragedy. It claimed that No. 2 had been bumping "in a small way every few weeks, tumbling coal off the face of the seam." It did not report that No. 2 had been killing people since the 1920s, including one miner in a bump in 1958 before the disaster. *Time* was a bit more honest, telling its readers that recently six major bumps had injured 14 miners, but it too failed to mention the longevity of No. 2's problems.

The terms which reporters unfailingly used ("fate," "luck," "destiny," "miracle"), referred to the town's misfortunes as though they were somehow beyond human control. "How much can one community take?" asked the *Chronicle-Herald*. "Surely this one has been dealt enough by fate." A cartoon by the *Herald's* Bob Chambers made the point perfectly. It shows a great lightning bolt descending from the heavens onto Springhill, and carries the caption, "Adversity's Focal Point." Only a few people pointed out the strange reasoning involved. "The Springhill mines' repeated disasters are no 'Acts of God,' " one letter to the *Chronicle-Herald* argued. "They are man-made tragedies. Who is to blame?" It was not a question the media felt at all inclined to ask.

For its part, Dosco handled the situation very well. The company's public relations effort was orchestrated by C. Arnold Patterson. Be on guard against rumours, Patterson warned reporters, and accept as gospel only those reports with the company name on them. Among the "rumours" that company officials were anxious to stop was one circulating among the miners that aligning the walls had brought on the bump. Louis Frost, Dosco's chief mining engineer, said that the new way was safest, besides being "a univeral mining practice." Harold Gordon also devoted some time on the CBC to this issue. The company's critics were not given anything like equal time or space.

The company's large donation to the disaster fund ($100,000) was mentioned in many news stories and won it special praise. It was also noted that generous donations of food had been made by Campbell's Soups and Weston Biscuits. It would not have suited the Springhill media package to report that the company and the union had battled each other for many months over alignment of the walls, so the story was neglected. A kind of excessively personal coverage took its place. General Manager Harold Gordon was made a star. Canadian Press said of him:

Many miners feel they owe their jobs to Gordon's determination to keep Springhill alive. Others don't always agree with his decisions. . . . The miners know Gordon and love him. A close friend, Dr. J.G.B. Lynch, says miners respect him as a man who asks no miner to go where he won't go or do more than he will do himself.

The *Chronicle-Herald* called Gordon "a miner's miner among those who know him." This kind of emphasis on personalities helped to blunt any criticisms the miners made, even after the disaster.

There were the usual exploitative photographs the news media feel they must get in a circumstance such as this. *Weekend Magazine* splashed a large photo of a crying woman above the caption, "By day the vigil goes on. Without self-consciousness, a woman wipes a tear from her eye." A photograph of a woman collapsing in tears as she left a church service was widely published over the caption, "Grief."

Unable to dig into the disaster or be critical of what they were told by the company, the media were reduced to reporting the number of coffee cups or to covering each other. The photographer from *Life* magazine was enthusiastic before the television cameras: it was the most exciting thing he'd ever put on film, he said.

There was no room in this interpretation for anger, no room for fear, no room for a conflict between company and men. When Calgary offered to adopt a Springhill family, and was told by Mayor Vaughan of Halifax that most of the miners would not want to leave Springhill, Mrs. Sterling Cameron of Springhill wrote: "We live next door to the mines and each time we see a man or men coming home before their shift is up, we cry and ask, 'Who's hurt or killed now?' Some life, isn't it Mayor Vaughan?" Such raw anger was rarely reported.

Strange as it may seem, the media turned the disaster into a happy story. Of course, the way events unfolded helped this happen. Springhill swung from despair to jubilation in the days of the disaster, as the rescue crews at long last began to bring up men instead of bodies. It made for a dramatic story. "Miracle" became the media watchword. "To be here will be an experience that will never be erased from our memory," said the CBC broadcaster at the pithead. "It's just a tremendously exciting succession of events here in Springhill that has thrilled and thrilled over again the people who are on the scene." It was a natural reaction to the discovery of survivors, but it shoved aside the greater number of families for whom all the news from the pithead was tragic.

After the last man alive was taken from the mine, an announcer asked, "Who wants to go home? Who's losing hope? Certainly not any more." It sounded like a football game. The area around the pithead looked like a bizarre circus, one reporter noted. "Floodlights from mobile units illuminated one end of the area. Marquees were set up alongside the roadway which had a glow of brilliance from flashing markers on the tops of police cars and ambulances patrolling or stationed in the area."

Miners' wives waiting for word from the pit would remember as the worst moment of their ordeal the announcement Gordon made over the radio and television during his fifth press conference, in which he said there was no more hope. Nobody seems to have considered the human costs of broadcasting such announcements.

The disaster the media portrayed did not raise any hard moral questions. There were no comments about a policy of resource development which had led a whole community into such an impasse, or about the methods of mining which had contributed to the bump. When men were finally rescued, John Diefenbaker said, "Courage paid off." For the *Reader's Digest*, the bump "taught the 7,000 townspeople that faith and determination can turn men dead into living, laughing human beings." But such comments neglected the harsh truth that most of the people who waited anxiously for word of their loved ones were disappointed. For the majority, there was no miracle, and in the flood tide of human interest stories, all the critical questions were left unasked.

The people who lived through it will never forget the moment when the trapped miners were discovered.

At 2:30 p.m. on Wednesday, October 29, 1958, the rescue crews were about 60 feet from the 13,000 wall. Chief Mine Surveyor Blair Phillips placed a light in the end of air pipe which had been uncovered in the level.

The light shone into the cavity housing the twelve miners, and Phillips heard six electrifying words: "There are twelve of us here." "Stay where you are!" he shouted. "We'll come as quickly as possible." The miners had no difficulty in staying where they were.

The news that twelve men had been found alive set the church bells ringing in Springhill and brought a huge crowd around the pithead. After a frantic search, some copper piping was found which could be used to bring liquids to the men through the air hole. The miners were sternly lectured by a doctor about consuming the liquids slowly. Independent as usual, they followed their own inclinations.

By 11:55 p.m. the miners were supplied with food, and by 3:25 a.m. the first of them reached the surface. By 5:05 all of the twelve men had been brought from the mine. The men were so gaunt and grimy that they could scarcely be recognized. One wife ran to a bedside and hugged the wrong man. Wide-eyed children found it hard to believe that the bearded faces before them belonged to their fathers.

On Saturday, November 1, 1958, the group of seven miners was found. When rescuers came upon Barney Martin, the isolated miner, he was dazed and his hands were raw from trying to scratch his way out of his coffinlike hole. By 9:15 a.m. the rescue of the other men was complete.

Everyone hoped there would be more "miracles," but as time went by this became less and less likely. The news agencies recalled their reporters for more pressing assignments. The lights came down, the tents were dismantled, and

Springhill moved off the front page.

On November 6, 1958, the last man was brought from the mine. The widow of this last victim of No. 2 had waited for the body of her husband at the pithead until the bitter end.

The media coverage of the bump, which everyone said had drawn Canadians together and made it impossible to believe Springhill would be allowed to become a ghost town, created unrealistic hopes. Most of the promises made to Springhill were betrayed.

In 1959 the Royal Commission called to investigate the causes of the bump reported that it was unable to find any such causes. It absolved the company and called for a heightened attack by researchers on the problem of bumps. The research team was promptly disbanded.

On November 12, 1958, the company issued this statement: "Dominion Coal Company Ltd. announces that, after careful consideration, it has been decided not to reopen the coal mines operated here by its wholly-owned subsidiary, the Cumberland Railway and Coal Company. The company will co-operate to the best of its abilities to meet with the government authorities to meet the difficult situation which the closing of these mines will cause in Springhill.''

The provincial government offered exceptional inducements to industry to locate in Springhill. Those which came did not approach a level of employment which would preserve the community.

Dosco's announcement struck some newspapers as a hard blow to a town they had come to admire. The *Globe and Mail*, noting the spirit of the people, editorialized, "A town which produces men like these ought not be casually dissolved. . . . What must be provided is simply the opportunity to make new, productive lives, and Canada will be the loser if that opportunity is not provided.'' The *Windsor Daily Star* was even more forthright. "Involved is the whole issue of the responsibility a company has to its employees,'' it noted. "Is a large powerful one justified in merely closing up shop or moving out of town, to leave its former workers and the community to fend for themselves?''

In the myth, the answer was no. The "family of Canadians'' would be so moved by the heroism of the town that its economic future was assured. In reality, the answer was a resounding yes. The company was perfectly within its rights to leave Springhill, and nobody in a position to do so put any roadblocks in its way. Whatever Springhill had given in the way of lives to the coal companies, in this mine founded by Confederation, mattered little. It was past history and did not appear on the present balance sheet.

"Courage paid off,'' Diefenbaker had said. Two or three years later the unemployment rate in Springhill was crippling and out-migration epidemic. Only a new correctional institution helped stem the tide—but nobody thinks this step preserved Springhill as the vibrant community it used to be. Compared with the sentiments expressed in 1958, the treatment of Springhill afterward was shabby. The population of Springhill fell sharply.

Barney Martin, who had spent over eight days trapped by himself in the mine, was cut off his compensation pay while he lay in a hospital bed. He got it back, only to have it cut off again for a nineteen-week period. When he finally got partial disability pay, he was cut off the disaster relief fund. After eight years of just making ends meet, his compensation was cut off completely.

Other survivors of the 1958 disaster joined the general exodus from Springhill. They found employment in Ontario and the United States. A few found local jobs.

In 1958, such a dismal outcome seemed unthinkable. It seemed impossible that so great a wave of public feeling would leave nothing in its wake. But the verdict on Springhill was brought in not by public opinion but by capital, and the pronouncement was simply the end of the town's economic usefulness. Against such verdicts, there is in our society no appeal.

The company escaped from Springhill unscathed, without even an apology. The disaster was for them an event which could easily be shoved aside. However, many people remember 1958 whether they want to or not. The community is still struggling to escape the consequences of the bump. The disaster reverberates yet in the terrible loneliness of people who mourn for the men who never came back. Its presence persists in the life of the town, blighting hopes, souring lives.

Outside Springhill, the disaster will live on—not as an event, but as a cruel revelation—in the minds of all those who have really grasped its significance. Springhill 1958 makes us face the dark and forbidding recesses of our entire way of life, and we look, still, for an escape.

Old Wounds:
Reopening the Mines of St. Lawrence

Alan Story

"**W**hy do you want to go back to work in the fluorspar mines of St. Lawrence, mines that have killed, by lung cancer and silicosis, more than 300 men out of the town's population of 1,800?" After being without any steady work for nearly two years, David Lambert, 41, says he doesn't find the question difficult to answer. "Why, well I guess it's just as well to die with money as live without," he replies. Lambert, who lost his father-in-law, two uncles, and a lot of friends to the old fluorspar mines in this isolated south-coast Newfoundland community, adds, "When they start up again, my brothers won't be going back; their wives won't let them."

Officials with Minworth Ltd., the British firm which will reopen the mines abandoned in the late seventies by the Aluminum Company of Canada Ltd. (Alcan), worried that the wives of most men in town won't "let them" go back underground. Lambert, a father of three, is one of almost 400 men who signed up for the 90-120 jobs that will be available next summer at Minworth's new fluorspar mines and processing mill.

"For Minworth or any other large outside corporation offering work, we are a captive people," says local parish priest Father John Maddigan sadly. He estimates that only about 140 men and women—or less than 15 percent of the labour force—now have a job in the essentially one-industry town of St. Lawrence. "Since Alcan pulled out, we've pretty much depended on Canada Works grants and social assistance," says Mayor George Doyle. The reopening of what will be Canada's only fluorspar mine will be "a godsend," says Doyle. Adds optimistic Leo Slaney, the town manager and, like Doyle, a former miner, "Minworth has given the town a chance to have a future again."

The problem, however, is that St. Lawrence is still a long way from getting over its past. Twenty years after this mining town slowly began to recognize that it was being decimated by one of most scandalous episodes of industrial disease in Canadian history, the memories remain fresh, and the deaths continue.

Mario Walsh, head nurse at the St. Lawrence Memorial Hospital, remembers how his father's face was always coated with a fine white powder when he came home after a shift drilling for fluorspar back in the 1940s and

This chapter is based on an article first published in *New Maritimes* (February 1986).

early 1950s. "My mother would wipe him off with a big dust cloth and then use it to clean the silverware. She said it worked better than silver polish," says Walsh. His father died at age 45 in 1954.

Much more than stone dust and "miner's TB," as the disease was first called, was killing St. Lawrence miners. Called in to probe the reasons why the town's death rate from lung cancer was 29 times the expected rate for a comparable Newfoundland community, several medical research teams working during the early and mid-1950s found the likely cause. For over three decades, veteran miners had been exposed to levels of radioactive radon gas that were between 2.5 and 10 times previously suggested working levels. In some sections of the mines, concentrations of radioactivity were 193 times recommended limits, another study found.

In short, St. Lawrence's mines had become death pits. By 1969, a provincial Royal Commission concluded 150 miners had already died and that as many as 100 others were permanently disabled with lung cancer, silicosis, and chronic obstructive lung diseases.

Since 1980, when he came to St. Lawrence, Father Maddigan has conducted 20-to-30 funerals a year for former miners, most of whom died after years of suffering. Said one widow to Father Maddigan about her once-robust husband, "He didn't die, he just wasted away."

Of course, the David Lamberts of St. Lawrence know that the upcoming fluorspar era is unlikely to reap the same scale of carnage as the first. Over the past 50 years, mine ventilation systems and inspection practices have been significantly upgraded. Yet, admits Lambert, "there will definitely be health hazards down there and some of us may die . . . but, tell me, what choice do I have?"

The hard-working people of St. Lawrence faced a very similar choice 50 years ago when fluorspar mining began at the height of the Depression. At the time, the economy was as bleak as the low, treeless hills that surround the town. A 1929 tidal wave had wiped out St. Lawrence's sole economic resource, its fishing fleet. Farming wasn't an alternative in this barren area where high winds and thick fog regularly sweep in from frigid Placentia Bay. Residents lived on welfare payments of $1.80 per person per month. Scurvy was rampant.

Enter Walter Seibert, a New York City accountant. Following up a tip from a local prospector, Seibert came to St. Lawrence and announced that boom times were right around the corner. St. Lawrence was sitting on top of one of the richest and highest-grade deposits of fluorspar in the world. The semihard industrial mineral, also known as calcium fluoride, is used as a metallurgical flux in aluminum smelting and in steel-making and as the basic raw material for hydrofluoric acid. It is mined on five continents, and Mexico is the leading world producer.

Seibert proposed opening a mine as soon as possible and, the next winter, a load of second-hand mining equipment arrived by freighter. Obliging local workers agreed to unload it for free and began work on Seibert's mine site with a promise that he would pay them if and when the fluorspar ore was sold. A year later, they were compensated at 15 cents an hour. Seibert's mine prospered and, by 1940, Alcan had moved in to open a second series of shafts.

In the beginning, no one allegedly knew what, 20 years later, would be the outrageous cost of this prosperity. Why no one knew seems almost incomprehensible.

The companies, at first, did not provide the miners with hard hats, safety boots, or safety lamps as they drilled underground in the narrow, damp, horizontal shafts, often measuring less than 2 by 5 metres. Miners "can tell you stories about working hundreds of feet underground in drifts so plugged with dust and smoke you couldn't see the man working beside you—you could only hear him," wrote journalist Ian Adams in a chapter on St. Lawrence in his 1970 book, *The Poverty Wall*. It took more than a decade before dry drills were replaced with more modern wet drills which sprayed water on the dusty mine faces. Most critically, ventilation was non-existent. Describing conditions in the mines to a 1956 government commission examining workers' compensation, mine captain (or foreman) Rennie Slaney said, "Myself and the men many times had to leave the (mine) faces and come to the shaft where we threw up for as high as an hour and the throwup would be mostly blood."

The first deaths began in 1940. Today as you walk through the town's cemetery, "an enormous brute of a thing," says Walsh, and the largest on the Burin Peninsula, you can see the gravestones recording the many deaths of miners during that era. Age 34 reads one, age 37 another, age 41 a third.

Seibert shut down his operations in 1958 and Alcan bought him out. In 1959 the first government health studies were completed which drew the link between the high rate of deaths and the leakage of radioactive radon gas into the fluorspar mines. Radon gas is an odourless gas derived from the breakdown of uranium, and often seeps into mines through the air or mine waters. Studies done in the 1970s confirmed that it was concentrations of radon gas which led to high rates of lung cancers in Elliot Lake and other Northern Ontario uranium-mining towns.

In 1960, Alcan began installing a ventilation system, though, as ex-miner Morris Doyle explains, "it's not easy to blow air into a mine that wasn't originally built for ventilation." "The theory," wrote Ian Adams, "was that the new (ventilation) machinery would exhaust the radon from the mine and bring the radioactivity down to the somewhat arbitrary level set by the federal Department of Health for workers exposed to radiation hazards." Adams continues: "The truth is that nobody really has very much information about the effects of radioactivity on health. When radon is inhaled, it is thought to deposit extremely fine radioactive particles in the lungs. These particles are suspected of causing lung cancer."

Amazingly, the St. Lawrence miners themselves were told none of this until five years after the first medical studies were released. By then, those still living were most concerned about trying to get workers' compensation for themselves and the numerous widows. Many weren't eligible and often the compensation payments were a pittance. When Slaney died in 1969, for example, his widow got $30 a month.

During the 1970s, the still working fluorspar miners conducted several lengthy strikes against Alcan demanding, among other things, wage parity with other Canadian hardrock miners. They never succeeded. With other supplies of fluorspar from Mexico available for its aluminum smelters, Alcan shut down the last mine in 1978.

There are disturbing signs that certain aspects of St. Lawrence's first experience with fluorspar are about to be repeated during the upcoming Minworth Ltd. era. As in 1933, the town's only other industry, fishing, faces uncertain times. In summer 1985, the local fish plant employed a mere 77 workers for 10 weeks, just long enough to collect unemployment insurance for the rest of the year. Although a new operator for the plant may be found, most of the jobs, as is traditional, will likely go to women workers. For the majority of men in the community, mining fluorspar is their only option.

Both the provincial and municipal governments were being almost as obliging to Minworth as the local unemployed workers were in 1934 when they unloaded Seibert's mining equipment for free. To reopen the mines, Minworth was given exclusive access to the fluorspar resources by the Peckford government and forgivable grants totalling $6.8 million. As well, the Newfoundland government provided equity financing of $1.5 million when Minworth couldn't find a Canadian partner. Transport Canada will spend $1.5 million to repair the local government wharf.

Before the project was started, Minworth's chief executive officer in England, Peter Mason, personally demanded—and won—concessions from the St. Lawrence town council. Headed by Mayor Doyle (who is now Minworth's local office manager), the council agreed that for the first three years the mine-mill complex operates, Minworth employees will work under the following conditions: (1) The wages (excluding benefits) will be approximately $9.00-$10.00 per hour. (This is about 40 percent below rates paid in Ontario's hardrock mines.) (2) If employees join a union, it must be a local, rather than a national or international union. (3) There will be no strikes. The legality of the deal is suspect. Charles Russell, general manager of St. Lawrence's Fluorspar Ltd. (the Minworth subsidiary operating the mine), says that because of labour unrest in the mines during the 1970s, "no company would move in here, without getting these assurances." Commenting on the deal, Father Maddigan says, "the people don't want to appear to be antagonistic."

Labour's response has been highly critical. "This has to be the most despicable attempt to sell the Newfoundland workers at bargain-basement prices," remarked Bill Parsons, President of the Newfoundland and Labrador Federation of Labour. Minworth's demand that there be promises of no strikes and no international unions added "insult to injury" for the people of St. Lawrence. Says Parsons, "The evidence of why workers need union representation lies in the graveyards of St. Lawrence," where more than 300 miners lie after dying of cancer and silicosis from the fluorspar mine before it was shut down by Alcan in 1978. "The safety and health of the workers must be the foremost consideration in any discussions of reactivating that mine, and the only assurance that this will be done is through working participation and representation by a trade union of the employees' choice."

The main concerns remain, of course, the safety of the new mines and the health of former and returning miners. It can hardly be reassuring to the community that the Newfoundland government is actively considering the phasing out of St. Lawrence's only hospital as a restraint measure, just as the new mine is about to open. About 70 former miners are still under active treatment for various lung ailments at the 27-bed hospital. If it's closed, the closest hospital for these men and future mine accident victims will be 40 km away.

As for the mines themselves, Premier Peckford promised during the April provincial election that they will be "safe." Russell promises the same. He says that radon gas levels will be closely monitored, that Minworth's "jacked up" ventilation systems will flush out gases and dust, and that miners will be required to have annual medical checkups. Russell also says the company probably won't institute a bonus system for the miners, agreeing that production bonuses can decrease respect for safety. At the same time, he makes the rather unbelievable claim that "there will be no dust at all in that mine." As for the earlier fluorspar era, Russell says "it's been overplayed how terrible the companies were." Adds Mayor Doyle, "there is no animosity in St. Lawrence to any of the companies that came before."

Loretta Walsh feels animosity. At least once a month she goes to St. Lawrence's cemetery to visit the graves of her three brothers, John J., Alonzo, and Frederick, who were all killed in the mines.

"I don't agree at all with opening them up again," she says. "If we didn't have the mines, we wouldn't have such a big cemetery."

Further Reading: Mining and Energy

History

Frank, David. "The Cape Breton coal industry and the rise and fall of the British Empire Steel Corporation." *Acadiensis* 7, No. 1 (Autumn 1977): 3-34.

Leyton, Eliot. *Dying Hard: The Ravages of Industrial Carnage* (Toronto, 1975).

Macgillivray, Don. "Henry Melville Whitney comes to Cape Breton: the saga of a gilded age entrepreneur, 1899-1914." *Acadiensis* 9, No. 1 (1979): 44-70.

Notley, Keith Roger. "Analysis of the Springhill Mine Disaster (October 23, 1958)." Ph.D. Thesis, Queen's University, 1980.

Seager, Allen. "Minto, New Brunswick: A Study in Canadian Class Relations Between the Wars." *Labour/Le Travailleur* 5 (1980): 81-132.

Current Perspectives

Belliveau, M. "Canso, Cabinda and the 'We Hurry' Boys: the Gulf Oil Story." *Round One*, No. 2 (February 1974).

House, J.D. "Big Oil and small communities in coastal Labrador: the local dynamics of dependency." *Canadian Review of Sociology and Anthropology* 18, No. 4 (November 1981): 433-52.

———. "The Mouse That Roars: New Directions in Canadian Political Economy—The Case of Newfoundland." In Robert J. Brym, ed., *Regionalism in Canada* (Toronto, 1986), pp. 161-96.

Kuusisto, N., and R. Williams. "Nova Scotia versus big gypsum." *Round One*, No. 4 (December 1974).

Senopi Consultants. *A Report on Noranda Mines Limited for Conseil Régional d'Aménagement du Nord* (Petit Rocher: mimeo, 1979).

Winson, Anthony, ed. *Oil and Gas Development in 'Have-Not' Regions: Some Lessons for Nova Scotia* (Halifax, 1984).

Is There Life after Underdevelopment? An Afterword

Rick Williams

To say a true word is to name the world.
—Paulo Freire

One conclusion emerges clearly from these chapters on the political economy of the Atlantic region: underdevelopment means not one but many things. It is high unemployment and underemployment. It is dependency on capital from outside for any new economic activity, and therefore dependency on decisions by outsiders about how, and even whether, our human and natural resources will be productively used. It is the poverty that saps energy and creativity from people and their communities. Most important, underdevelopment is a state of mind, a social consciousness, which leads people to demand less and less of themselves and of those who exercise power over them and on their behalf.

It would be wrong to try to equate in quantitative or qualitative terms the kinds of problems we face in the Atlantic region with underdevelopment in Third World countries. However, the word *underdevelopment* is being used more and more frequently by mainstream commentators as well as by the left to describe conditions in the Atlantic region. Terms such as *regional disparities* and *the have-not provinces* are dissatisfying because of their seeming innocuousness and complacency, and there is a growing need in the region to express alarm at the depth and severity of the economic crisis and its widespread social, psychological, and cultural consequences.

Yet, the concept of underdevelopment has not caught the popular imagination in the Atlantic region. In this sense it is not a "true word" with which to express profound insight into the real meaning of our collective experience. True words, when they come, will not be borrowed from the experiences of others or implanted in our minds by experts. They will arise from the vernacular of struggle, and they will give expression to the act of seizing the day.

At this early stage in the development of such a vernacular, *New Maritimes* is a critically important venture. It is one of the few vehicles through which the many dissident voices of the region—workers, artists, feminists, environmentalists, minority group members, peace activists, primary producers, both new recruits and wise veterans of struggle—are and amplified. The magazine is rooted in the region as a whole, having successfully avoided the urban and academic biases which could have fatally isolated it. Although *New Maritimes* has its antecedents in popular journalistic inquiry and protest, it is opening new ground within the dynamics of crisis and resistance in the current epoch.

None of the preceding chapters set out to make a grand or definitive statement about the nature of the crisis in the region. Few were written by professional journalists. Each began with a concrete situation or issue and was primarily concerned with informing the sympathetic reader about what is happening and why it matters for others in the region. The writers implicitly addressed themselves to a sympathetic readership because they knew the great majority of people who read *New Maritimes* are themselves engaged in struggles for change of one kind or another within the region. It is this assumption of a shared engagement that frees *New Maritimes* from dominant ideology, from the spurious "objectivity" and fetishistic "balance" of the mainstream media, and makes it an instrument for the building of solidarity and collective self-consciousness in the Maritimes and Newfoundland.

What have these chapters told us about the underlying nature of what, for lack of a true word, we will continue to describe as underdevelopment in the Atlantic region? Four general themes seem to emerge. One is the need to more deeply understand how regional capitalists have adapted themselves to underdevelopment, making of it a source of wealth and local power, rather than organizing themselves and their communities to overcome it. A second is the critically important role of the Canadian state in shaping, directing, and perpetuating the historical process of underdevelopment. Third is the central role of primary industries and producers in the regional identity and in the possibilities for significant economic, social, and political transformation. Fourth is the range of difficulties primary producers face in attempting to organize, and in attempting to resist the intensifying threats to their industries and ways of life.

Orthodox theorists define the problem of underdevelopment as an absence of capitalism or the presence of an underdeveloped capitalism. They argue that the conditions needed for a private ownership–based economy to take root and thrive must be put in place if development is to proceed. In the case of the Atlantic Region, this view is obviously faulty. In the Maritimes in particular there was a period of very successful indigenous capitalist development in the last century, and since then every conceivable effort short of literally enslaving the work force has been made by the state to facilitate expanded accumulation. Simply put, it is the very "success" of capitalism, first on the local level and then on the national and international levels, that has generated the problem of underdevelopment in this and other peripheral areas.

If underdevelopment simply meant the absence of capitalism, a vacuum, then the population would be free to choose another route to development if it saw fit to do so. In fact, despite its many failures, capitalism is still all-powerful in the Atlantic region. Other options are not readily available, and people are not free to choose or create them. There is no vacuum; multinational capital (Stora Kopparbergs, Shell Oil, Michelin, Hawker-Siddeley, U.S. Gypsum), national capital (Noranda, Husky–Bow Valley, Alcan, the banks, Eaton's), and regional capital (the McCains, the Irvings, the Sobeys, the Jodreys) do what they do very well and make very large profits. In fact, the better they have done in their own terms, the deeper the crisis of regional underdevelopment.

How does the indigenous capitalist class survive and prosper despite severe economic decline in the region? These chapters have provided ample information with which to address this question. In many cases, local businessmen concentrate their investments in service-sector enterprises and real estate, where foreign investment and, more importantly, the tremendous inflow of government transfer spending virtually guarantee them ample returns. They organize trust companies and other financial institutions to move money to safer ground outside the region and to pool it for service-sector ventures and the use of foreign investors locally.

In goods-producing industries such as agribusiness, pulp and paper, and fishing, they use their political leverage to undermine trade unions and producer organizations, to ensure "friendly" environmental, resource-management, and health-and-safety legislation, and to avail themselves of overly generous grants, loans, and tax concessions. As in the service sector, they often organize their enterprises specifically to exploit low-wage, unorganized, and seasonal labour—predominantly women. They use their control of the mass media to shape and constrain the popular discussion of politics and economic affairs. When all else fails, they sell out to outside interests and retreat to the safety of their trust companies.

Multinational companies are generally very clear about their motives and intentions. They come and take what they want, and when it is gone or they no longer need it, they go somewhere else. They dictate their terms, and pretty much get their way, but still their influence and penetration within the regional society is limited. They remain outsiders. The indigenous capitalist class, on the other hand, is a ruling class in the full sense of the word. Its influence pervades all aspects of life in the region, from educational and cultural institutions to the mass media to politics and religion. The indigenous capitalists' very substantial economic investments in the processes and structures of regional underdevelopment are therefore a major barrier. Their power is the first obstacle to be overcome in any struggle for real development in the region.

A second general theme of regional underdevelopment is the heavy legacy of state policy, traced out in sector after sector by the preceding chapters. In the face of postwar economic decline in the Atlantic region, the Canadian state had two basic options. It could simply move viable industries into the region and "level the playing field" of access to markets, or it could support the greater concentration and centralization of the Canadian economy, providing the losers with welfare in one form or another. From the 1950s to the 1970s it pursued the latter course, thereby generating the profound political and economic dependence that so characterizes the region today. In the 1980s, despite the vast wealth accumulating in the centre, it has been decided that this "solution" for the poorer regions is far too expensive. Dependence is suddenly a "bad thing." Cuts will have to be made, belts will have to be tightened. The belts are around poor people, unemployed people, marginalized people, and the biggest belt is around the throat of the Atlantic region.

Dependence has long been identified as a primary dimension of underdevelopment, and the fact that the fate of the region rests in the hands of federal politicians is ample testimony to the validity and relevance of the theory. Close to three out of every ten jobs in the region are government jobs of one kind or another. Business spokespersons, deeply concerned that the rug will be pulled from under their "safe" investments, point out that 80 percent of gross domestic expenditure in the region originates with government. The federal government has been spending some $6 billion a year over and above total revenues in the region, and an estimated 60 cents of every transfer dollar immediately returns to central Canada via consumer spending.

Government is the overwhelmingly dominant economic actor in the region, and yet its power in no sense constrains or counteracts the activities of local or foreign capital, nor is it a source of greater self-determination or "consumer sovereignty" for the people of the region. State policies at the national level have not provided an antidote, but have only created a temporary safety net in relation to regional underdevelopment. Welfare spending, public enterprises, and subsidies to private corporations are integral dimensions of the deeper problem. Policies of fiscal restraint and benign neglect now merely intensify the processes of economic, political, and social breakdown in the region.

In this context, primary production has a central role in the economy of the region. Although primary production is not itself the biggest direct employer in the Atlantic region, it provides the base for secondary production and the lion's share of export earnings. Fishing, forestry, mining, and agriculture have been such central elements in the social and economic history of the region that our shared cultural identity is deeply rooted in them. There is a growing awareness that, if we are to regain control of our situations and to pursue economic development options that actually make sense in terms of environment, settlement patterns, and natural and human resources, primary industries will play an even greater part in our futures.

It is precisely that future which is so much at risk in the current crisis. Controlling corporate interests jeopardize the long-term viability of primary industries through their drive to maximize production while minimizing investments in the nurturing of renewable resources. Destructive ecological practices further jeopardize both the resources and the human settlements around them. The insatiable corporate need to control production results in a sustained attack on independent producers. The fishing, forestry, and agribusiness companies impose minimal prices upon independents while expanding their own production in order to maintain the general oversupply which holds prices down. At the same time, the companies provide credit and sell machinery and supplies to small producers, thus strengthening control over their production and draining off more of their limited surpluses.

Historically, capitalist development implied the decline of rural populations and the creation of labour-hungry urban industrial centres. In the Atlantic region and, indeed, in Canada, no such major expansion of "smokestack industries" or other labour-intensive endeavours is likely in the future, given the realities of automation, deindustrialization, and the emergence of what is complacently called the "post-industrial society."

Independent producers have been able to remain in their industries because of their "occupational pluralism," the wage-earning activities of spouses, and supplementary income from transfer payments, notably unemployment insurance. Now such crucial supports for rural communities are threatened by reversals in state policies and a shrinking government role in the regional economy. Like the resource base, the population base for primary industries is in serious jeopardy—it is a death of a thousand cuts, as schools close, rural postal services are withdrawn, extension services are "defunded," staffing is reduced in hospitals, grants for municipal services are reduced, and so on and on.

Faced with the overwhelming evidence of decline and disaster in sector after sector, the reader may well come away from this book with a sense of despair. One after the other, the authors have documented the fate of the region and the hardships underdevelopment has imposed on its people. The depressing problems mentioned in this volume cannot be avoided. No simple, obvious solution to them exists within Canadian capitalism. Even though rational analysis tells us that economic resources should now be flowing back into rural areas to stabilize populations and renewable-resource bases and to develop rural economies, the opposite is occurring and will continue as long as economic policy aims only to maintain the profitability of obsolete and destructive corporate operations.

The only way out of a sense of despair about the future of the Atlantic region is to think of ways in which this trajectory can be changed. Any major social transformation requires a "historical subject." Some broad base of people with energy, organization, and vision must seize hold of this crisis situation and create new ways of organizing economic activity, political decision-making, and social relations. Who could play this role in challenging capitalist underdevelopment in the Atlantic region and in mobilizing broad popular support for an alternative future?

There are many groups who can play a part and who clearly have a direct interest in building a different kind of society here in the region. The traditional heavy industries—shipbuilding, steel, railways, coal, etc.—can be revitalized if there is a dynamic economy in the region to generate immediate and stable demand. The non-commercial service sector—health, education, and social services—has much to offer to the quality of life if there are tax revenues to support it, which again implies a healthy regional economy. The commercial service sector can also be restructured so that it more effectively circulates goods within the regional economy, instead of simply draining off the available cash flow. Workers' struggles in these sectors will continue to be important, but perhaps even more important would be the establishment of popular control over, and the radical redevelopment of, primary industries.

There are signs of hope in the organization of the region's primary producers, although, as always, our hopes for genuine development must be tempered with realism. These chapters have suggested that the news on the struggles of primary producers is not altogether encouraging. On the positive side, we find little evidence of political stagnation or passivity in the face of the deepening crisis. In forestry, mining, fishing, and farming alike, events are moving quickly and people are responding actively and often militantly in defence of their perceived interests. In response to environmental issues, there has been widespread protest and organization-building.

Despite these factors, however, there is clearly a lot more to be accomplished before any new historical subject can begin to flex its muscles. What is to be done? Two things are missing: strong, broadly based primary-producer organizations committed to popular control and real development in their industries, and effective linkages among primary producers and workers within primary-industry sectors.

Strong producer organizations are necessary because the capitalist organization of primary industries effectively pits producers against each other through the "normal" workings of corporate-controlled markets. In what Hobbes called the "war of each against all," inequality among producers constantly increases and their numbers are continually reduced through competition to sell more and more at less and less real return. At each stage the survivors think the system really works for them, until their turn comes. The real winner is monopoly capital, which benefits whether catches or crops are good or bad, whether the markets are up or down, or whether the number of producers increases or decreases.

We have had two strong primary-producer organizations in the Maritimes, the National Farmers Union (NFU) and the Maritime Fishermen's Union (MFU), and there is also an effective woodlot owners' asociation in New Brunswick. None of these bodies, after many years of hard work, has made a breakthrough in regrouping all of its potential members, but each has demonstrated the value of organization and the major gains that can be made when producers act in concert. In addition to the open resistance to producer organizations by governments and corporations, an important barrier seems to be the resilience of small-capitalist ideology in the face of ever-mounting evidence that capitalism no longer really works for the little guy, and that radical new structures are needed if independent producers are to survive in their industries.

Effective collaboration between producers and workers in primary industries is also a risky proposition under current conditions. We can readily find instances of conflict, as manifested in recent strikes in some of the larger co-operatives, and in the lack of solidarity with workers shown by woodlot owners during pulp-mill strikes. Nevertheless, there are a few developments that indicate potential for change in the future.

In Newfoundland, the Newfoundland Fishermen, Food and Allied Workers Union (NFFAWU) has brought small producers, offshore crews, and plant workers into one dynamic organization that bargains for all of them. Sectoral conflicts can be worked out among union members before the companies can divide and rule. Although the inshore fishermen tend to be less well mobilized within the union because of their scattered settlements and the unique nature of their working conditions, the union as a whole still puts a strong emphasis on stabilization of the small-producer sector in its political campaigns for fisheries development.

Another important example to look at is the reopening on the Miramichi River in New Brunswick of a liner-board mill now jointly owned by the plant-workers' union, the woodlot owners, and a management team. If the current interest in co-operatives and worker-controlled enterprises takes root and spreads, there will be many more instances where workers and primary producers will have to go beyond mere expressions of mutual support to develop concrete forms of interdependence and shared control.

When workers and primary producers get together, a very interesting and creative chemistry can develop. Workers know about organizational unity and discipline, about bargaining collectively and using the power of their productivity to force concessions from the opposition. Primary producers are more "political," in the sense that they are accustomed to running their own operations and to taking an active interest in policymaking and the overall industrial-management practices of government and the companies. Fishermen, farmers, and woodlot owners are somewhat more likely to think about how to make their industries work as a whole, and have often had a lot of experience in struggles to change such structural elements as resource-management policies, marketing practices, licensing arrangements, and so on.

What we might hope for is that in combining worker and producer groups, the strengths of both sectors would prevail. Organizational skill and unity would combine with political imagination and assertiveness to create demands for popular control of the industry and for a radical restructuring of its operations, and also create the social mobilization necessary to press home these demands. In some cases, opportunities for such undertakings will fall into the hands of producers and workers as corporate interests simply fold up and leave industrial operations that are not sufficiently profitable for them. Rather than government-owned "lemon socialist" enterprises, workers, primary producers, and others in their communities will opt to run the plants themselves, to make them work, and to keep the economic surpluses within the industry and the region.

The more important test will be, however, when workers and primary producers combine their efforts to take on state policies and dominant corporate interests on issues of survival and development in healthy, surplus-producing industries. The MFU, the NFU, the NFFAWU, and other organizations have been fighting such battles largely in isolation, and from positions of relative weakness, for several years. As the issues become more clearly defined, and conditions for workers and producers become more critical, the possibilities and needs for a wider unity become manifest and impossible to ignore. It is through this key dynamic that struggles against capitalist underdevelopment will take shape.

Communication is an essential element in the expansion of regional struggles against underdevelopment. We each need to know what others are doing, and we all have to learn from each other's experiences so that the same mistakes are not endlessly repeated. We need to celebrate our victories, suffer our defeats, declare and redeclare our commitments—together. The absence of such communication is a primary charactristic of our underdevelopment.

The survival and growth of *New Maritimes* is itself an important achievement in the struggle against underdevelopment. It is a vehicle, a meeting place, and a sounding board. It does not set itself up as the arbiter of correct analysis. It takes positions but encourages debate and recognizes a plurality of views within the struggle. It seeks ways to give voice to and empower the many people who are not heard or seen in the mainstream media, and to do so without the patronizing style that so typifies the region's mass media.

We have a place to create and to share true words. We have a massive challenge ahead in struggling with the heavy legacy of underdevelopment. There is no alternative, for those who care about the region, to fighting for change and continuing this tradition. This volume shows how much *New Maritimes* has contributed to our understanding of the region in its five years of publication. It also points the way forward, to the many struggles we will face in the region in the years to come, building on this foundation of solid analysis and political commitment. To name the world and to change it—in our region, this is the only way our collective survival can be ensured.

The Contributors

Mary Boyd is the Director of Social Action for the Catholic Diocese of Charlottetown.

Marie Burge works as a research and education resource person with the National Farmers Union and, since 1984, has also been involved with the Cooper Institute, a popular education and research institution in P.E.I. She is past chairperson of the Board of Directors of *New Maritimes*.

Gary Burrill helped to organize the unemployed in Nova Scotia in the 1970s and early 1980s before becoming managing editor of *New Maritimes*.

Bernie Conway works for the Maritime Fishermen's Union in Charlottetown.

Bruce Livesey is a free-lance journalist living in Toronto specializing in labour and business issues. He formerly worked for the Irving-owned *Daily Gleaner* of Fredericton.

Christopher Majka is a biologist, writer, and filmmaker based in Halifax.

Darrell McLaughlin has a farm near Aroostook, N.B., and is an active member of the National Farmers Union.

Julia McMahon is currently working as a writer and editor in Montreal.

Ian McKay is a social historian at Dalhousie University and an editor of *New Maritimes*.

Tom Murphy, a well-known Fredericton activist, wrote for alternative publications such as *The Mysterious East* and *Nuclear Reaction* and now is pursuing doctoral work at Cornell University on the politics of agricultural research in Canada.

Eleanor O'Donnell of Halifax has written extensively on international development, the media, and the Sobeys empire and has made important contributions to investigative journalism in the Atlantic region.

Brian O'Neill works in Halifax for Oxfam-Canada and has done extensive research on oil and gas development at Saint Mary's University.

Aaron Schneider of Baddeck, N.S., is a freelance writer, poet, and a director of the Coalition for Alternatives to Pesticides.

Alan Story is Halifax bureau chief of the *Toronto Star*.

Rick Williams teaches political economy at the Maritime School of Social Work in Halifax and has done research for the Maritime Fishermen's Union.